VITAL SIGNS

VITAL SIGNS

The trends that are shaping our future

1995
1996

Lester R Brown
Nicholas Lenssen
Hal Kane

WORLDWATCH INSTITUTE

EARTHSCAN
Earthscan Publications Ltd, London

> **Worldwatch Database Diskette**
>
> *The data from all graphs and tables contained in this book, as well as from those in all other Worldwatch publications of the past year, are available on diskette for use with IBM-compatible or Macintosh computers. This includes data from the* Vital Signs *series of books, Worldwatch Papers,* World Watch *magazine, and the Environmental Alert series of books. The data are formatted for use with spreadsheet software compatible with Lotus 1-2-3 version 2, including all Lotus spreadsheets, Quattro Pro, Excel, SuperCalc, and many others. For IBM-compatibles, both $3\frac{1}{2}$- and $5\frac{1}{4}$-inch diskettes are supplies. To order, send check or money order for £60 (excl VAT), or credit card number and expiration date to Earthscan Publications, 120 Pentonville Road, London N1 9JN (tel 44 171 278 0433, fax 44 171 278 1142).*

First published in the UK in 1995 by
Earthscan Publications Limited
120 Pentonville Road, London N1 9JN

Copyright © Worldwatch Institute, 1995

All rights reserved

A catalogue record for this book is available from the British Library

ISBN: 1-85383-276-6

Printed and bound in Great Britain by
Biddles Ltd, Guildford and King's Lynn

Earthscan Publications Limited is an editorially independent subsidiary of Kogan Page Limited and publishes in association with the International Institute for Environment and Development and WWF-UK.

CONTENTS

ACKNOWLEDGMENTS 9
FOREWORD 11
OVERVIEW: THE
ACCELERATION OF
HISTORY 15
   Economy Picks Up 16
   Energy Use Growing 16
   Warming Trend Resumes 17
   Food Supplies Tighten 18
   Disturbing Health Trends 18
   Computerizing the World 19
   Environmental Issues Shaping
     History 20

Part One: KEY INDICATORS

FOOD TRENDS 25
   Grain Production Rebounds 26
   Soybean Production Jumps 28
   Meat Production Takes a Leap 30
   Aquaculture Boosts Fish Catch 32
   World Feedgrain Use Up Slightly 34
   Grain Stocks Decline Again 36

AGRICULTURAL RESOURCE
TRENDS 39
   Fertilizer Use Continues Dropping 40
   Grain Yield Remains Steady 42

ENERGY TRENDS 45
   Oil Production Up 46

   Natural Gas Production Stalls 48
   Coal Use Remains Flat 50
   Nuclear Power Flat 52
   Wind Power Soars 54
   Solar Cell Shipments Expand
     Rapidly 56
   Compact Fluorescents Remain
     Strong 58

ATMOSPHERIC TRENDS 61
   CFC Production Plummeting 62
   Global Temperature Rises Again 64
   Carbon Emissions Resume Rise 66

ECONOMIC TRENDS 69
   World Economy Expanding Faster 70
   Third World Debt Still Growing 72
   World Trade Climbing 74
   Television Continues to Spread 76

TRANSPORTATION TRENDS 79
   Bicycle Production Rising 80
   Auto Production on the Rise 82

ENVIRONMENTAL TRENDS 85
   Sulfur and Nitrogen Emissions Fall Slightly 86
   Nuclear Waste Still Accumulating 88
   Environmental Treaties Grow in Number 90

SOCIAL TRENDS 93
   Population Growth Steady 94
   Cigarette Production Up Slightly 96
   HIV/AIDS Cases Rise at Record Rates 98
   Urbanization Spreading 100
   Refugee Flow Unabated 102

MILITARY TRENDS 105
   Nuclear Arsenals Decline Again 106
   Peacekeeping Expenses Reach New High 108
   Wars Reach a Plateau 00

Part Two: SPECIAL FEATURES

ENVIRONMENTAL FEATURES 115
   Tropical Forests Vanishing 116
   Soil Erosion's Toll Continues 118
   Amphibian Populations Take a Dive 120
   Water Tables Falling 122
   Dam Starts Up 124
   Lead in Gasoline Slowly Phased Out 126
   Steel Recycling Rising 128

NOTES 148
THE VITAL SIGNS SERIES 175

SOCIAL FEATURES 131
   Computers Multiplying Rapidly 132
   Women Slowly Accepted as Politicians 134
   Breast and Prostate Cancer Rising 136
   Cigarette Taxes Show Ups and Downs 138
   Access to Safe Water Expands 140
   Homelessness Remains a Problem 142
   Income Gap Widens 144
   Hunger Still Widespread 146

ACKNOWLEDGMENTS

As with all Worldwatch projects, the staff at Worldwatch are not the only ones who deserve credit. A host of others not only make the publication possible, they help make it an even richer source of information.

Core funding for researching and writing *Vital Signs* comes from three sources: The Surdna Foundation provided initial funding for this annual report, thanks to its executive director, Ed Skloot, who in 1992 encouraged us to take on the project. In 1993, Surdna was joined by the W. Alton Jones Foundation, a major supporter of Worldwatch. And in 1994, the U.N. Population Fund, which has long supported activities here at the Institute, joined in providing project support for *Vital Signs*.

In addition, thanks go to our other principal funders, as *Vital Signs* draws on the highly developed information-gathering system that has evolved to support the Institute's overall research program. These supporters include the Cummings, Geraldine R. Dodge, Energy, George Gund, Homeland, John D. and Catherine T. MacArthur, Andrew W. Mellon, Curtis and Edith Munson, Edward John Noble, Pew Memorial Trust, Turner, Wallace Genetic, Weeden, and Winslow foundations, the Lynn R. and Karl E. Prickett Fund, the Rockefeller Brothers Fund, and Rockefeller Financial Services.

Assistance for *Vital Signs* also comes from people outside the Institute who not only provide us with information but also review early drafts of the entries. This year we express our thanks to Jared Blumenfeld, Dirk Bryant, Daniel Campbell, David Fisher, Paul Gipe, Bill Heenan, Peter Johnson, Pantelis M. Kledaras, Milton Leitenberg, Birger Madsen, Luc Martial, Paul Maycock, Mack McFarland, Judith McGuire, D.M. Parkin, Maurizio Perotti, Christine Pintat, Matt Sagars, Michael Stoops, David Sweanor, Daniel Tarantola, Valerie Thomas, F.A. Vogelsberg, Jr., Michael Walsh, and the staffs at the Declining Amphibian Populations Task Force in Milton Keynes, England; the Economic Research Service at the U.S. Department of Agriculture; the Environmental Law and Institutions Programme Activity Centre at the U.N. Environment Programme; the Global AIDS Policy Coalition in Massachusetts; and the Surveillance, Epidemiology, and End Results Program at the National Cancer Institute in Maryland. We also thank Jane Dignon of the Lawrence Livermore National Laboratory in California for supplying data on global emissions of sulfur and nitrogen oxides.

Of course, no Worldwatch book would come to fruition without the guidance of independent editor Linda Starke, who has been responsible for all 4 editions of *Vital Signs* as well as 12 editions of *State of the World*. Ross Feldner of New Age Graphics unfailingly produced the graphs once again, and under even tighter time constraints than normal. And we also appreciate the contributions of two former colleagues—Megan Ryan, who was able to complete the section on chlorofluorocarbons before departing on a fellowship to Sri Lanka,

Acknowledgments

and Howard Youth, who supplied a piece on amphibian populations.

Finally, we are grateful to Iva Ashner and Andrew Marasia, and to their colleagues at W.W. Norton & Company, for accelerating the book's production process in order to release *Vital Signs 1995* a month earlier than initially planned.

Lester R. Brown
Nicholas Lenssen
Hal Kane

FOREWORD

During the three years since the *Vital Signs* series was launched in 1992, it has gained steadily in translations and sales. In the United Kingdom, sales have overtaken those of *State of the World*, the Institute's flagship publication.

One reason *Vital Signs* is used so widely throughout the world is that it identifies and follows key trends—often ignored or overlooked—that are essential to charting a sustainable future. The book provides a one-stop shop for the government decision maker, the reporter on deadline, or the grassroots activist who needs the latest data on trends affecting the environmental health of the planet, the state of the economy, or social conditions.

At a time when many international organizations and national governments are facing increasingly tight budgets, the constellation of global trends in *Vital Signs* becomes even more valuable. Pressures are growing on governments to cut programs, including data-gathering and publishing efforts.

In *Vital Signs*, Worldwatch continues to cover such key indicators as the condition of the planet's atmosphere, the productivity of its primary biological systems, and investments in social and military sectors. Astute readers will also notice that each year we update our databases, taking into account revisions in historical series made by the United Nations, the World Bank, the U.S. Department of Agriculture, and other sources.

As the world becomes more complex, the need to include more indicators in *Vital Signs* increases. Among the 15 new entries this year are the use of lead in gasoline, the status of amphibian populations, the availability of safe drinking water, the condition of groundwater tables, and the growing global proliferation of both televisions and computers.

The use of lead in gasoline is a useful indicator of human health, particularly of children, since they disproportionately suffer the ill effects—including mental retardation—of lead ingestion. The recent decline in amphibians, meanwhile, indicates a deterioration of the ecosystems they inhabit.

The spread of television has perhaps as much effect, both environmental and social, as automobiles do, given that the growing use of this medium is closely tied to the adoption of western-style consumerism—and despite the positive role television can and does play. Likewise, the information-processing potential of computers can be turned into a constructive tool or a destructive one, depending on its application, in the effort to forge a sustainable future.

As with the growth in indicators being tracked, the reach of *Vital Signs* continues to expand, too. The book has now appeared in some 14 languages, including French, German, Italian, Japanese, Korean, and Spanish, with an additional 3 translations, including Chinese, in prospect.

It is often said that the best compliment is imitation, and efforts to replicate at the na-

Foreword

tional level what *Vital Signs* does internationally have surfaced in a number of countries. In the United Kingdom, for example, a coalition of nongovernmental organizations has published a book of key national indicators, and the Japanese government has contracted with a private firm to develop a similar product. The Royal Society of Canada has also initiated an effort to collect and publicize international environmental trends viewed in a Canadian context.

Following repeated requests from academics, government officials, and scientists for the data used to develop the graphics in *Vital Signs*, we released a diskette in mid–1993. The subsequent reaction to what became the Worldwatch Database Diskette (which includes data from *State of the World* and all other Worldwatch publications) has greatly surprised us. Sales, which reached 160 in 1993, jumped to nearly 1,000 in 1994. We are now offering the database as a subscription that will be regularly updated.

The popularity of the Worldwatch Data Diskette has encouraged us to explore other ways to provide information electronically, perhaps in CD-ROM format or on the Worldwide Web. We welcome your suggestions on how we can best achieve this, as well as on how we could improve *Vital Signs 1996*.

Lester R. Brown
Nicholas Lenssen
Hal Kane
March 1995

Worldwatch Institute
1776 Massachusetts Ave., N.W.
Washington, D.C. 20036

VITAL SIGNS 1995

OVERVIEW
The Acceleration of History

Lester R. Brown

The pace of history is accelerating as soaring human demands collide with the earth's natural limits. Collisions with the sustainable-yield limits of fisheries, forests, aquifers, and soils and with the capacity of the earth's ecosystem to absorb carbon dioxide are occurring with increasing frequency. National political leaders are spending more and more time dealing with the consequences of these collisions—with collapsing fisheries, falling water tables, food shortages, increasingly destructive storms, a steadily swelling international flow of refugees, and the many other effects of overshooting natural limits.

History is about change, not about the status quo. Throughout most of human history, the growth of population, the rise in income, and the development of new technologies were so slow as to be imperceptible during an individual life span. In contrast, the pace of change in all three during the last several decades has been breathtaking.

Population growth rates of the sort we know today have no historical precedent. Throughout most of our existence as a species, our numbers were measured in the thousands. Today, they are measured in the billions. Those of us born before the middle of this century have seen more growth in population during our lifetimes than occurred during the preceding 4 million years of our existence. Evolution has prepared us to compete with other species, to survive, and to multiply, but it has not equipped us well to deal with the threat we pose to ourselves by the uncontrolled growth in our own numbers.

As population has more than doubled since mid-century, so too has income per person. The combination of population growth and rising incomes has expanded the world economy fivefold during this period. (See pages 70–71.) The growth in output of goods and services in just one decade, from 1984 to 1994, totalled more than $4 trillion—more than from the beginning of civilization until 1950.

In the earlier stages of the Industrial Revolution, economic expansion was slow, rarely exceeding 1–2 percent a year. Countries industrializing now are doing so much faster simply because they do not have to invent the technologies needed by a modern industrial society, such as automobiles, refrigerators, and power plants. Instead, they can import them. As a result, the countries that are successfully industrializing in the late twentieth century are expanding at an extraordinary rate.

Economic growth in East Asia has averaged 8 percent annually in recent years. In China, it has been even faster: in 1992, 13 percent; in 1993, 13 percent; in 1994, 11 percent; and for

---

Units of measure throughout this book are metric unless common usage dictates otherwise. Historical population data used in per capita calculations are from the Center for International Research at the U.S. Bureau of the Census. Data in *Vital Signs* are updated each year, incorporating any revisions in series done by the originating organizations.

Overview: The Acceleration of History

1995, a projected 10 percent. If the latter growth rate materializes, the Chinese economy will have expanded by a staggering 56 percent in just four years. Income per person for 1.2 billion people will have risen by half.

The enormous growth in the world economy, reflecting both population growth and rising affluence, is taking place on a planet that is finite. It is no larger today than it was when we evolved some 4 million years ago, when agriculture began some 10,000 years ago, or when the Industrial Revolution began two centuries ago. One of the consequences of placing ever growing human demands on the natural systems and resources of a finite planet is that sustainable-yield thresholds are being crossed in every country. Against this backdrop, we can keep the trends of the last year in perspective.

ECONOMY PICKS UP

In 1994, the 3-percent growth in world output of goods and services marked the end of a protracted slowdown during the early nineties. (See pages 70–71.) Economic expansion moved ahead of population growth for the first time since 1990.

The industrial world grew at roughly 2.5 percent in 1994, compared with 5–6 percent for the developing world. Asia, led by China, expanded 8 percent. Western Europe emerged from the economic doldrums to expand by more than 2 percent. The United States (at 3.7 percent) and Canada (at an even more robust 4.1 percent) put North America in the lead within the industrial world.

In Central and Eastern Europe, some economies are expanding; those still struggling to reform are declining. Poland achieved its third year of growth, expanding by 4.5 percent. The Baltic states of Latvia, Lithuania, and Estonia, along with the Czech Republic, also achieved substantial gains. Russia, the largest economy in Eastern Europe, declined again—shrinking by an estimated 12 percent. The Ukrainian economy also continued its free-fall. Both these economies shrunk by nearly half between 1990 and 1994.

Economic growth in Africa, spurred largely by rising commodity prices, reached 3.3 percent, exceeding population growth for the first time in some years. Within Latin America, overall economic growth slowed slightly, from 3.4 percent in 1993 to 2.8 percent in 1994.

These economic data, compiled by the International Monetary Fund, are the conventional means of measuring progress. But they fail to reflect the loss of ecological capital involved in achieving this growth. At some point, this loss of capital will begin to affect not only national economic expansion but global trends as well.

ENERGY USE GROWING

In 1994, production of natural gas was essentially flat due to declines in Russia. Oil was up by just over 1 percent. Coal production was unchanged. (See pages 46–51.) Further increases in all three fossil fuels are likely as the economies of Central and Eastern Europe revive and as the Third World continues to boom. The bottom line is that increased fossil fuel use will boost carbon emissions further, bringing disruptive climate change ever closer.

With nuclear power, new plants still coming on-line were partially offset by the closing of older plants, holding the growth in nuclear power generation to 0.8 percent. (See pages 52–53.) In the not too distant future, the closing of older plants will exceed the dwindling number of new completions, leading to a decline in nuclear power.

The most dynamic energy sector in 1994 was renewable energy, particularly wind and photovoltaics. In 1994, wind power generation expanded by a remarkable 22 percent. (See pages 54–55.) The addition of 660 megawatts of generating capacity in 1994 is the largest on record. With more than 25,000 wind turbines hooked up to electrical grids, wind power is now supplying millions of consumers with electricity.

In 1994, the growth in new wind capacity was dominated by Germany, which accounted for 300 megawatts. India, now a hotbed of foreign investment in wind power, moved into second place in terms of 1994 additions. More important than the growth in 1994 is the evidence that many countries are beginning to invest heavily in wind power, suggesting that growth will accelerate sharply in the years immediately ahead.

Closely trailing the growth in wind power was that in photovoltaic cells: factory shipments climbed by more than 15 percent in 1994. (See pages 56–57.) At the end of 1994, some 250,000 households in developing countries were relying on solar cells for their electricity.

In many rural areas of the Third World where electrical grids do not exist, solar cells are now a competitive source of power. With some 2 billion people still without electricity, and many of these not near an electrical grid, the market for solar cells is promising, to say the least.

In more and more situations, wind and solar cells can compete economically with traditional sources. Wind farms under development in Scotland and Wales, for example, will produce electricity for less than that generated by coal-fired plants. This extraordinary growth in both wind power and solar cells is a promising step in the effort to build an energy economy that will not disrupt the earth's climate system.

WARMING TREND RESUMES

The sharp rise in the earth's temperature in 1994 underlined the need to shift from a carbon-based energy system to environmentally benign renewable sources. Average world temperature in 1994 was 15.32 degrees Celsius, up sharply from the 15.20 degrees Celsius of 1993. (See pages 64–65.) This increase made 1994 the fifth warmest year recorded since official recordkeeping began around 1860. And with the rise in temperature came a rise in the anxiety level of government officials responsible for maintaining adequate food supplies.

The world's temperature has been rising gradually for more than a century, but most of this has happened since the late seventies. Indeed, the 10 warmest years since recordkeeping started have all occurred since 1980.

The hottest year on record was 1990, at 15.47 degrees Celsius. Rising temperatures in early 1991 were heading for yet another record when Mount Pinatubo, the Philippine volcano, erupted in June. The enormous explosive force of the volcano pushed some 20 million tons of sulfate aerosols into the upper atmosphere. These quickly spread around the planet, producing a thin reflective layer that bounced a tiny amount of sunlight back into space, preventing it from reaching the earth's surface.

This in turn led to a cooling effect that abruptly dropped the temperature in 1992 to 15.13 degrees Celsius. Inadvertently, Mount Pinatubo provided a short-term test of the computer climate models that are used to simulate the effects of rising concentrations of greenhouse gases on global temperature. The models predicted that the amount of sulfate aerosols ejected into the upper atmosphere from the volcano would reduce global temperature by nearly a half-degree Celsius, which is exactly what happened.

By early 1994, the sulfate aerosols had largely settled out, signaling an end to the sabbatical from global warming. The high world temperature in 1994 suggests that the warming trend that was becoming so pronounced in the eighties and early nineties is resuming. The Intergovernmental Panel on Climate Change, which involves hundreds of the world's leading scientists, projects that if fossil fuel use continues to grow, global temperatures will rise to somewhere between 16 and 19 degrees Celsius by 2050.

Such a potentially rapid warming is of great concern because it will likely bring with it climatic extremes, including floods, droughts, and greater storm intensity. These events may be influenced by human activity in the future, raising the question as to whether they should still be called "natural" disasters.

Rising temperatures, causing water in the oceans to expand and some polar ice to melt, could push sea levels up by 6 centimeters (2.3 inches) per decade, eventually inundating low-lying coastal areas. With much of humanity clustered in coastal regions, and with much of the world's rice produced on the river floodplains of Asia, this is a matter of keen concern.

Stabilizing climate means reducing carbon emissions by some 60 percent, reversing a trend that began with the Industrial Revolu-

Overview: The Acceleration of History

tion. In 1860, carbon emissions from fossil fuel burning were estimated at 93 million tons per year. By 1950, they had climbed to 1.62 billion tons, and in recent years, they have averaged some 6 billion tons. (See pages 66–67.) As a result of this, along with a more modest contribution from deforestation, atmospheric levels of carbon dioxide (CO_2) have risen from an estimated 316 parts per million in 1959, when systematic measurement began, to 359 in 1994, a gain of nearly 14 percent. If the rise in fossil fuel use of 1994 is sustained in the years ahead, it will add to the trend of rising atmospheric CO_2 concentrations that is driving climate change.

FOOD SUPPLIES TIGHTEN

World consumption of grain exceeded production again in 1994, lowering world grain stocks for the second year in a row. (See pages 36–37.) Measured in days of consumption, carryover stocks of grain have dropped from 66 days in 1994 to an estimated 62 days in 1995. This key indicator, which measures the amount of grain in the bin when the new harvest begins, is at its lowest level in 20 years. In 1973, when stocks dropped to 56 days of consumption, world grain prices doubled.

If the rise in temperature that prevailed from the late seventies through 1990 resumes, the risk of weather-reduced harvests from severe heat and droughts will escalate. For example, if the United States were to experience a summer like that of 1988, when severe heat and drought dropped grain production below consumption, it would not be able to export grain to many of the more than 100 countries that depend on it. Such a reduced harvest today, with world grain stocks already at a precariously low level, could easily lead to chaos in world grain markets.

World grain production rebounded from the depressed harvest of 1993 (see pages 26–27), but not enough to keep up with the growth in consumption, which was spurred by the fastest economic growth in five years. This same economic expansion encouraged more meat production in 1994, pushing it above population growth for the first time in many years.

(See pages 30–31.) Production of pork expanded some 3 percent, further widening the gap between it and beef, the second most popular meat. Production of poultry, the most efficient converter of grain into meat, grew 6 percent in 1994. If these recent trends continue, world poultry production will overtake that of beef within the next few years.

The world fish harvest picked up in 1994, recovering the losses since 1989, reaching a new high of 101 million tons. (See pages 32–33.) Growth in China's fish harvest of some 2.5 million tons—mainly from aquaculture—accounted for much of the gain. Although the total fish catch has regained the level of the late eighties, per capita seafood supply is still 7 percent below the peak it reached in 1988.

DISTURBING HEALTH TRENDS

Some of the most destructive health trends in the world today can be traced wholly or partly to life-style choices and behavioral patterns. Among these are the spread of the HIV virus, the growing incidence of breast and prostate cancer, and cigarette smoking.

In 1994, the number of people estimated to be infected with the HIV virus increased to 26 million, up from 22 million in the preceding year. (See pages 98–99.) Of this rise of 4 million, 1.9 million occurred in Africa, the epicenter of the AIDS pandemic. New infections in Asia totalled 1.7 million. With the number of new infections in Africa apparently plateauing and the number in Asia still climbing, Asia may overtake Africa in the near future.

The number of people with full-blown AIDS climbed from 6.9 million to 8.5 million. And an estimated 1.5 million people died of AIDS in 1994, four fifths of them in sub-Saharan Africa.

In some African countries, the incidence of the HIV virus is frighteningly high, and it is estimated that AIDS will eventually cut average life expectancy by some 25 years. In Zambia, at least 20 percent of the women aged 15 to 49 are HIV-positive. In many African hospitals, most beds are now occupied by people with AIDS. One reason for the massive drop in life expectancy is the high number of infants born with the virus. As population densities build and as international transportation systems expand, linking even the most remote regions, infectious viruses are transmitted much more easily.

Some of the more common forms of cancer have also been increasing during the last several decades. For example, the incidence of breast cancer has been rising 1–2 percent annually since 1930. (See pages 136–37.) The incidence of prostate cancer is likewise increasing. Both forms of cancer primarily affect older people. Worldwide, breast cancer is expected to take nearly 1 million lives by the year 2000. Although similar estimates are not available for prostate cancer, it now claims 110,000 men a year in industrial countries alone.

A third social trend affecting human health is smoking. The good news is that world cigarette production has plateaued during the nineties. In per capita terms, cigarettes smoked per year have declined from the historic high of 1,029 in 1988 to 946 in 1994, a drop of 8 percent. (See pages 96–97.)

While smoking is declining in western industrial countries, it is increasing in most developing countries, including China. The gradual reduction in cigarettes smoked for the world as a whole means that the decline in western industrial countries is slightly outweighing the rise in China and other developing countries.

Many industrial countries are now using high taxes to actively discourage cigarette use. (See pages 138–39.) Denmark is leading the way with a tax of $3.88 per pack, followed by Norway ($3.44) and the United Kingdom ($3.27). Germany and France tax cigarettes at $2.25 and $1.94 per pack, respectively. The United States, which in some ways seems to have the world's most health-conscious population, has an average cigarette tax of just 56¢ per pack, one of the lowest in the world.

In terms of the human toll, cigarette smoking is by far the most costly. In the United States, it claims 417,000 lives per year, compared with 46,000 from breast cancer, a smaller number for prostate cancer, and roughly 70,000 from AIDS. Worldwide, smoking is claiming 3 million lives per year, compared with 1.5 million from AIDS. But the AIDS toll is rising much more rapidly and could overtake cigarette deaths by the end of this century.

COMPUTERIZING THE WORLD

In contrast to the lack of recent progress on the biological front in raising cropland productivity or checking the spread of infectious diseases, gains in computer technology have been spectacular. By 1994, there were an estimated 173 million computers in use worldwide, up from 4 million in 1981. (See pages 132–33.) Of these, 166 million were personal computers. When the history of the last two decades of the twentieth century is written, this will undoubtedly be seen as a period in which the computer ceased to be a novelty and became an everyday part of people's lives.

In 1981, there was one computer for every thousand people in the world; by 1993, the figure was 31. Computer ownership is highly uneven, with most of the machines concentrated in industrial countries. The United States leads the world in computer use. With 75 million computers, or 287 per thousand people, the United States dominates cyberspace in much the way that it dominated world automobile ownership a generation ago.

Given the rapid spread of computers to other countries, however, this dominance will not long continue. Countries with high levels of computer use include Australia, Canada, and the United Kingdom, all having between 150 and 200 computers per thousand population. In Japan, the figure is nearly 100 computers. Yet China and India, with scarcely one computer per thousand people in each case, are just entering the computer age.

Although computer use has certainly grown rapidly since 1981, this trend understates the computational capacity of computers, which has increased fifteenfold during the last seven years. Unfortunately, although the capacity of computers to process and analyze data has increased dramatically in the last decade, the capacity of the human mind to absorb and process information and to generate an effective social response to the threats facing society remains essentially unchanged.

ENVIRONMENTAL ISSUES SHAPING HISTORY

As the nineties unfold, environmental issues are taking center stage. Governments that do not stabilize the populations of their countries before demands outrun the sustainable yield of local life-support systems run the risk of being overwhelmed by the consequences of their failures. Nowhere is this clearer than with ocean-based food supplies. The prospect of maintaining seafood supply per person will be shaped largely by the capacity of national governments to halt population growth and adopt sustainable-yield practices for the fisheries within their 200-mile offshore zone.

Land-based food sources are threatened by the loss of topsoil. (See pages 118–19.) When soil erosion begins to exceed natural soil formation, gradually depleting the topsoil, inherent land productivity begins to fall and people go hungry. The costs of failing to check soil losses can be seen in countries such as Ethiopia and Haiti—agrarian societies that have lost so much soil they can no longer feed themselves even in years of good weather. With an estimated 30 percent of the world's cropland now losing productivity from soil erosion, the list of countries joining Ethiopia and Haiti could lengthen rapidly.

With the human demand for fresh water exceeding the sustainable yield of rivers and aquifers in more and more areas, water scarcity is becoming a national concern and an international issue. In North China and the Middle East, deficits are being satisfied in the short run by depleting aquifers. (See pages 122–23.) Once the aquifers are depleted, the pumping of water will fall sharply, dropping to the level of aquifer recharge. At that point, supply and demand of water can only be balanced through rationing, increased efficiency, or population migration. Where aquifers are shared by more than one country, this growing scarcity may lead to conflict over management.

Of all the environmental policy challenges facing national governments, few have elicited such an inept response as global warming. At some point, the costs of temperature rises will become unacceptably high. Within the insurance industry, companies providing coverage for property damage are all too aware of the costs of increasing storm intensity. When Hurricane Andrew tore through Florida in 1991, it took down not only thousands of homes and commercial buildings, but also seven insurance companies. The survival of such firms depends on accurately assessing the effects of rising atmospheric levels of greenhouse gases. If they underestimate the risks, they will face bankruptcy.

Like insurance companies, national governments also need to assess the economic risks associated with climate change. Dealing with the consequences of failing to stabilize climate—whether it be severe droughts, increasingly destructive storms, or the migration forced by rising sea level—seems certain to absorb a great deal of political time and energy in the decades ahead.

Aside from the growth of population itself, the dominant demographic trend of the last half-century has been the movement of people from countryside to city. (See pages 100–01.) From 1950 to 1995, the world's urban population climbed from just over 700 million to 2.6 billion. If this trend continues, shortly after the turn of the century we will pass a major social milestone and become a predominantly urban species.

In China alone, an estimated 120 million villagers have left their homes during the last few years, travelling to cities in search of employment. When they fail to find it, they move from city to city. The result is a huge floating population, one equal to the total population of Japan. Few trends concern officials in Beijing more than the potentially destabilizing effect of this mass movement of people.

National governments are faced with socially and politically difficult questions as job-seeking moves to the next stage: international migration from poor to rich countries. (See pages 102–03.) Algerians in France, Turks in Germany, and Mexicans in the United States have become a major political issue as indigenous populations see migrants as a threat to their culture, to their jobs, or to both.

All the trends discussed here, such as overfishing, soil erosion, water scarcity, and rising global temperatures, affect the food prospect. With natural constraints beginning to impinge on the expansion of food production in many countries, food security may soon become the principal preoccupation of many governments. Perhaps more than anything else, spreading food insecurity will symbolize the widespread failure of population and environmental policies.

These issues seem certain to occupy much of the time of national governments and the United Nations in the future. The dominant role of military concerns in international negotiations in the form of military treaties and alliances during the century's third quarter is being supplanted by the growing attention claimed by environmental treaties. Dealing with issues ranging from trade in endangered species to efforts to protect the ozone layer, the list of environmental treaties reached 173 in 1994. (See pages 90–91.)

Governments are hard-pressed to deal effectively with the seemingly endless number of issues associated with the collisions between ourselves and the natural systems on which we depend. Among the more important challenges are the need to stabilize population, to minimize climate change, and to protect the diversity of plant and animal life.

Any one of these challenges would be hard for a generation to handle. We are facing many of them simultaneously. It is perhaps not surprising that political leaders appear overwhelmed by the complex environmental issues that confront us.

Part ONE

Key Indicators

Food Trends

Grain Production Rebounds

Lester R. Brown

The 1994 world grain harvest, at 1,747 million tons, was up 2.9 percent from the depressed 1993 harvest of 1,697 million tons.[1] (See Figure 1.) Despite this rise, the harvest was still smaller than the 1990 bumper crop of 1,780 million tons that began the decade.[2]

The increase in 1994 was sufficient to boost output per person to 311 kilograms, up from 305 kilograms the year before, a gain of 2 percent.[3] (See Figure 2.) Compared with the 1984 historical high of 346 kilograms per person, however, the latest harvest was down 10 percent, a fall of 1 percent annually over the last decade.[4]

Thus far in the nineties, world grain production has shown no clear trend up or down. With grain area down slightly and yield up slightly, the two trends have essentially offset each other, leaving production static.

Of the big three grains, wheat production dropped sharply in 1994, rice was unchanged, and corn climbed dramatically.[5] (See Figure 3.) The 1994 wheat harvest, the smallest thus far during the nineties, fell in part because of the shrinking harvest in the former Soviet Union.[6] For example, in Russia, which continues to struggle in its effort to reform and modernize the farm sector, the wheat harvest has dropped by nearly one third since 1990—from 50 million tons to 35 million.[7]

In contrast, agriculture in Central Europe has been recovering from the disruptions associated with economic reforms in each of the last two years. The wheat harvest in 1994 of 33.5 million tons was up more than one fifth from the post-reform low point of 26.4 million tons reached in 1992.[8]

Perhaps the most dramatic decline came in Australia, where the wheat harvest dropped in half—from 17 million tons in 1993 to 8 million tons in 1994.[9] Faced with a crop failure brought on by one of this century's worst droughts, Australia was not a major factor in world wheat exports during the 1994/95 marketing year.

The world rice harvest, 90 percent of it produced in Asia, has been remarkably stable in recent years, with the last five harvests (1990–94) fluctuating narrowly between 350 million and 353 million tons.[10] This static production trend is the result of a shrinkage in the rice land area of nearly 2 percent since 1990 being offset by a yield rise of roughly 2 percent.[11]

In Asia, the loss of cropland to industrialization is nullifying the efforts to boost the rice harvest. Much of the loss of rice land is occurring in China, but losses are beginning to show up in India and Indonesia as well.[12] The continuing loss of cropland to industrialization reduced China's rice harvest for the second year in a row, dropping it from 123 million tons in 1992 to 115 million tons in 1994, a drop of more than 6 percent.[13] India, meanwhile, with near-ideal growing conditions in the last two years, boosted its harvest from 72 million tons in 1992 to 77 million tons in 1994.[14]

The 1994 world corn harvest rebounded strongly from the depressed one of 1993, which suffered heavily from flood damage to the U.S. harvest. With the United States accounting for at least 40 percent of the world corn harvest, any severe setback to the U.S. crop substantially lowers the world harvest.[15] But with the 1994 U.S. harvest at an all-time record, the world corn harvest came in at 556 million tons, far exceeding the record of 533 million tons set in 1992.[16]

The global corn yield of nearly 4 tons per hectare is well above that of both wheat and rice.[17] The production of corn in 1994 moved above that of wheat, traditionally the leading grain crop, for only the second time. The first occurred in 1979, when the wheat harvest dropped while the corn harvest was surging.[18]

That the world grain harvest has not increased thus far during the first four years of the current decade is not too surprising. Both the land planted to grain and fertilizer use have fallen since 1990.[19] With water scarcity continuing to spread, and more and more irrigation water being diverted to the cities, particularly in the United States and China—the two leading food producers—the irrigated area is increasing slowly, if at all.[20]

Grain Production Rebounds

WORLD GRAIN PRODUCTION, 1950–94

YEAR	TOTAL (mill. tons)	PER CAPITA (kilograms)
1950	631	247
1955	759	273
1960	847	279
1961	822	267
1962	864	276
1963	865	270
1964	921	281
1965	917	274
1966	1,005	294
1967	1,029	295
1968	1,069	301
1969	1,078	297
1970	1,096	296
1971	1,194	316
1972	1,156	299
1973	1,272	323
1974	1,220	304
1975	1,250	306
1976	1,363	328
1977	1,337	316
1978	1,467	341
1979	1,428	326
1980	1,447	325
1981	1,499	331
1982	1,550	336
1983	1,486	317
1984	1,649	346
1985	1,664	343
1986	1,683	341
1987	1,612	321
1988	1,564	306
1989	1,685	324
1990	1,780	336
1991	1,696	315
1992	1,776	316
1993	1,697	305
1994 (prel)	1,747	311

SOURCES: USDA, *World Grain Database* (unpublished printout) (Washington, D.C.: 1991); USDA, "Production, Supply, and Demand View" (electronic database), Washington, D.C., November 1994; USDA, "World Agricultural Supply and Demand Estimates," Washington, D.C., January 1995.

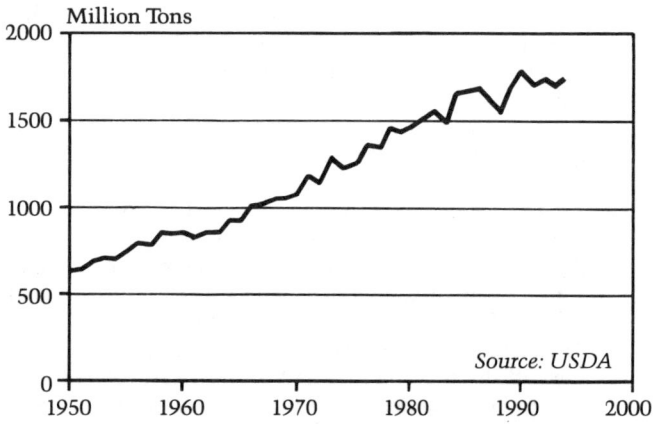

Figure 1: World Grain Production, 1950–94

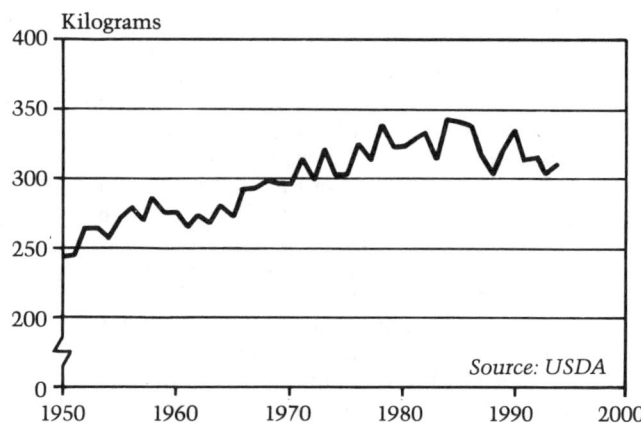

Figure 2: World Grain Production Per Person, 1950–94

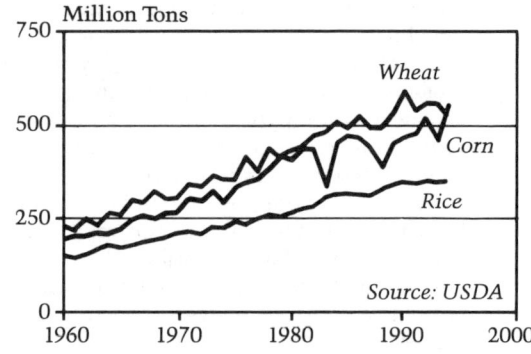

Figure 3: World Production of Wheat, Corn, and Rice, 1960–94

Soybean Production Jumps — Lester R. Brown

The 1994 world soybean harvest of 133 million tons was the largest ever, a staggering 14 percent above the previous record of 117 million tons in 1993.[1] (See Figure 1.) Almost all of the gain was due to a bumper harvest in the United States, where superb weather and improved varieties raised yields per hectare to a new high.

The dramatic rise in the 1994 world harvest led to a substantial increase in the harvest per person, boosting it to 23.6 kilograms per person, up from 20.8 in 1993.[2] (See Figure 2.) From 1978 until 1993, this figure fluctuated between 18 and 21 kilograms, making the 1994 harvest the first to break out of this narrow range. The years since 1979 contrast sharply with the preceding decade and a half, when soybean production per person doubled—climbing from 11 kilograms in 1965 to 21 kilograms.[3]

Soybean production is concentrated in just a few countries. The United States accounts for half the harvest.[4] Brazil, Argentina, and China—where the crop originated—account for another 40 percent of the total.[5] Although the consumption of soybean oil and soybean meal is widely distributed around the world, production is more geographically concentrated than for any other major crop.

Worldwide, seven commercially important oilseeds are grown for their vegetable oils and for their protein. In addition to soybeans, these include cottonseed, peanuts, sunflowers, canola, coconut oil, and palm oil. Soybeans are totally dominant, however, supplying as much oil and protein meal as the other six combined.[6]

Of the world soybean harvest, 85 percent is crushed to separate the oil from the meal.[7] The oil is used widely for cooking purposes. As incomes among low-income people have climbed, particularly in Asian countries, such as China and India, the demand for cooking oil has climbed in tandem. For this reason, many market analysts have described this year's crush of beans as an oil-driven crush as opposed to one driven by the demand for protein meal.[8]

Historically, soybeans were grown for their oil content. But in the early postwar period, as the demand for livestock products in Europe, the United States, and Japan climbed, so too did the demand for the protein meal needed to supplement grain in livestock diets.

As recently as 1964, one fifth of the world soybean harvest was consumed as food.[9] But over time this share slowly declined. Since 1984, it has been less than one tenth.[10] For the 1994 harvest, it is estimated at 8 percent.[11] Most soybeans consumed for food are eaten in East Asia as bean curd in various forms, principally as tofu.

Since mid-century, the enormous growth in world consumption of livestock products—meat, milk, cheese, yogurt, and eggs—has created a growing market for soybean meal. The world harvest, which totalled 18 million tons in 1950, increased nearly eightfold to reach the 1994 figure of 133 million tons.[12] This compares with the world fish catch, which went from 22 million to 101 million tons during the same period, a gain of 4.6-fold.[13]

Long-term growth in the soybean harvest depends on the availability of additional land on which to plant soybeans, since yields rise very slowly. With little new land available for soybean production in the United States and China, much of the growth in area since 1970 has occurred in Brazil and Argentina.[14]

Soybean carryover stocks, which had dropped to less than 18 million tons following the depressed U.S. harvest in 1993, recovered to a somewhat more secure level of 26 million tons in 1994.[15] This increase in stocks has slightly weakened prices for soybeans and soybean oil meal, although not nearly as much as might be expected given the growth in the harvest. As soybean prices have fallen somewhat, the demand for soybeans, both oil and meal, has increased.

Despite the bumper world soybean harvest in 1994, soybean oil prices were higher in early 1995 than a year earlier.[16] This raises the question of what happens to soybean oil prices if the world produces a smaller harvest in 1995.

Soybean Production Jumps

WORLD SOYBEAN PRODUCTION, 1950–94

YEAR	TOTAL (mill. tons)	PER CAPITA (kilograms)
1950	18	7
1955	21	8
1960	27	9
1961	31	10
1962	31	10
1963	32	10
1964	32	10
1965	37	11
1966	39	11
1967	41	12
1968	44	12
1969	45	12
1970	46	12
1971	48	13
1972	49	13
1973	62	16
1974	55	14
1975	65	16
1976	59	14
1977	72	17
1978	77	18
1979	93	21
1980	81	18
1981	86	19
1982	93	20
1983	83	18
1984	93	19
1985	97	20
1986	98	20
1987	103	21
1988	95	19
1989	106	21
1990	103	20
1991	106	20
1992	116	21
1993	117	21
1994 (prel)	133	24

SOURCES: USDA, *World Oilseed Database* (unpublished printout) (Washington, D.C.: 1992); USDA, "Production, Supply, and Demand View" (electronic database), Washington, D.C., November 1994; USDA, "Oilseeds: World Markets and Trade," Washington, D.C., January 1995.

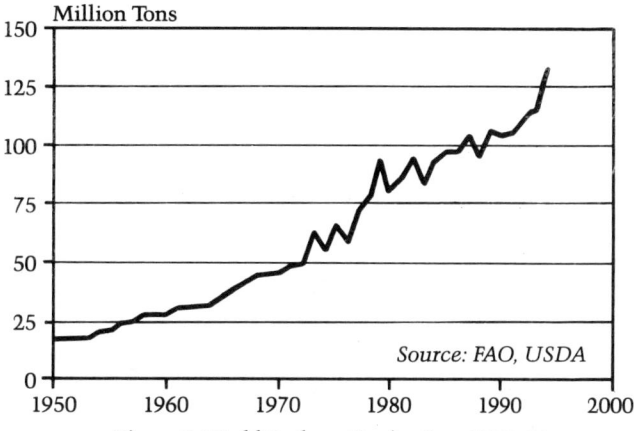

Figure 1: World Soybean Production, 1950–94

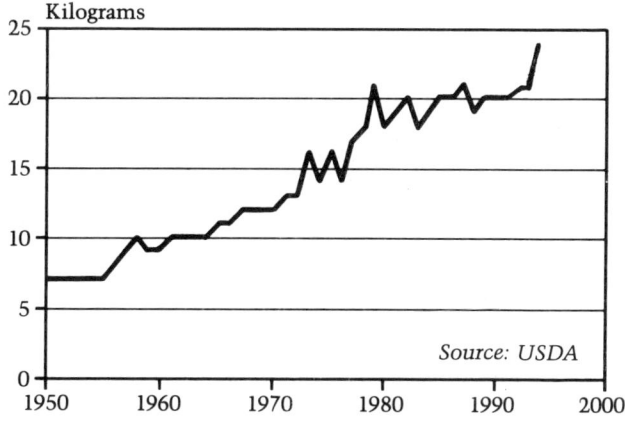

Figure 2: World Soybean Production Per Person, 1950–94

Meat Production Takes a Leap — Lester R. Brown

World meat production in 1994 totalled 184 million tons, up from 177 million tons in 1993.[1] (See Figure 1.) Almost all of this 3.4-percent gain—one of the largest on record—was accounted for by pork and poultry. The impressive gain in overall output boosted per capita production to 33 kilograms, the highest ever achieved.[2] (See Figure 2.) During the preceding six years, meat output per person fluctuated narrowly around 32 kilograms.

With pork production gaining nearly 3 percent and beef production scarcely 1 percent, pork continued to widen its lead over beef as the world's most popular meat.[3] (See Figure 3.) Mutton production was essentially unchanged. Poultry production continued to be by far the most dynamic subsector of the meat industry, increasing by more than 6 percent.[4]

The 1-percent gain in world beef production was led by a 5-percent gain in the United States, which accounts for one fourth of world beef production.[5] China, which ranks a distant fourth, registered a dramatic 16-percent gain.[6] The number of cattle in China increased from 103 million head in 1991 to 113 million head in 1994.[7] Almost as important as the increase in numbers were improvements in feeding practices and the upgrading of cattle for beef production. The latter was achieved largely through the use of artificial insemination with imported semen from high-grade beef breeds in North America and Europe.[8]

Partially offsetting these impressive gains in beef output in the United States and China were declines of 2 percent in South America and Europe, and of 5 percent in the former Soviet Union.[9]

Mutton production in 1994 was essentially unaltered from 1993. The principal changes were concentrated in the former Soviet Union and China, with declines in the former largely offsetting gains in the latter.[10]

In 1994, pork production reached 74.8 million tons, up nearly 3 percent from the previous year.[11] This growth was led by gains of more than 5 percent in China and of 3 percent in the United States.[12] Partially offsetting these were declines in Eastern Europe—led by drops of 17 percent in Poland, 9 percent in the Ukraine, and 5 percent in Russia.[13]

No country dominates production of any meat as much as China does that of pork, accounting for 43 percent of world output.[14] With nearly 400 million pigs, China has one pig for every 3 persons. The rest of the world has 340 million pigs, or one for every 13 persons.[15]

Most of the gain in world poultry output came in the United States, China, and Brazil. In the United States, which accounts for 31 percent of world poultry production, output climbed 6 percent.[16] In China, now the world's second ranking poultry producer, it was up a phenomenal 15 percent.[17] And in third ranking Brazil, output climbed by an impressive 8 percent.[18]

Early signs of economic recovery in Eastern Europe can be seen by gains of poultry production in Poland of 10 percent and in Romania of 12 percent.[19] In Russia, output dropped some 6 percent, the smallest decrease in several years.[20] Hefty gains were registered in some middle-sized countries, such as Egypt and Thailand, which posted increases of 15 and 5 percent, respectively.[21]

The longer-term trends in meat production reflect an interesting interaction of environmental and economic trends. For example, the production of beef, the leading source of meat throughout most of the postwar period, was overtaken by pork in the late seventies, opening a lead that has continued to widen since then.[22] The widening of the gap has been particularly impressive since 1990, when beef production levelled off.[23]

Production of beef, along with that of mutton, is constrained by the lack of rangeland. Once farmers and ranchers are forced to turn to grain for additional production of beef, the more efficient converters of grain, such as pigs and chickens, gain an advantage.

If grain prices rise in the years ahead, as now seems likely, poultry and pork will gain an even greater advantage over beef. Quite soon, possibly as early as 1997, poultry will also overtake beef production, moving into second place behind pork.

Meat Production Takes a Leap

WORLD MEAT PRODUCTION, 1950–94

YEAR	TOTAL (mill. tons)	PER CAPITA (kilograms)
1950	44	17.2
1955	58	20.7
1960	64	21.0
1961	66	21.6
1962	69	22.0
1963	74	23.0
1964	76	23.3
1965	81	24.2
1966	84	24.5
1967	86	24.5
1968	88	24.8
1969	92	25.5
1970	97	26.2
1971	101	26.7
1972	106	27.4
1973	104	26.8
1974	107	26.6
1975	109	26.7
1976	112	26.9
1977	117	27.6
1978	121	28.2
1979	126	28.8
1980	130	29.1
1981	132	29.2
1982	134	29.0
1983	138	29.4
1984	142	29.7
1985	146	30.1
1986	152	30.8
1987	157	31.2
1988	164	32.1
1989	166	31.9
1990	171	32.4
1991	173	32.1
1992	175	31.9
1993	177	31.9
1994 (prel)	184	32.7

SOURCES: FAO, *1948–1985 World Crop and Livestock Statistics* (Rome: 1987); FAO, *FAO Production Yearbooks 1988–1991*; USDA, FAS, *Livestock and Poultry: World Markets and Trade*, Washington, D.C., October 1994.

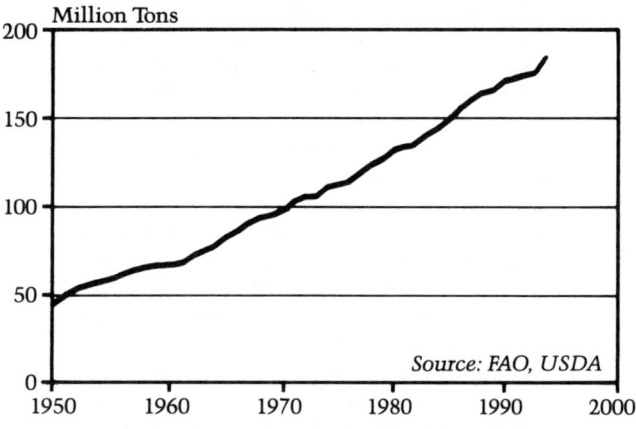

Figure 1: World Meat Production, 1950–94

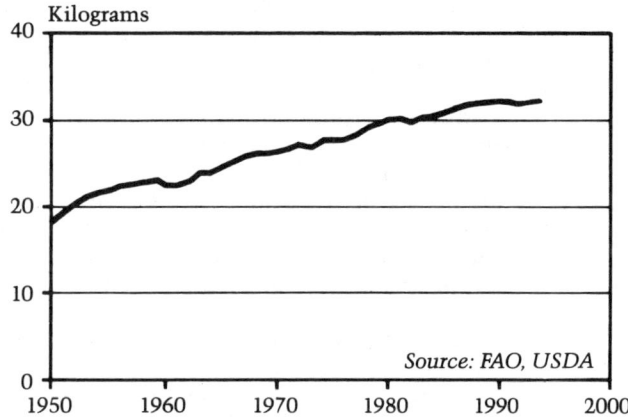

Figure 2: World Meat Production Per Person, 1950–94

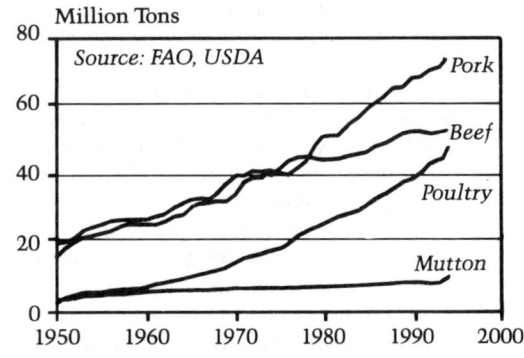

Figure 3: World Meat Production by Type, 1950–94

Vital Signs 1995   31

Aquaculture Boosts Fish Catch — Anne E. Platt

In 1994, total fish catch was an estimated 101 million tons, matching the previous year's catch.[1] (See Figure 1.) But steady population growth lowered the amount of fish available per person to an estimated 18.0 kilograms in 1994, down from a peak of 19.4 kilograms in 1988.[2] (See Figure 2.)

From 1950 through the early seventies, the total world fish catch grew by about 6 percent annually.[3] After the crash of Peruvian anchovy stocks, growth continued at 2 percent a year.[4] After years of overinvestment in fishing vessels, the sector is now overburdened with too many boats and too many fishers. Returns from fisheries across the globe are diminishing.

In the last 15 years, the fastest growing part of fish production has been in aquaculture (fish farming).[5] This now accounts for 13.9 million tons of the global fish catch, with more than four fifths of it coming from Asia.[6] China had the largest increase in 1993—2.5 million tons—and most of that was from aquaculture.[7]

For many fish farmers, shrimp have become the latest cash crop. In 1992, India received $425 million in World Bank loans for shrimp and fish farming.[8] Aquaculture provides an alternative to the marine catch, but it has some high environmental costs, such as using large amounts of water and feed.

The total marine catch has stagnated at 84 million tons, but levels of production have declined in many countries. The catch in the former Soviet Union dropped by 53 percent in five years, from 11.3 million tons in 1988 to 5.3 million in 1993.[9] Japan, the Republic of Korea, and Chile all recorded declining production for 1993. Mexico lost 18 percent of its catch in four years.[10] Peru, Thailand, and Vietnam, on the other hand, all registered increases in total catch of at least 1 million tons in 1993.[11] Peru's catch went up by 3.2 million tons between January and November 1994.[12]

Within the overall catch, there have been shifts from higher-valued to lower-valued species. The traditional dietary mainstays such as cod, haddock, and tuna have been decimated, only to be replaced with smaller, pelagic (schooling) species such as mackerel, pilchard, and pollock.[13] In 1990, the World Conservation Union classified 3.5 percent of all fish species as threatened (713 species) and 1.8 percent as endangered (368 species).[14] As overfishing continues and fish are caught at younger stages in development, stocks are unable to recover fully and the depletion of stocks continues.

The year 1994 was an absymal one in terms of international attempts to protect fisheries. The United States failed to improve and reauthorize its national fisheries law, while the European Union's Fisheries Ministers permitted France, Italy, Ireland, and the United Kingdom to continue using driftnets in violation of the 1992 international moratorium.[15]

In November, the U.N. Law of the Sea Treaty entered into force, 12 years after initial negotiations.[16] The convention is designed to promote compromise, but confusion over territorial waters, which may be extended to 12 miles, and the exclusive economic zone (EEZ), which coastal states are entitled to extend to 200 miles, is likely to cause disputes. In areas of overlapping jurisdiction, such as the South China Sea, access to fisheries has become a national security issue.[17] In the Aegean Sea, Turkey has threatened to go to war if Greece claims its 12-mile territory.[18]

The U.N. Conference on Straddling Fish Stocks and Highly Migratory Fish Stocks met in March and August to address the conservation of species such as tuna, marlin, and swordfish on the high seas and in areas adjacent to national EEZ territories.[19] Despite several sessions and heated debates, no consensus was achieved in 1994.

The increasing number of conflicts between fishers and the growing demand for fish supplies guarantee economic devastation for those whose livelihoods and nutrition depend on fisheries. In June, delegates to the International Collective in Support of Fishworkers representing 30 countries met in the Philippines and called for a complete ban on bottom trawling in tropical waters, areas dominated by small-scale fishers.[20]

Only with effective long-term planning, short-term cutbacks, and a frank discussion of social and economic trade-offs will fisheries continue to be an important source of food and jobs into the twenty-first century.

Aquaculture Boosts Fish Catch

WORLD FISH CATCH, 1950–94

YEAR	TOTAL (mill. tons)	PER CAPITA (kilograms)
1950	22	8.6
1955	29	10.4
1960	38	12.5
1961	42	13.6
1962	45	14.4
1963	48	15.0
1964	53	16.2
1965	54	16.1
1966	57	16.7
1967	60	17.2
1968	64	18.0
1969	63	17.4
1970	66	17.8
1971	66	17.5
1972	62	16.1
1973	63	16.0
1974	67	16.7
1975	66	16.2
1976	69	16.6
1977	70	16.5
1978	70	16.3
1979	71	16.2
1980	72	16.2
1981	75	16.6
1982	77	16.7
1983	77	16.4
1984	84	17.6
1985	86	17.7
1986	93	18.8
1987	94	18.7
1988	99	19.4
1989	100	19.2
1990	97	18.3
1991	97	18.0
1992	99	18.1
1993	101	18.2
1994 (prel)	101	18.0

SOURCES: FAO, *Yearbook of Fishery Statistics: Catches and Landings* (Rome: various years); 1993 and 1994, FAO, Rome, private communication, January 19, 1995.

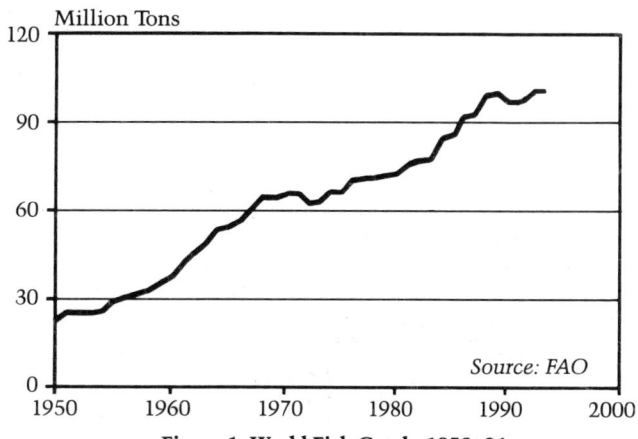

Figure 1: World Fish Catch, 1950–94

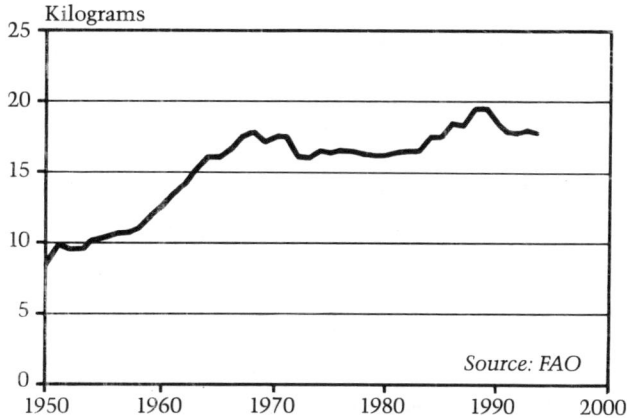

Figure 2: World Fish Catch Per Person, 1950–94

World Feedgrain Use Up Slightly
Lester R. Brown

For 1994, the world use of grain for feed was estimated at 665 million tons, up from 652 million tons in 1993.[1] (See Figure 1.) The 3-percent growth in the world economy in 1994, the fastest thus far during the nineties, strengthened the demand for livestock products, boosting the use of grain for feed.[2]

The historical rise in the per capita use of grain for feed has been reversed in recent years. (See Figure 2.) After climbing by nearly one third between 1960 and its all-time high in 1986, it has declined by more than one tenth during the eight years since then.[3]

With 665 million tons of grain used for feed in 1994 out of a total world consumption of 1.76 billion tons, the feed share came to nearly 38 percent.[4] For the last seven years, this figure has fluctuated narrowly between 37 and 39 percent. The consumption of grain for food is driven primarily by population growth, while that for feed is largely driven by rising affluence. The unchanging share of grain used for feed in recent years means that growth in the use of grain for food and for feed are increasing at the same rate.

Historically, the share of grain used for food increased from mid-century until the early seventies, when it reached an all-time high of 41 percent before starting to edge downward.[5] The reversal after 1972 coincides with a decelerating rate of world economic growth since then.[6]

In China, the world's largest grain consumer, the share of grain used for feed has climbed from 7 percent in 1978, the year economic reforms were launched, to 22 percent in 1994.[7] Most of the increase went to boost pork production, raising per capita pork production in China to levels approaching those in western industrial countries.[8]

In the United States, the feed share of grain use peaked at 81 percent in 1972.[9] Gradually declining since then, it was an estimated 67 percent in 1994.[10] In the European Community, the share for feed peaked at 62 percent in 1973, and declined to an estimated 57 percent in 1994.[11]

The feed share of grain use has also reached its highest point in the former Soviet Union, but this happened some years later than in western industrial countries. It peaked at 64 percent in 1979 and was down to 57 percent in 1994.[12]

In India, only 4.9 million tons of a harvest of 167 million tons is consumed as feed.[13] While this 3 percent is extraordinarily low, the amount has actually doubled from 2.4 million tons a decade ago.[14] Most of this rise reflects growth in the poultry and egg industry.[15]

In Latin America, the feed share of grain use is climbing steadily. In Brazil, it exceeded half for the first time in 1978 and was estimated at 60 percent for 1994.[16] In Mexico, the feed share of grain use has been climbing steadily since 1960, going from 5 percent to 36 percent in 1994.[17]

In the quantity of grain used for feed, the United States easily leads the world, at 163 million tons.[18] This compares with 98 million tons in the former Soviet Union, 85 million tons in the European Union, and 78 million tons in China.[19] If recent trends continue, China will overtake the former Soviet Union and Europe within a matter of years, moving into second place behind the United States.

Although the amount of grain used for feed is now the same as in 1990, the production of livestock products has continued to increase slowly.[20] This is due both to a shift toward breeds of livestock and poultry that convert grain into meat, milk, and eggs more efficiently and to a shift toward the more grain-efficient forms of livestock products. For example, the production of feedlot beef, which uses relatively large amounts of grain, is no longer increasing appreciably.[21] In fact, world beef production has actually declined some 4 percent since 1990.[22] Pork production has been gaining at the expense of beef.[23] And poultry, which converts grain into meat even more efficiently, has been gaining even faster.[24]

Over the longer term, the demand for livestock products is projected to rise, pulling the use of feedgrain upward.[25] So, too, is the demand of grain for food. If grain supplies tighten during the late nineties, as now seems likely, then the share of grain used for feed may well decline further.

World Feedgrain Use Up Slightly

WORLD GRAIN USE AND SHARE FED TO LIVESTOCK, 1960–94

YEAR	TOTAL GRAIN USE (mill. tons)	GRAIN USED FOR FEED (mill. tons)	SHARE (percent)
1960	820	294	36
1961	821	294	36
1962	843	295	35
1963	852	292	34
1964	905	315	35
1965	940	348	37
1966	958	361	38
1967	991	376	38
1968	1,022	397	39
1969	1,079	422	39
1970	1,113	432	39
1971	1,153	467	41
1972	1,178	483	41
1973	1,241	496	40
1974	1,196	453	38
1975	1,216	459	38
1976	1,283	488	38
1977	1,321	511	39
1978	1,396	556	40
1979	1,423	571	40
1980	1,456	560	38
1981	1,461	574	39
1982	1,484	592	40
1983	1,519	583	38
1984	1,569	610	39
1985	1,576	620	39
1986	1,633	652	40
1987	1,652	661	40
1988	1,637	627	38
1989	1,683	649	39
1990	1,719	666	39
1991	1,721	657	38
1992	1,731	652	38
1993	1,749	652	37
1994 (prel)	1,767	665	38

SOURCES: USDA, "Production, Supply, and Demand View" (electronic database), Washington, D.C., November 1994; USDA, "World Agricultural Supply and Demand Estimates," Washington, D.C., January 1995.

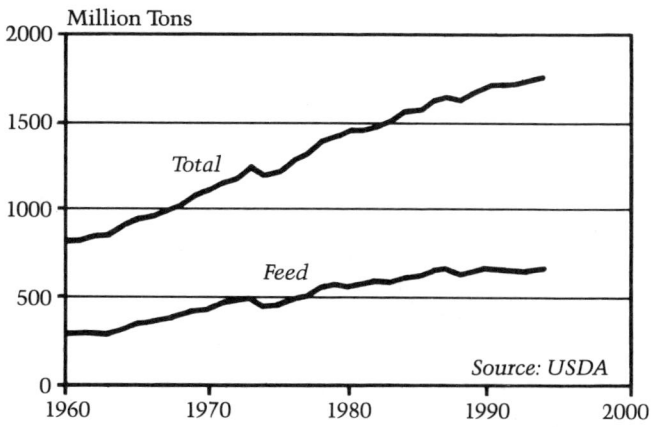

Figure 1: World Grain Use, Total and for Feed, 1960–94

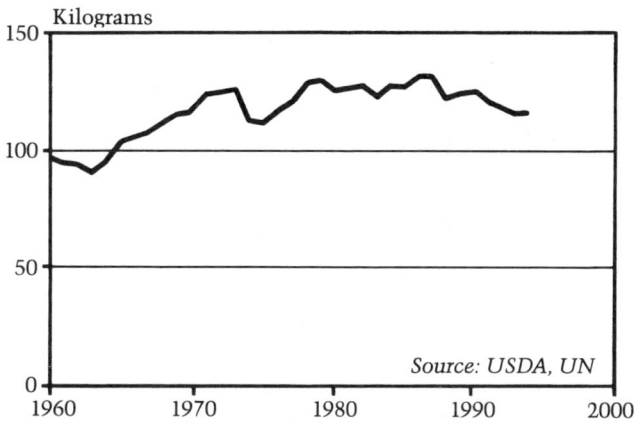

Figure 2: World Per Capita Use of Grain for Feed, 1960–94

Grain Stocks Decline Again — Lester R. Brown

World carryover stocks of grain in 1995 are projected at 298 million tons, down from 317 million tons in 1994 and from 369 million tons in 1993.[1] (See Figure 1.) This drop of nearly 20 percent during the last two years has brought stocks to the lowest level since 1975, measured in days of world consumption.[2]

Stocks dropped from 78 days of consumption in 1993 to a projected 62 days for 1995.[3] (See Figure 2.) This decline is occurring even though the United States harvested the largest grain crop on record.[4]

Carryover stocks of grain, the amount in the bins when the new harvest begins, are a key measure of world food security. For part of humanity, the ago-old challenge of making it to the next harvest remains a central preoccupation.

World wheat stocks are expected to be at their lowest level in 20 years, down close to that in the early seventies, when wheat prices doubled.[5] With area and yield both down in 1994, production dropped from 559 million tons to 527 million.[6] The resulting higher price for wheat is reducing consumption to 553 million tons, but this is still exceeding production by a wide margin.[7]

With rice, world consumption exceeded production for the fourth consecutive year. The result was another decline in stocks, bringing them to the lowest level in 20 years.[8] Since 1990, the world rice area has shrunk by close to 2 percent while the yield has risen by roughly the same amount.[9] The result is a standstill in production. With production not increasing and consumption continuing to rise, stocks are being drawn down.

For coarse grains, dominated by corn, stocks are expected to recover slightly in 1995, based on the record U.S. harvest.[10] Compared with wheat and rice, where yields have gained little during the nineties, corn yields are continuing to rise.

The world corn harvest in 1994 totalled 556 million tons, up sharply from the unusually low 1993 harvest of 467 million tons and well above the previous record of 533 million tons in 1992.[11] The record U.S. corn harvest contrasted sharply with the flood-depressed harvest of 1993.[12]

Normally a bumper world grain harvest like that of 1994 would lead to a dramatic rebuilding of stocks, but with consumption up by nearly 14 percent since 1990, stock rebuilding is limited.[13] Measured in days of consumption, stocks have been lower in only three years of the last three decades.

As a result of the record U.S. corn harvest that depressed both U.S. and world prices in the fall of 1994, the U.S. Department of Agriculture asked farmers to set aside 7.5 percent of their corn land in 1995.[14] For farmers to be eligible for price supports, they must hold this share of their corn land out of production. This contrasts with wheat and the other grains, where there are no commodity program restrictions on area planted for the 1995 crop.

In looking ahead, the world is facing continuing steady growth in grain demand, assuming no dramatic rise in grain prices. Demand is being driven by the addition of nearly 90 million people per year and by a recovering world economy.[15]

With carryover stocks at such a low level, the world grain market is delicately balanced, a nervous market. Any news of weather-induced decline in output in a major grain-producing region of the world can send prices climbing. Similarly, any unanticipated import demand for grain in a large country can also push prices upward.

The key question for world political leaders is whether grain stocks can easily be rebuilt. With more and more governments reducing or eliminating fertilizer and irrigation subsidies and reducing price supports that are well above the world market, inefficient production is being reduced or, in some cases, eliminated.

When world grain carryover stocks dropped to 56 days of consumption in 1973, grain prices doubled.[16] Once stocks drop below 60 days of consumption, the likelihood of disruptive grain price rises increases rather dramatically.

Grain Stocks Decline Again

WORLD GRAIN CARRYOVER STOCKS, 1963–95[1]

YEAR	STOCKS (mill. tons)	(days use)
1963	190	82
1964	193	83
1965	194	78
1966	159	62
1967	189	72
1968	213	78
1969	244	87
1970	228	77
1971	193	63
1972	217	69
1973	180	56
1974	192	56
1975	200	61
1976	220	66
1977	280	80
1978	279	77
1979	328	86
1980	315	81
1981	288	72
1982	308	77
1983	357	88
1984	304	73
1985	366	85
1986	435	101
1987	465	104
1988	410	91
1989	319	71
1990	304	66
1991	346	73
1992	323	69
1993	369	78
1994	317	66
1995 (est.)	298	62

[1] Data are for year when new harvest begins.
SOURCES: USDA, *Grain: World Market and Trade*, Washington, D.C., January 1995; USDA, "Production, Supply, and Demand View" (electronic database), Washington, D.C., November 1994.

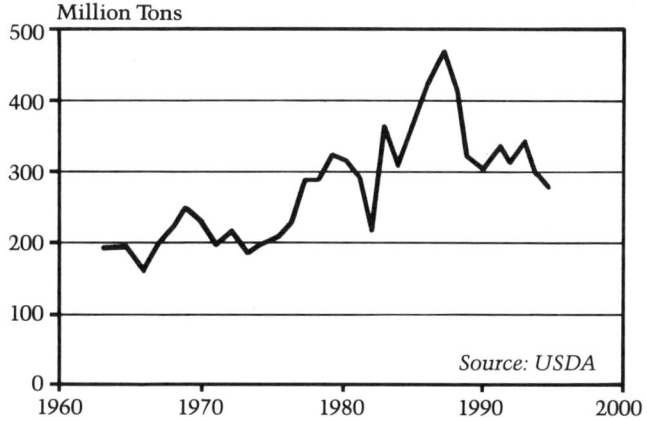

Figure 1: World Grain Carryover Stocks, 1963–95

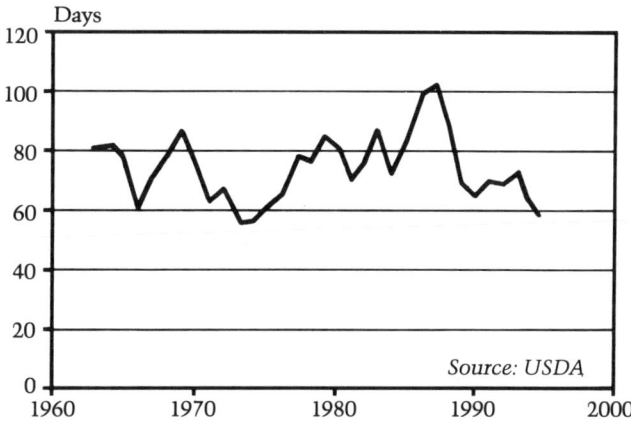

Figure 2: World Grain Carryover Stocks as Days of Consumption, 1963–95

Agricultural Resource Trends

Fertilizer Use Continues Dropping — Lester R. Brown

The world's farmers used 121 million tons of fertilizer in 1994, down from 126 million tons in 1993.[1] (See Figure 1.) This was the fifth consecutive annual decline since the historical peak of 146 million tons in 1989.[2]

Several factors have contributed to this unanticipated decline. After decades of finding that increased fertilizer use led to higher yields, farmers had assumed that this trend would continue indefinitely. Unfortunately, in many countries available crop varieties began to approach the agronomic limits of the response to fertilizer.

Simply put, scientists were no longer able to breed varieties that would respond to ever heavier applications of fertilizer. As farmers began to realize that the relationship between increased fertilizer use and higher yields was no longer holding, they stopped using more. In cases where fertilizer use at the margin had become unprofitable, they actually reduced use.[3]

Also, within the last several years a number of major food-producing countries, such as the Soviet Union, India, and China, have reduced or eliminated fertilizer subsidies. In the former Soviet Union, the agricultural reforms that led to a shift to world market prices for fertilizer had the effect of dramatically boosting fertilizer prices.[4] The August 1992 decision by the government of India to withdraw subsidies on both potash and phosphate fertilizer helped check the growth in consumption in that country.[5]

In China, which now leads the world in fertilizer use, farmers increased their reliance on fertilizer from 28.6 million tons in 1993 to 29.2 million tons in 1994.[6] (See Figure 2.) This gain was quite modest compared with the huge jumps in consumption that occurred during the decade immediately following agricultural reforms in 1978.[7]

Consumption in the United States in 1994 was up slightly, from 18.3 million tons in 1993 to 19.0 million tons in 1994.[8] (See Figure 3.) This level of fertilizer use is still one tenth below that during the early eighties.[9]

India, too, boosted consumption—from 12.2 million tons in 1993 to 12.8 million in 1994, a gain of 5 percent.[10] This means that India has now replaced the former Soviet Union as the number three user of fertilizer. But the recent cut in subsidies has slowed the growth in fertilizer use in India, holding it between 12 million and 13 million tons in each of the last five years.[11]

Fertilizer use in the former Soviet Union declined again in 1994, the seventh consecutive year of decline.[12] During the last two years, however, the drop has been rather modest compared with 1988–92. From the peak use of 27.4 million tons in 1987 to the 12.4 million tons of 1994, Soviet fertilizer use has fallen by more than half.[13]

In Western Europe, a combination of lower commodity prices and the prospect of reduced European Union support of agricultural prices as the result of global trade negotiations led to a decline in fertilizer use in 1994.[14] Without much higher world grain prices, there does not seem to be any reason to expect a substantial recovery in fertilizer use within Europe in the years immediately ahead.

Eastern Europe has experienced a decline in fertilizer use during the last three years similar to that in Western Europe—and for some of the same reasons.[15] A combination of depressed commodity prices, uncertain land tenure, and the shift from a system of allocated fertilizer to one where fertilizer is available only on the market have all contributed to the drop.

Among the exceptions to the overall global trend of stagnant or declining fertilizer use during the nineties is Brazil, where usage has continued to grow several percent a year.[16] It is expected that this trend will continue for the foreseeable future, particularly as marginal land is brought under cultivation.

It seems likely that the global decline in fertilizer use of the last five years is about to end. The combination of economic recovery in several East European countries, low world grain stocks, and somewhat higher prices for wheat and rice may have set the stage for the restoration of a slow but steady gain in fertilizer use. It will, however, take many years for fertilizer use to regain the historical high of 1989.

Fertilizer Use Continues Dropping

WORLD FERTILIZER USE, 1950–94

YEAR	TOTAL (mill. tons)	PER CAPITA (kilograms)
1950	14	5.5
1955	18	6.5
1960	27	8.9
1961	28	9.1
1962	31	9.9
1963	34	10.6
1964	37	11.3
1965	40	12.0
1966	45	13.2
1967	51	14.6
1968	56	15.8
1969	60	16.5
1970	66	17.8
1971	69	18.2
1972	73	18.9
1973	79	20.1
1974	85	21.2
1975	82	20.1
1976	90	21.6
1977	95	22.5
1978	100	23.2
1979	111	25.3
1980	112	25.1
1981	117	25.8
1982	115	25.0
1983	115	24.5
1984	126	26.4
1985	131	27.0
1986	129	26.1
1987	132	26.3
1988	140	27.4
1989	146	28.0
1990	143	27.0
1991	138	25.7
1992	134	24.5
1993	126	22.7
1994 (prel)	121	21.6

SOURCES: FAO, *Fertilizer Yearbook* (Rome: various years); International Fertilizer Industry Association, 62nd Annual Conference, May 9, 1994; Worldwatch Institute.

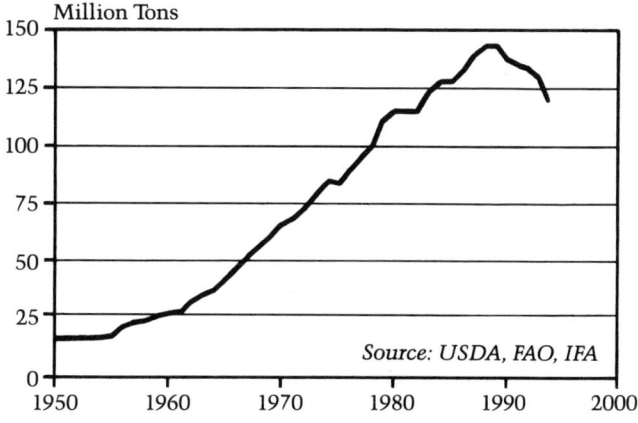

Figure 1: World Fertilizer Use, 1950–94

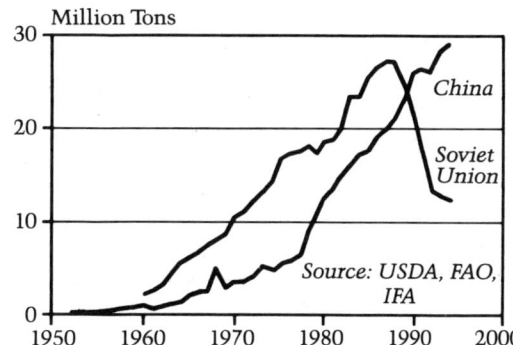

Figure 2: Fertilizer Use in China and the Soviet Union, 1950–94

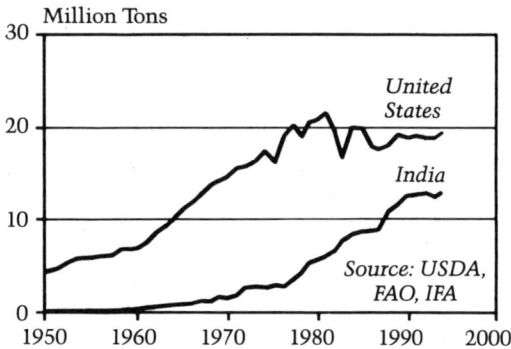

Figure 3: Fertilizer Use in the United States and India, 1950–94

Grain Yield Remains Steady

Lester R. Brown

World grain yield in 1994 averaged 2.60 tons per hectare, passing the previous record set in 1992.[1] (See Figure 1.) Although up from the 2.50 tons per hectare of 1993, when the world harvest was depressed by severe flooding in the U.S. Corn Belt, the bountiful 1994 yield per hectare was just 2 percent above the 2.54 tons per hectare with which the decade began in 1990.[2]

With each passing year, accumulating evidence indicates that the rapid sustained rise in land productivity that characterized the period from mid-century onward may be coming to an end. This slowdown is evident when the worldwide data are disaggregated by cereal and by country.

An analysis of global trends for each of the three major cereals—wheat, rice, and corn—shows that since 1990, neither wheat nor rice yields have shown a strong upward trend.[3] Only corn still shows a substantial rise in yield per hectare.[4]

Of the three cereals, corn has the highest world average yield, coming in at roughly 4 tons per hectare in recent years, compared with 2.5 tons for wheat.[5] (See Figure 2.) Corn's 60-percent advantage over wheat is not so much because of an inherently better yield potential, but rather because most of the world's wheat is produced on semiarid land, such as the Great Plains of the United States and Canada.[6] Where wheat is well watered, as in the United Kingdom and France, yields average close to 8 tons per hectare, essentially the same as corn in the United States.[7]

With the global average of 2.4 tons per hectare in recent years, rice yields are almost exactly the same as wheat.[8] (See Figure 3.) But since the great bulk of the world's rice is grown on irrigated land, this means it is inherently less productive than either wheat or corn. A new type of rice being worked on at the International Rice Research Institute in the Philippines, which should be ready for widespread commercial use around the end of this decade, has the potential to raise yields by an estimated 20–25 percent.[9] If this increase materializes, it will bring the inherent yield potential of rice much closer to that of wheat.

An analysis of trends by country shows the slowdown in grain yields is most pronounced in agriculturally advanced countries. In Japan, for example, there have been no gains at all in rice yields during the last decade.[10] Since Japan was the first country to initiate a sustained rise in yield, beginning a century ago, it is not surprising that it now has difficulty sustaining this trend. Rice yields in China, by far the largest producer of rice, are now approaching those in Japan.[11]

In the United States, a technological leader in world agriculture, the slowdown in grain yields has become increasingly evident during the last two decades. During the fifties and sixties, average grain yields increased at an extraordinary rate of nearly 4 percent a year.[12] During the seventies, this slowed to roughly 2 percent, and in the eighties, to 1 percent.[13]

Growth in the use of irrigation water and fertilizer—the two inputs that account for most of the gain in world cropland productivity—has slowed dramatically or actually declined.[14]

The growth in world irrigated area during the third quarter of this century was extraordinarily rapid, averaging some 3 percent a year.[15] After 1978, however, growth slowed as the number of appropriate sites for new dams dwindled and as the pumping from underground sources in many areas approached or exceeded the sustainable yield of aquifers.[16] In effect, the growth of scarcely 1 percent per person in world irrigated area since 1978 suggests that the supply of irrigation water per person is also declining.[17]

The use of fertilizer, which has been the key to raising land productivity since mid-century, has been declining since 1989. In effect, two natural limits—the sustainable water yield of aquifers and the physiological limits on the amount of fertilizer that existing crop varieties can use—are both beginning to affect the rise in land productivity.

Grain Yield Remains Steady

WORLD GRAIN YIELD PER HECTARE, 1950–94

YEAR	YIELD (tons)
1950	1.06
1955	1.18
1960	1.28
1961	1.31
1962	1.26
1963	1.31
1964	1.40
1965	1.40
1966	1.52
1967	1.54
1968	1.59
1969	1.60
1970	1.65
1971	1.77
1972	1.74
1973	1.84
1974	1.76
1975	1.76
1976	1.90
1977	1.87
1978	2.05
1979	2.00
1980	2.00
1981	2.04
1982	2.16
1983	2.10
1984	2.31
1985	2.32
1986	2.38
1987	2.36
1988	2.28
1989	2.43
1990	2.54
1991	2.46
1992	2.58
1993	2.50
1994 (prel)	2.60

SOURCES: USDA, "Production, Supply, and Demand View" (electronic database), Washington, D.C., November 1994; USDA, *World Grain Database* (unpublished printout) (Washington, D.C.: 1992); USDA, "World Agricultural Supply and Demand Estimates," Washington, D.C., January 1995.

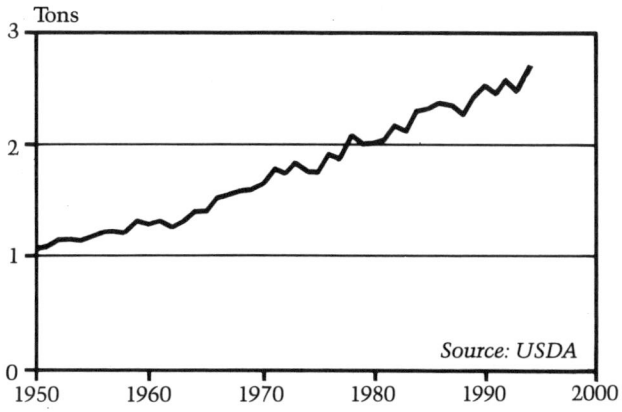

Figure 1: World Grain Yield Per Hectare, 1950–94

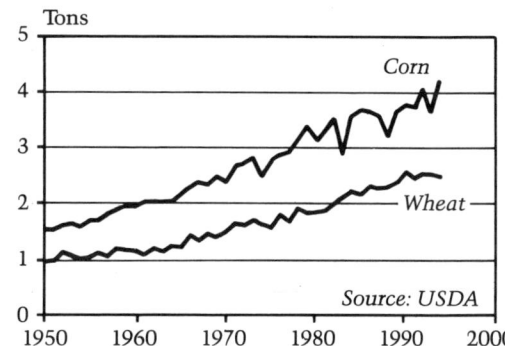

Figure 2: World Wheat and Corn Yield Per Hectare, 1950–94

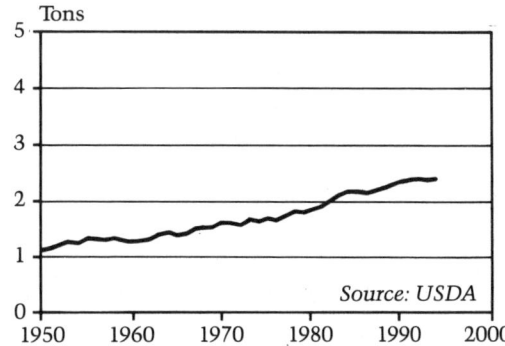

Figure 3: World Rice Yield Per Hectare, 1950–94

Energy Trends

Oil Production Up

Christopher Flavin

World oil production rose 1.1 percent in 1994, to 2,953 million tons (59.0 million barrels per day), according to preliminary estimates—the first significant increase in five years.[1] (See Figure 1.) This still leaves output well short of the record 3,122 million tons recorded in 1979.[2]

The largest single increase in oil production in 1994 was in Western Europe, where output was up 18 percent, reaching record levels of more than 5 million barrels a day.[3] Most of the increased production came from North Sea producers Norway and the United Kingdom.[4]

Growth in oil production during the past two years was driven by rapid increases in demand in North America and Asia, due to increased car and truck traffic. Additional growth occurred in Latin America and Europe. Still, excess production capacity was ample to keep a lid on world oil prices, which at roughly $16 per barrel were (in inflation-adjusted terms) lower than at any time since 1973.[5] (See Figure 2.)

Preliminary figures show U.S. oil use up 3.3 percent in 1994, the largest increase since 1988, and growing much faster than the 1-percent rise recorded in 1993.[6] U.S. oil production meanwhile fell 3 percent in 1994, to 6.6 million barrels a day.[7] U.S. consumers relied on more than 7 million barrels of imports each day to meet 52 percent of their crude oil needs in 1994—both of which are records.[8]

Oil use continued to boom in Asia during the past two years. It was up 4 percent for the region as a whole in 1993, but in individual countries, the growth was far faster: up 8.1 percent in Indonesia, 8.6 percent in South Korea, 11.1 percent in China, and 13.8 percent in Thailand.[9] In 1993 and 1994, China became a net importer for the first time since the seventies.[10] Calculations show that if China were to use as much oil per person as Japan now does, it would absorb nearly 60 million barrels per day.[11]

In 1994, oil production in the former Soviet Union was down by about 10 percent, but by late in the year, production was levelling off for the first time since it began to collapse in the late eighties.[12] If this region's output had not dropped nearly 50 percent since 1988, world oil production in 1994 would have been 5 million barrels a day higher—above the record reached in 1979.[13]

The apparent stabilization of oil markets in this region suggests that global oil production and use will rise by as much as 2 percent annually in the next few years, reaching a new record as early as 1997.

Although the oil market still had 3–4 million barrels per day of unused production capacity in 1994, a growing world economy could absorb all that and more. Indeed, with net oil exports outside the Middle East likely to be about flat in the next few years, the world may need 5–8 million additional barrels of Middle Eastern oil each day by 2000.[14]

The prospects for meeting this demand are uncertain. Some 2 million barrels a day will be available once Iraq returns fully to the world market, and several other Persian Gulf countries could increase production somewhat.[15] But even the abundant oil fields of the Middle East are beginning to reach their limits. Production costs are rising, and future increases in capacity are likely to be modest and expensive.[16]

Saudi Arabia, which has the greatest potential to raise output, is now spending $2 billion a year just to maintain its current daily capacity of 10 million barrels.[17] A 1993 study by the Center for Global Energy Studies, headed by former Saudi oil minister Sheik Yamani, suggests that Saudi Arabia may never supply the 12–15 million barrels of oil a day that many politicians and industrialists seem to be counting on.[18]

If an all-out effort to increase Middle Eastern production is needed just to keep up with demand, this leaves little room for unexpected political turmoil. Saudi Arabia, the traditional "swing" producer, may soon have the production accelerator all the way to the floor—whether it wants to or not.

The last time that was needed, in 1979, a modest disruption in Iran's oil flow resulted in a near tripling of prices.[19] Concern is heightened by the fact that the major oil-producing countries are marked by large wealth disparities, high rates of population growth, and burgeoning financial problems.

Oil Production Up

WORLD OIL PRODUCTION, 1950–94

YEAR	WORLD (mill. tons)
1950	518
1955	767
1960	1,049
1961	1,115
1962	1,210
1963	1,300
1964	1,408
1965	1,509
1966	1,638
1967	1,743
1968	1,937
1969	2,050
1970	2,281
1971	2,410
1972	2,547
1973	2,779
1974	2,803
1975	2,659
1976	2,901
1977	2,988
1978	3,023
1979	3,122
1980	2,976
1981	2,779
1982	2,644
1983	2,619
1984	2,701
1985	2,659
1986	2,774
1987	2,754
1988	2,881
1989	2,918
1990	2,963
1991	2,928
1992	2,936
1993	2,922
1994 (prel)	2,953

SOURCES: API, *Basic Petroleum Data Book* (Washington, D.C.: 1993); Worldwatch estimates based on BP and *Oil & Gas Journal*.

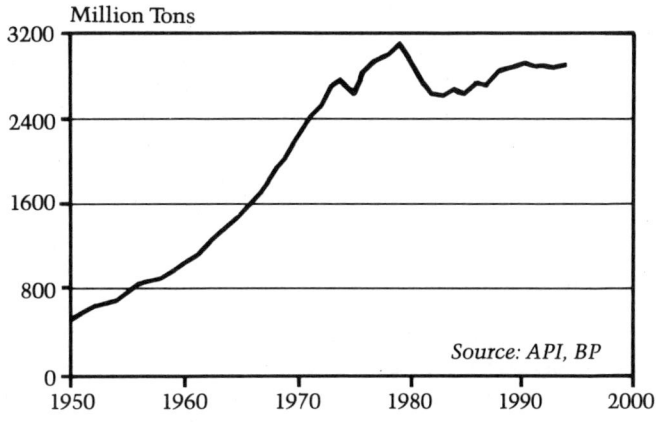

Figure 1: World Oil Production, 1950–94

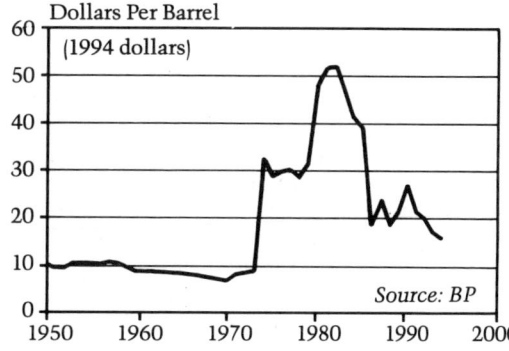

Figure 2: Price of Oil, 1950–94

Vital Signs 1995

Natural Gas Production Stalls — Christopher Flavin

World production of natural gas rose just 0.3 percent in 1994, according to preliminary estimates.[1] (See Figure 1.) The global figure was depressed, however, by a 6-percent decline in the former Soviet Union in 1994—in stark contrast to the major increases in other regions.[2] Excluding that region, global gas production and use are on a 4-percent growth path—about twice the underlying rate of growth in oil.[3]

The sharp decline in Russian gas production in 1994 was driven by falling demand fueled by a 12-percent decline in the Russian economy.[4] As much as 40 percent of the gas provided in 1994 by Gasprom, the Russian gas monopoly, was never paid for.[5] Gasprom is now cutting off customers who do not pay—in Ukraine and other Central European countries as well as Russia.[6] This is driving production down, a trend that may continue in 1995.

Still, natural gas exploration and infrastructure projects are proceeding rapidly in Siberia as well as in Kazakhstan and Turkmenistan, which have enormous resources.[7] The problem for these nations is to get their gas to market, which requires crossing seas, mountain ranges, and the politically unstable Middle East and Caucasus regions. In 1994, a major pipeline was announced that will carry gas from Turkmenistan across Iran to the booming Turkish market.[8] One study estimates that production in the former Soviet Union could be nearly double the 1994 level by 2010.[9]

An even bigger boom is under way in the Far East, where huge resources have been identified, many of them offshore. One project, in Indonesian waters, will build a gas gathering and liquefaction plant on a small island in order to ship liquefied methane to other Asian countries.[10] Farther north, a major offshore field will be tapped near the Philippines, and a pipeline will carry the fuel to the fast-growing Manila region.[11] This will be the first time natural gas has been used in the Philippines.

Although China is known for its coal, its natural gas potential is huge. The Chinese government neglected this in the past, but has recently opened several areas to exploration, and is building long pipelines and a distribution system in Beijing.[12] If China were to exploit its reserves at the same rate that the United States does, it could meet all current energy needs, or half the projected needs of 2010.[13] The International Energy Agency said in a 1994 report that China is on the verge of a gas boom.[14]

Production is expanding even on the continent where natural gas reserves have been most heavily exploited: North America.[15] Technology has lowered the cost of finding new gas, tripling the yield per effort in the past decade, according to one estimate.[16] Recent U.S. reserve additions were larger than expected, and estimates of the total resource base continue to grow.[17]

In both Europe and the United States, gas prices have generally followed a slow downward trend in the past few years, staying below the declining price of oil.[18] (See Figure 2.) U.S. prices were up in 1993 and 1994, but fell sharply at the end of the year—to the equivalent of less than $11 per barrel of oil, despite a 3-percent rise in demand.[19] Even so, U.S. gas production is up 18 percent since 1986, while oil output is down 20 percent.[20]

Low and stable prices suggest that gas supplies in North America and elsewhere are abundant. Estimating the ultimate scale of global resources is still difficult, but better information is becoming available. The U.S. Geological Survey has counted 12,000 exajoules of "conventional resources" that are economically accessible using today's technologies.[21]

This represents 145 years of supply at the current level of world production. But some geologists believe that even these figures understate the resource by a factor of three or more, since they exclude potential gas in many unexplored areas, as well as much of the "tight" gas, "deep" gas, and "coalbed" gas that may exist in many parts of the world.[22]

Major production increases appear near certain in the coming years, driven in part by the fuel's environmental advantages over oil and coal. At the recent underlying growth rate of 4 percent, gas production could triple over the next three decades, which appears well within reach, given current resource estimates. As OPEC Secretary-General Subroto said in 1993, "The writing is on the wall. Gas will replace oil."[23] Indeed, current trends suggest that gas will be number one by 2010.

Natural Gas Production Stalls

WORLD NATURAL GAS PRODUCTION, 1950–94[1]

YEAR	PRODUCTION (mill. tons of oil equivalent)
1950	180
1955	287
1960	442
1961	480
1962	523
1963	550
1964	598
1965	640
1966	690
1967	743
1968	820
1969	895
1970	989
1971	1,066
1972	1,127
1973	1,195
1974	1,211
1975	1,214
1976	1,262
1977	1,295
1978	1,332
1979	1,423
1980	1,459
1981	1,502
1982	1,489
1983	1,497
1984	1,634
1985	1,691
1986	1,728
1987	1,812
1988	1,900
1989	1,964
1990	2,005
1991	2,064
1992	2,081
1993	2,122
1994 (prel)	2,128

[1] Includes natural gas liquids production.
SOURCES: U.S. Department of Energy, Energy Information Agency, *Annual Energy Review 1992* (electronic database); Worldwatch estimates based on DOE, API, UN, and government sources.

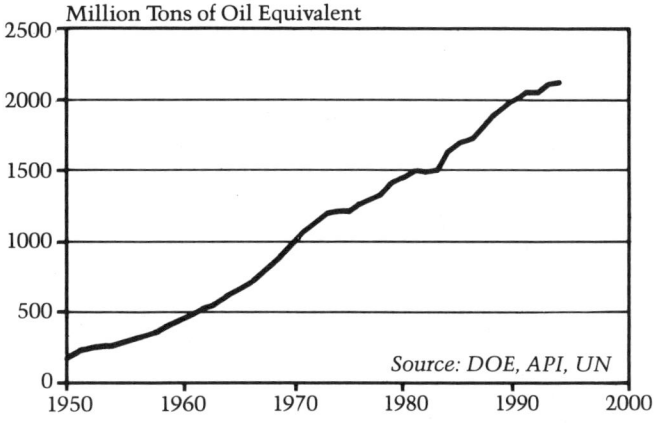

Figure 1: World Natural Gas Production, 1950–94

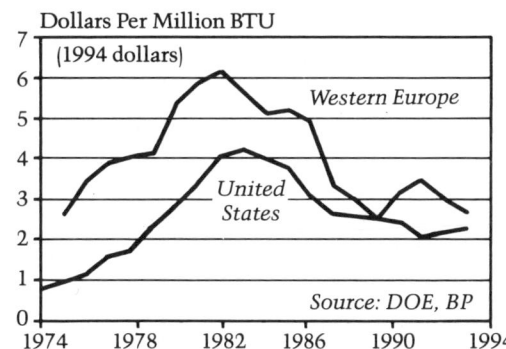

Figure 2: Price of Natural Gas in the United States and Western Europe, 1974–93

Coal Use Remains Flat

Nicholas Lenssen

The use of coal worldwide remained flat in 1994 for the sixth consecutive year, according to preliminary estimates, and remains 5 percent below the 1989 peak. (See Figure 1.)[1] There are distinct, regional variations, with coal use rising in some areas, falling in others, and remaining flat elsewhere in recent years. (See Figure 2.)[2] However, it is clear that the steady global growth in coal use that occurred during the previous four decades has come to an end.

Wide-ranging differences can be found in industrial countries. Whereas coal consumption in the United States has risen more than 5 percent since 1989, its use has slipped by 18 percent in the European Union during the same period.[3]

The United Kingdom has led the European fall, with a 24-percent decline, as the government continued pulling subsidies from the industry and as electricity producers substituted North Sea natural gas for coal.[4] Likewise, coal use has fallen in recent years in France, Italy, the Netherlands, and Spain. In Germany, the country's high court ruled in December that the government's controversial means of subsidizing domestic coal production—through an 8.5-percent tax on electricity—was unconstitutional. That subsidy is likely to be withdrawn over the next decade, which will tend to reduce coal use in Germany.[5]

Coal use is still falling rapidly in the former Eastern bloc countries, with an additional 10-percent decline in 1994, bringing the total drop since 1987 to 38 percent.[6] The collapse has come as uneconomical state industries have shut down, and as governments have discontinued subsidies. In Russia, outstanding debts to the coal industry came to some $320 million by early 1995, leaving coal miners without paychecks and on the verge of massive strikes.[7]

The use of coal continues to grow rapidly in developing countries, however, where total use has more than doubled since 1980.[8] China is now the largest coal user and its use is growing rapidly, as are India's and South Africa's.[9] Here and elsewhere in the Third World, coal is used extensively for home heating and cooking as well as to fuel factories, run railroads, and generate electricity.

Coal accounts for 76 percent of China's commercial energy supply, and government planners hope to double coal use in the next two decades.[10] But as this huge nation's experience already shows, using coal as the primary energy source for development is fraught with problems. It is expensive to develop. Seventeen percent of China's total investments were for coal-related projects in 1990.[11] Altogether, this country now spends 10 percent of its gross national product on coal production, transport, and use—a major drain on other areas of the economy.[12]

Likewise, coal extracts a heavy human and ecological toll, particularly when burned without adequate pollution control equipment, as it generates substantial amounts of sulfur dioxide, nitrogen oxides, and particulates. These create severe air pollution and cause acid rain, leading to crop and forest damage in scores of countries. In China, the area affected by acid rain has increased by 60 percent between 1985 and 1993.[13]

Coal pollution leads to eye irritations, respiratory disorders, and heart ailments. According to an extrapolation from U.S. data by Keith Florig of Resources for the Future, more than 900,000 Chinese may be dying each year as a result of pollution-related lung disease, a number likely to increase as the cumulative effect of decades of polluted air is felt.[14]

Although the way coal is mined and burned can be changed to reduce much of its environmental impact, its contribution to global warming is less amenable to a technical solution. Coal contains 80 percent more carbon per unit of energy than natural gas, and it already contributes 36 percent of the world's annual carbon emissions.[15]

Coal Use Remains Flat

World Coal Use, 1950–94

YEAR	WORLD (mill. tons of oil equivalent)
1950	884
1955	1,045
1960	1,271
1961	1,174
1962	1,199
1963	1,251
1964	1,280
1965	1,299
1966	1,321
1967	1,255
1968	1,317
1969	1,357
1970	1,359
1971	1,355
1972	1,355
1973	1,413
1974	1,434
1975	1,450
1976	1,525
1977	1,581
1978	1,615
1979	1,681
1980	1,708
1981	1,732
1982	1,751
1983	1,804
1984	1,877
1985	1,980
1986	2,001
1987	2,062
1988	2,183
1989	2,189
1990	2,109
1991	2,074
1992	2,091
1993	2,081
1994 (prel)	2,083

SOURCE: UN, *World Energy Supplies, Yearbook of World Energy Statistics,* and *Energy Statistics Yearbook* (New York: various years); 1993 and 1994 are Worldwatch estimates based on UN, BP, DOE, *Energy Economist,* and private communications and printouts.

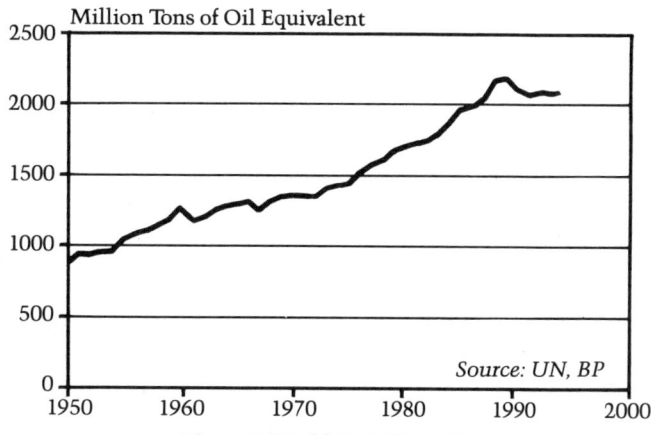

Figure 1: World Coal Use, 1950–94

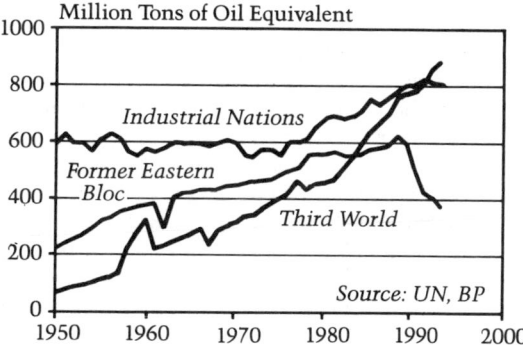

Figure 2: Coal Use in Industrial Nations, Former Eastern Bloc, and Third World, 1950–93

Nuclear Power Flat

Nicholas Lenssen

In 1994, total installed nuclear generating capacity inched up to a new high, from 337,000 megawatts to just below 340,000 megawatts, a gain of less than 1 percent.[1] (See Figure 1.) New plant openings outnumbered closures by two, yet given the dearth of new orders, worldwide nuclear capacity is still likely to peak before the turn of the century.

The small gain in global nuclear capacity in 1994 came from the completion of single units in China, Japan, South Korea, and Mexico.[2] At the same time, reactors were closed down in France and the United Kingdom, bringing to 83 the number of reactors that have been retired after an average service life of less than 17 years.[3] (See Figures 2 and 3.)

In 1994, construction started on just two new reactors, both in China.[4] Worldwide, some 40 plants (with a combined capacity of 30,000 megawatts) are under active construction, the fewest in more than a quarter-century.[5] Most are scheduled to be completed in the next few years, though delays in construction continue to plague the industry.

In the United States, where just one plant remains under construction, it has been 17 years since a nuclear reactor has been ordered, and 22 years since one was ordered and not subsequently cancelled.[6] Indeed, between 1972 and 1994, a total of 123 nuclear plants were cancelled by utilities there, representing 135,677 megawatts of generating capacity—well above the country's total current nuclear capacity (109 reactors and 99,000 megawatts).[7]

No reactors are being built in Canada, and five are being constructed in Western Europe.[8] Sweden's newly elected government has called for the closure of one reactor within the next four years.[9]

With contracts scarce in western countries, nuclear vendors there have turned to Asia and the former Eastern bloc for business. Asian contracts are still few and far between, as only South Korea has ordered a western reactor in the past five years.[10] In 1994, Thailand retreated on its plan to order as many as six reactors, while Indonesia and Taiwan continue to move slowly on orders long anticipated by vendors.[11]

Western companies have managed to sign contracts in the Czech Republic, Russia, and Slovakia to service existing reactors or build new ones in recent years.[12] Meanwhile, efforts to gain agreement from Ukraine for the closure of the two remaining reactors at Chernobyl were stymied again in 1994, as Ukrainian officials announced that they do not intend to close the units in the foreseeable future despite their earlier statements to the contrary.[13]

Surprisingly, South Korea has the most active nuclear construction program in the world, with six reactors being built.[14] Japan accounts for five additional reactors in the works, and India, another five.[15] Altogether, Asian countries account for half of all plants under construction.

India is one country that could use international assistance but has not received it for more than 20 years due to its refusal to sign the Nuclear Non-Proliferation Treaty. The country's reactors had a capacity factor of only 39 percent in 1993, far below the 60–80 percent average of most countries.[16] Meanwhile, a 130-ton concrete slab of the containment dome collapsed at a reactor under construction at Kaiga in 1994, increasing uncertainties about the safety of India's nine operating nuclear reactors.[17]

Although India has been penalized for its efforts to develop nuclear weapons, North Korea was in a sense rewarded in 1994 for just such an undertaking. Western governments, led by the United States, have promised North Korea as much as $400 million worth of fuel oil and two large western-style reactors (still capable of producing plutonium that can be used in nuclear weapons) in exchange for a pledge to curtail nuclear weapons development.[18]

In addition to proliferation concerns, the rising cost of decommissioning retired facilities continues to cloud the industry's future. The Yankee Rowe reactor in western Massachusetts, which cost $186 million (in 1993 dollars) to build in 1960, was closed in 1991.[19] To fully dismantle the plant will cost some $370 million.[20] If governments and utilities have had a difficult time justifying the cost of building and operating reactors, closing them could be an even harder sell.

Nuclear Power Flat

WORLD NET INSTALLED ELECTRICAL GENERATING CAPACITY OF NUCLEAR POWER PLANTS, 1960–94

YEAR	CAPACITY (gigawatts)
1960	0.8
1961	0.9
1962	1.8
1963	2.1
1964	3.1
1965	4.8
1966	6.2
1967	8.3
1968	9.2
1969	13.0
1970	16.0
1971	24.0
1972	32.0
1973	45.0
1974	61.0
1975	71.0
1976	85.0
1977	99.0
1978	114.0
1979	121.0
1980	135.0
1981	155.0
1982	170.0
1983	189.0
1984	219.0
1985	250.0
1986	276.0
1987	297.0
1988	311.0
1989	321.0
1990	329.0
1991	326.0
1992	328.0
1993	337.0
1994 (prel)	339.0

SOURCES: Worldwatch Institute database, compiled from the International Atomic Energy Agency and press reports.

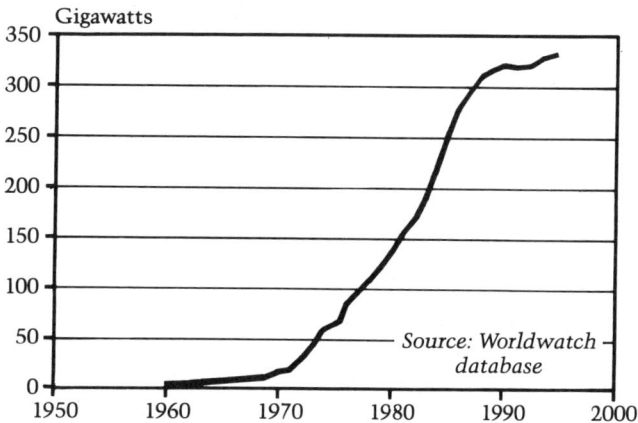

Figure 1: World Electrical Generating Capacity of Nuclear Power Plants, 1960–94

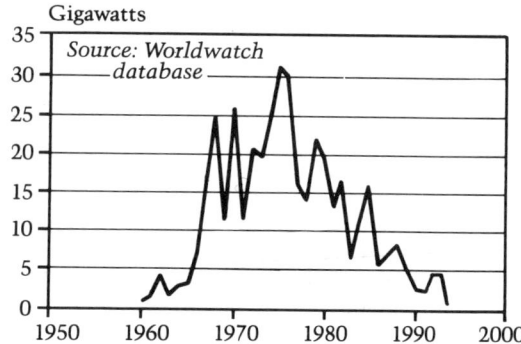

Figure 2: World Nuclear Reactor Construction Starts, 1960–94

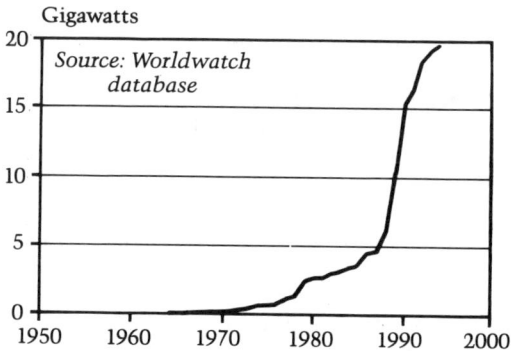

Figure 3: Cumulative Nuclear Generating Capacity Decommissioned, 1964–94

Wind Power Soars
Christopher Flavin

Global wind power generating capacity jumped 22 percent in 1994, to 3,710 megawatts, according to preliminary estimates.[1] (See Figure 1.) The net increase of 660 megawatts represents an all-time record for the wind industry. (See Figure 2.) Altogether, more than 25,000 wind turbines are now hooked up to the world's electric power systems.[2]

In 1994, the wind power industry was dominated by Germany, which by itself added about 300 megawatts of capacity, nearly half the world total.[3] Although Germany's wind industry was virtually nonexistent in 1990, it has taken off in the last three years as a result of strong government incentives at the state and federal levels.[4] Following the pattern established by Denmark in the eighties, Germany's wind turbines are located singly or in small clusters amid the farms of the north German plain, a sharp contrast to the giant wind farms pioneered in California.

About 100 megawatts of capacity were added in the rest of Europe in 1994, and several countries are poised for a takeoff like Germany's.[5] Spain has 900 megawatts of capacity being planned in the northwestern province of Galicia alone, and rapid growth is expected in 1995.[6] Greece, too, has a large wind energy potential, and recent policy changes suggest rapid development in 1995 and beyond. Altogether, wind generation in Europe is likely to pass that in North America in 1995.[7]

The United Kingdom has Europe's greatest wind energy potential, and in a major development in 1994, a U.K. power auction yielded some 500 megawatts of new wind projects, sufficient to quadruple the country's wind generating capacity.[8] The new projects, located mainly in windy parts of Wales and Scotland, have an average cost of just 6¢ per kilowatt-hour—less than coal and on a par with gas.[9]

Not surprisingly, given the market trends, European manufacturers dominate the global wind power industry, producing an estimated 80 percent of the wind turbines manufactured in 1994.[10] Denmark continues to lead, with more than half the global market, while the fast-growing German industry is in the number two position. Wind power installations in 1994 represent about $700 million in new business, while wind turbines in place generated $250 million worth of electricity.[11]

The U.S. wind industry has been in the doldrums in the nineties. U.S. wind generating capacity increased by less than 50 megawatts in 1994, and is not much higher now than it was in 1991.[12] The chaos entailed in restructuring the U.S. power industry has slackened utility interest in new technologies for the time being. Nevertheless, wind power projects are being developed in several states, including Maine, Minnesota, Montana, and Texas.[13] The Electric Power Research Institute has identified 2,600 megawatts of wind capacity being planned.[14]

Canada has enormous wind potential, but with its abundant fossil fuels and commitment to nuclear and hydropower, planners had ignored wind power until the early nineties. In 1994, a federal task force recommended a shift in the country's energy R&D priorities from nuclear to wind.[15] Most remarkable was Hydro Quebec's 1994 announcement that it will abandon the huge Great Whale hydro project and begin developing 100 megawatts of wind power.[16]

In India, a wind boom was launched in 1994, as the government opened the power grid to independent developers and offered tax incentives for renewable energy.[17] About 115 megawatts of wind turbines were added in India in 1994, bringing total capacity to more than 180 megawatts.[18] India is already the world's second most active wind market, and another 100 megawatts were expected to be in place by the end of March 1995.[19]

Most of the Indian projects involve joint ventures with European and U.S. turbine manufacturers who are building assembly plants thanks to government efforts to lower trade barriers and permit foreign investment in the Indian economy. India's wind potential is estimated at 20,000–50,000 megawatts.[20]

Elsewhere, the wind power industry continues to gain a foothold in Argentina, Bolivia, Brazil, Chile, China, Egypt, Indonesia, Mexico, and Morocco.[21] Overall, developing countries appear to have a good chance of dominating global wind power by the end of the decade.

Wind Power Soars

WORLD WIND ENERGY
GENERATING CAPACITY, 1980–94

YEAR	CAPACITY (megawatts)
1980	10
1981	25
1982	90
1983	210
1984	600
1985	1,020
1986	1,270
1987	1,450
1988	1,580
1989	1,730
1990	1,930
1991	2,170
1992	2,510
1993	3,050
1994 (prel)	3,710

SOURCE: Birger Madsen, BTM Consult, Ringkobing, Denmark, private communication, February 23, 1995; Paul Gipe, Gipe and Associates, Tehachapi, Calif., private communication, February 22, 1995.

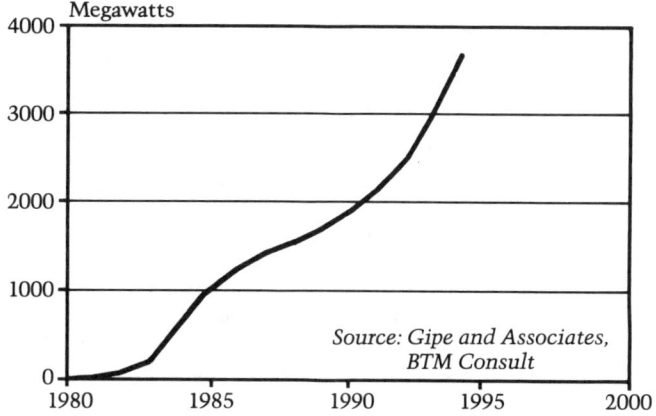

Figure 1: World Wind Energy Generating Capacity, 1980–94

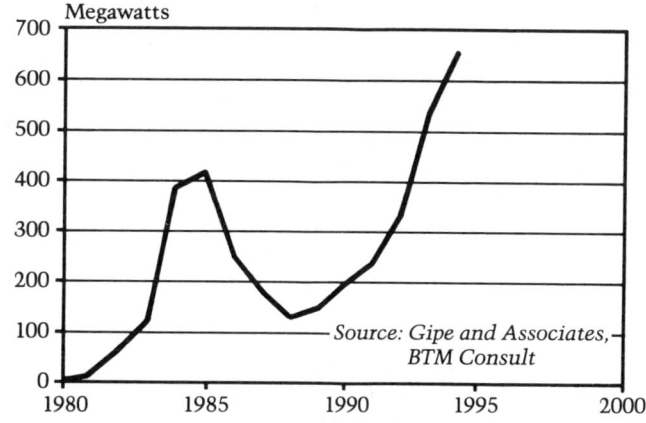

Figure 2: Net Annual Additions to World Wind Energy Generating Capacity, 1980–94

Solar Cell Shipments Expand Rapidly
Nicholas Lenssen

World shipments of photovoltaic cells, the small, silicon-based chips that directly produce electricity from sunlight, jumped by more than 15 percent in 1994, to nearly 70 megawatts.[1] (See Figure 1.) The rise was the first double-digit growth in three years, as the global economic slowdown of the early nineties had depressed sales. Cumulative output of photovoltaic cells, also known as solar cells, grew to more than 500 megawatts globally. (See Figure 2).[2]

The cost of solar cells fell by nearly 9 percent in 1994, reaching $4 a watt for delivery from the factory.[3] (See Figure 3.) Since 1985, technological improvements and expanding production have brought the cost of solar cells down by more than 50 percent. Overall, for each cumulative doubling of shipments of cells, costs have fallen by nearly one third.[4]

The United States continued to be the largest producer in 1994, raising its output by 14 percent from the previous year.[5] Some nominally U.S. companies are actually foreign-owned, however; the world's largest company (Siemens Solar) is owned by the German electronics giant Siemens. In 1994, two additional U.S. firms, including Mobil Oil's solar subsidiary, were purchased by German and Japanese companies. (The sale by Mobil leaves just three oil companies invested in solar cells: Amoco, British Petroleum, and Royal Dutch/Shell.)[6]

Even excluding the output from U.S.-based operations, European production grew by more than 30 percent in 1994, and for the first time surpassed that of Japan.[7] Japanese output fell for the third straight year, despite a new government initiative launched in 1994 that has a goal to install some 62,000 home solar units by the end of the decade.[8] By the end of 1994, 577 projects had received approval for the government subsidy, but only some 200 systems were in place apparently.[9]

Developing-country producers boosted their output of solar cells by more than 27 percent, though they still claim just 8 percent of total shipments.[10] Yet these countries remain an important market. India alone purchased some 12 percent of global shipments in 1994.[11]

The biggest market for these devices is supplying electricity to the more than 2 billion people in developing countries whose homes lack it.[12] By the end of 1994, some 250,000 Third World households were using solar cells to provide power for such uses as lighting, televisions, and pumping water.[13] Sales of photovoltaics for rural electrification could grow by more than threefold during the next five years, according to analysts.[14]

Even large development institutions have recently found that using solar cells is a cost-effective way to bring electricity to rural areas. A 1994 study by the World Bank discovered that 20,000 Kenyan homes had been electrified using solar cells in the past few years, compared with only 17,000 homes that were hooked up to the central power grid by subsidized government programs during the same period.[15]

In industrial countries, building-integrated photovoltaics are also an expanding market, involving not just rooftop panels but also roofing shingles or tiles that incorporate solar cells, and even glazing for commercial buildings. In one effort, a consortium of 86 U.S. electric utilities launched a six-year, 50-megawatt effort.[16] The Sacramento Municipal Utility District in California installed more than 100 home systems for the second consecutive year, while bringing the cost to below 20¢ a kilowatt-hour.[17]

As markets heat up, expansion, acquisitions, and mergers among manufacturers are regularly occurring. Siemens Solar announced in early 1995 that it had expanded its production capacity by nearly 50 percent.[18]

Meanwhile, the world's second largest solar cell maker, Amoco Oil's Solarex, merged in late 1994 with a subsidiary of ENRON Corp., the largest U.S. natural gas company.[19] The new firm's first initiative was to offer the U.S. government solar electricity for 5.5¢ a kilowatt-hour, to be produced by a solar power plant in Nevada by the turn of the century. It also plans to install 10-megawatt manufacturing plants to produce solar cells in a number of developing countries.[20] If these and similar plans come to fruition, photovoltaics could soon become one of the world's largest industries, as well as one of its most ubiquitous energy sources.

Solar Cell Shipments Expand Rapidly

WORLD PHOTOVOLTAIC SHIPMENTS, 1971–94

YEAR	SHIPMENTS (megawatts)
1971	0.1
1975	1.8
1976	2.0
1977	2.2
1978	2.5
1979	4.0
1980	6.5
1981	7.8
1982	9.1
1983	17.2
1984	21.5
1985	22.8
1986	26.0
1987	29.2
1988	33.8
1989	40.2
1990	46.5
1991	55.4
1992	57.9
1993	60.0
1994 (prel)	69.4

SOURCES: Paul Maycock, *PV News*, February 1995, February 1992, February 1985, and February 1982.

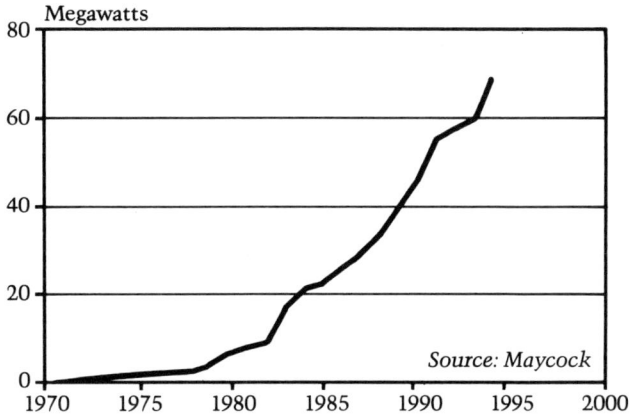
Figure 1: World Photovoltaic Shipments, 1971–94

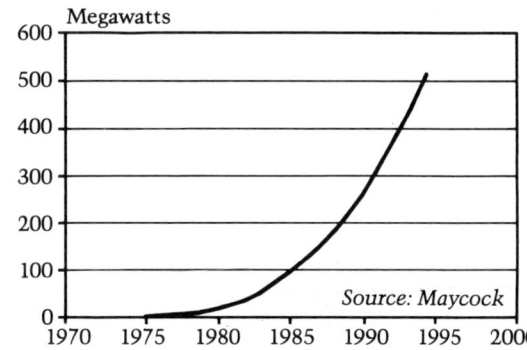
Figure 2: World Photovoltaic Shipments, Cumulative, 1975–94

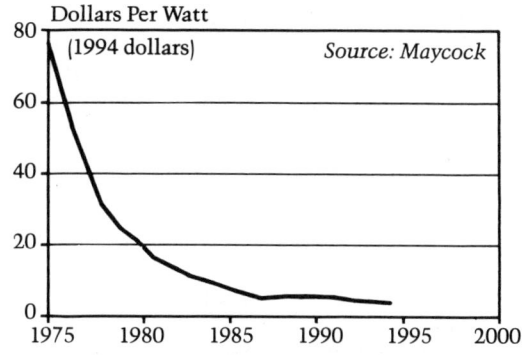
Figure 3: Average Factory Price for Photovoltaic Modules, 1975–94

Compact Fluorescents Remain Strong — David Malin Roodman

Sales of the compact fluorescent lamp (CFL) reached 195 million in 1994, according to preliminary estimates, which means that they have increased fourfold in six years.[1] (See Figure 1.) Some 500 million CFLs are probably now installed around the world. If they were all being used at the same time, they would save as much electricity as 28 large coal plants would generate—about 28,000 megawatts.[2] For comparison, the world added 50,000 megawatts of coal, oil, and gas-fired generating capacity in 1992.[3]

The compact fluorescent is just the latest installment in a centuries-old story of improvements in lighting technology. The incandescent bulb is 70 times as efficient as a candle, while lasting 100 times as long, and is 20 times as efficient as an oil lamp, while providing higher-quality illumination.[4] The compact fluorescent is four times as efficient again, lasts 10 times longer still, and produces light of comparable quality.[5]

Like its technological predecessor, the compact fluorescent has lowered the cost of lighting. In the United States, light from a CFL now costs about half as much as light from an incandescent (and an extraordinary 0.4 percent of what lighting cost in 1800).[6] This is because over its 10,000-hour lifetime, each 75-watt CFL eliminates the need to purchase 10 incandescents and 560 kilowatt-hours of electricity.

In the United States, using a CFL to replace an incandescent will save $30, even after subtracting up to $20 for the price of the lamp itself. In Japan, where electricity costs 65 percent more, net savings average about $55 per bulb.[7] As a result, not surprisingly, the Japanese get more than 80 percent of their home lighting from CFLs.[8]

Initial appearances to the contrary, the new lamp has actually claimed a significant share of the lighting market. About 50 incandescents are made for every compact fluorescent, but since each CFL matches the output of 10 incandescents over its lifetime, the CFL has now actually taken one sixth of the world market from incandescents in terms of hours of lighting capacity.[9] Western Europe accounted for nearly half of CFL sales in 1992, and North America claimed another quarter. (See Figure 2.)

In most parts of the world, the high up-front cost of CFLs has been a major obstacle to sales, despite their long-term cost-effectiveness. In response, many governments and government-regulated utilities have adopted policies to encourage the use of energy-efficient technologies, primarily through cash rebates and high-profile consumer education campaigns.[10] The CFL owes much of its initial success to these programs.

U.S. utilities now spend $3 billion a year encouraging energy efficiency, much of it on lighting programs.[11] The utilities pass the costs of these programs, with a profit margin, back to consumers through slightly higher electricity prices. Participants still come out ahead because they buy much less electricity for lighting. Similar utility programs are now found in Western Europe, Canada, Mexico, Brazil, and Thailand.[12]

The experience with CFLs demonstrates the many benefits of energy efficiency. By using less electricity, the CFL helps reduce environmental side effects of energy use, such as climate change risk, acid rain, and the generation of toxic metals such as lead and arsenic from coal burning. And generating electricity involves the construction and maintenance of large infrastructures to extract, deliver, and use the energy, all of which generate waste. Thus, it is estimated that plugging in a CFL in the United States will eventually cut solid waste generation by 90 kilograms, simply by lessening the need for industrial activity to generate electricity.[13]

The success of the CFL is just one example of recent progress in energy efficiency. By displacing some of the need for new fuel supplies, gains such as these are in effect making efficiency one of the world's largest sources of energy.

Compact Fluorescents Remain Strong

WORLD SALES OF COMPACT FLUORESCENT BULBS, 1988–94

YEAR	SALES (million)
1988	45
1989	59
1990	80
1991	115
1992	139
1993	168
1994 (prel)	195

SOURCE: Evan Mills, Lawrence Berkeley Laboratory, Berkeley, Calif., private communication, February 3, 1993; Nils Borg, National Board for Industrial and Technical Development, Stockholm, Sweden, private communication, February 10, 1995.

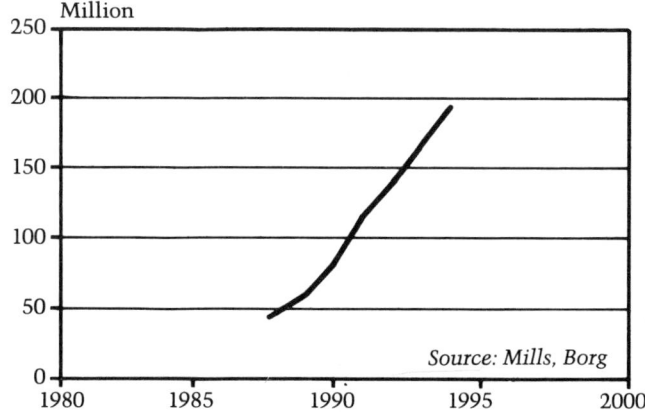

Figure 1: World Sales of Compact Fluorescent Bulbs, 1988–94

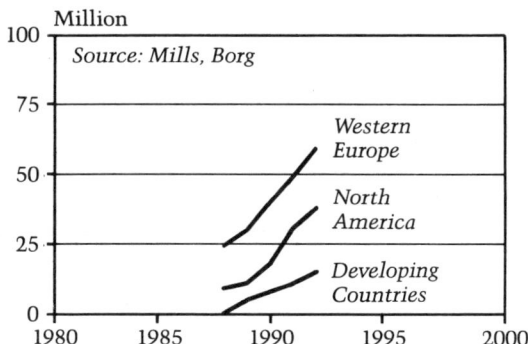

Figure 2: Sales of Compact Fluorescent Bulbs, Western Europe, North America, and Developing Countries, 1988–92

Atmospheric Trends

CFC Production Plummeting

Megan Ryan

Global chlorofluorocarbon (CFC) production declined further in 1994, falling for the sixth consecutive year and bringing total production levels down by 77 percent from their peak in 1988, according to preliminary estimates.[1] (See Figure 1).

This year represented another milestone in global efforts to eliminate production of a family of chemicals that has been depleting the stratospheric ozone layer. As a result of diplomatic efforts that began with the Montreal Protocol in 1987, and were strengthened in 1990 and 1992, industrial countries agreed to eliminate CFC production by December 31, 1995.[2] Developing countries that have signed the treaty—which has been endorsed by 146 of the world's nations—have an additional 10 years to halt production.[3]

Although CFC production in developing nations has been lower than in industrial ones, the demand for products that use these chemicals has grown, becoming a more significant share of the global total. For example, although CFC use in China, India, and other developing economies stood at less than half that in the United States in 1992, consumption there is increasing at nearly double-digit rates.[4] (See Figure 2.)

To aid developing countries in moving away from CFCs, industrial nations have set up a fund to help them establish CFC-free production techniques. But payments into the fund have consistently fallen short of commitments, with donor countries putting in only two thirds of the $393 million they pledged for 1991–94.[5]

Another impediment to eliminating production is that a black market for CFCs has developed. This stems partially from the collapse of the Soviet economy and the resulting need for hard currency. Illegal imports into the European Union in 1994 from Russia and Estonia were estimated at 2,500 tons—equal to 10 percent of the Union's legal total.[6] In the United States, a large excise tax on CFCs has further enticed opportunistic traders, with an estimated 10,000 tons—10 percent of total U.S. production—illegally imported in 1994.[7]

Despite these continuing challenges, however, efforts to protect the ozone layer are making a large difference. A 1994 panel of more than 200 leading atmospheric scientists from around the world concluded that efforts to date to reduce CFC production would mean that concentrations of chlorine and bromine—the chemical agents that react to destroy ozone—would peak in the lower atmosphere in 1994.[8]

Given the three- to five-year time lag before these chemicals make it into the upper atmosphere, stratospheric ozone depletion will continue to get worse until roughly 1998. Thereafter, however, if countries comply with their treaty obligations, the atmosphere will begin to heal. By about 2050, chlorine levels should return to where they were when the Antarctic ozone hole first appeared in the late seventies.[9]

The link between CFCs, bromine, and other ozone-depleting substances and the destruction of the stratospheric ozone layer has been well established. Depletion is most pronounced over Antarctica, where recent ozone amounts during October were less than 50 percent of the levels observed in the seventies.[10] In 1994, the ozone hole registered ozone levels as low as 102 Dobson Units—better than 1993's record low of 91 Dobson units, but higher than scientists had predicted during recovery.[11] Although less severe, ozone depletion has been observed everywhere else except the tropics.

Ozone depletion is known to cause increases in biologically damaging ultraviolet (UV-B) radiation reaching the earth's surface if all other factors (such as cloudiness and local pollution) remain constant.[12] Laboratory and epidemiological studies show that increases in UV-B can have a variety of human health and ecological effects, including non-melanoma skin cancer and decreased productivity of food crops.[13] This information, combined with observed ozone depletion and the long lifetimes of the gases causing this depletion, provided a sound basis for the Montreal Protocol.

To the credit of the international policy community, decision makers acted on the precautionary principle to avert a large-scale catastrophe that scientific information indicates could have happened if analysts had waited for documentation on actual health or ecological impacts of the disappearing ozone layer.

CFC Production Plummeting

ESTIMATED GLOBAL CFC PRODUCTION, 1950–94

YEAR	TOTAL[1] (thousand tons)
1950	42
1955	86
1960	150
1961	170
1962	210
1963	250
1964	290
1965	330
1966	390
1967	440
1968	510
1969	580
1970	640
1971	690
1972	790
1973	900
1974	970
1975	860
1976	920
1977	880
1978	880
1979	850
1980	880
1981	890
1982	870
1983	950
1984	1,050
1985	1,090
1986	1,130
1987	1,250
1988	1,260
1989	1,150
1990	820
1991	720
1992	630
1993	520
1994 (prel)	295

[1]Includes all CFCs (CFC-11, CFC-12, CFC-113, CFC-114, and CFC-115). The totals are increasingly uncertain because of a growing percentage of use occurs in regions where data are not readily available.
SOURCES: 1950 and 1955, Worldwatch estimates based on Chemical Manufacturers Association; 1960–94 from E.I. du Pont de Nemours, Wilmington, Del., private communications.

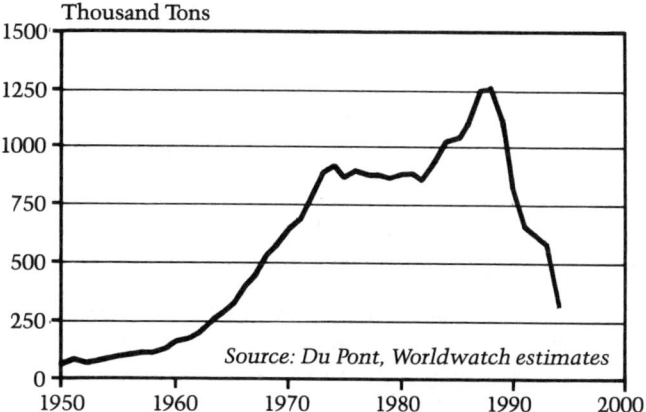

Figure 1: World Production of Chlorofluorocarbons, 1950–94

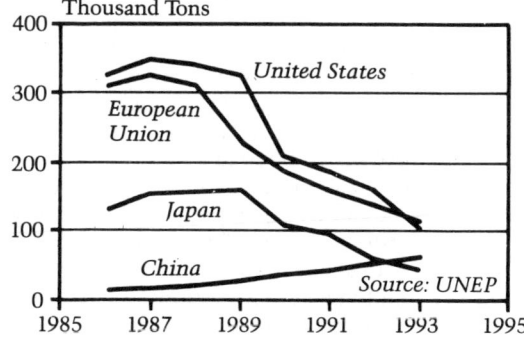

Figure 2: CFC Consumption, Selected Regions, 1986–93

Global Temperature Rises Again

David Malin Roodman

The average temperature of the lower atmosphere was 15.32 degrees Celsius in 1994, according to preliminary estimates. This made 1994 the warmest year since 1991, when Mount Pinatubo erupted in the Philippines, and placed it in a tie with 1987 as the fifth-warmest on record.[1] (See Figure 1.)

Year-to-year changes in the average temperature of the lower atmosphere—like day-to-day temperature changes in weather anywhere—are quite erratic, and difficult to interpret. During the last century, though, the clear trend has been upward. Global temperature is today 0.3–0.6 degrees Celsius above what it was in 1880.[2] The 10 warmest years ever recorded have all occurred since 1980.[3]

The eruption of Mount Pinatubo—the largest volcanic eruption in a century—injected millions of tons of dust into the upper atmosphere, which spread around the globe and blocked enough sunlight to depress temperatures in the lower atmosphere by about half a degree Celsius.[4] But these particles slowly fell to earth during the following two years; by early 1994 the volcano's effects had apparently ended, and temperatures began to return to their pre-Pinatubo highs.[5]

Climatologists are now monitoring the data streaming in from temperature-measuring stations around the world to see what happens next. Most believe that the warming trend will eventually resume in response to the continuing buildup of greenhouse gases in the air, particularly carbon dioxide (CO_2). It is less clear when this will happen, and how much.

Over a longer time scale, global temperature has tracked remarkably closely the amount of carbon dioxide in the air.[6] (See Figure 2.) Though there is no proof that changes in CO_2 levels directly cause temperature changes, or vice versa, the two are clearly related. And since the mid-eighteenth century, levels of CO_2 (as well as other greenhouse gases) have reached concentrations unprecedented in the last 160,000 years.[7] This suggests that humanity has now embarked on a large experiment in which the habitability of the planet for centuries may be at stake.

Around the world, teams of physicists, geologists, chemists, biologists, ecologists, and computer scientists are now at work trying to synthesize a more sophisticated analysis of the risk, gathering large amounts of information and continually improving their computer models.[8] So far, their work has supported the conclusion that the risk is significant.

The Intergovernmental Panel on Climate Change (IPCC), sponsored by several U.N. agencies, coordinates the work of hundreds of scientists studying global change. The IPCC projects that if fossil fuel use continues its steady long-term rise, global temperature will reach between 16 and 19 degrees Celsius by 2050—an extremely rapid warming by past standards.[9]

The eruption of Mount Pinatubo actually provided a natural test of scientists' climate models, allowing them to confirm certain assumptions about the short-term dynamics of the atmosphere.[10] Many key variables remain uncertain, however. The detailed workings of such complex phenomena as cloud formation, polar ice melting, and the ocean's ability to absorb carbon will most likely remain unclear for some time to come.[11]

A warming of the extent foreseen by the IPCC would have a variety of impacts, though how much each part of the globe would be affected is hard to predict. Higher temperatures would cause ocean waters to expand and some polar ice to melt, raising sea levels by a projected 6 centimeters per decade and inundating some coastal areas.[12] Global warming would also likely alter local climate patterns (including precipitation, soil moisture, and the lengths of seasons). This could lead to the fragmentation or destruction of many ecosystems, threatening thousands of species.[13]

Climate change would have major impacts on people as well. It could shift prime food-growing regions in a matter of decades, placing additional adjustment stresses on a global agricultural system that will already be struggling to keep up with a skyrocketing human population.[14] Of equal concern is the possibility that climate change could increase the occurrence of extreme events such as hurricanes, droughts, and floods, which could also destabilize agriculture or destroy some human settlements.[15]

Global Temperature Rises Again

GLOBAL AVERAGE TEMPERATURE, 1950–94

YEAR	TEMPERATURE (degrees Celsius)
1950	14.86
1955	14.94
1960	14.98
1961	15.08
1962	15.02
1963	15.02
1964	14.74
1965	14.85
1966	14.91
1967	14.98
1968	14.88
1969	15.03
1970	15.04
1971	14.89
1972	14.93
1973	15.19
1974	14.93
1975	14.95
1976	14.79
1977	15.16
1978	15.09
1979	15.14
1980	15.28
1981	15.39
1982	15.07
1983	15.29
1984	15.11
1985	15.11
1986	15.16
1987	15.32
1988	15.35
1989	15.25
1990	15.47
1991	15.41
1992	15.13
1993	15.20
1994 (prel)	15.32

SOURCES: H. Wilson and J. Hansen, "Global and Hemispheric Anomolies," in Boden et al., eds., *Trends '93;* James Hansen, Goddard Institute for Space Studies New York, private communication, January 30, 1995.

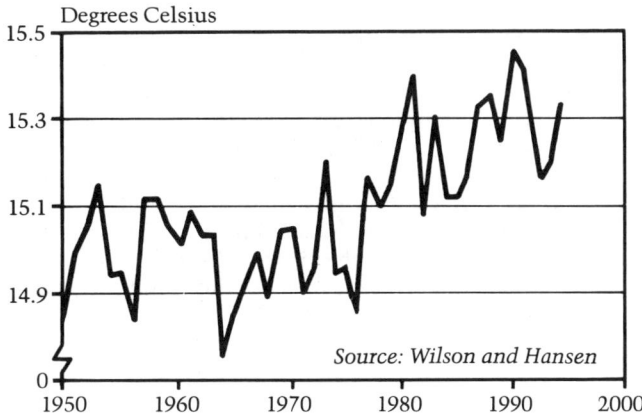

Figure 1: Global Average Temperature, 1950–94

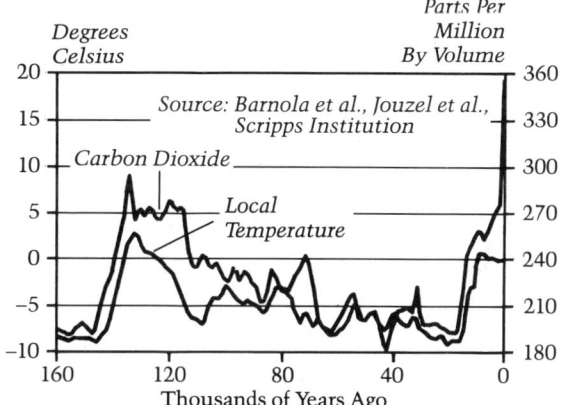

Figure 2: Local Temperature* and Atmospheric Carbon Dioxide Concentrations at Vostok, Antarctica, 158,000 B.C. to Present

* *Relative to today's average of –55 degrees Celsius in Vostok.*

Vital Signs 1995   65

Carbon Emissions Resume Rise — David Malin Roodman

The amount of carbon pumped into the air by fossil fuel burning rose slightly in 1994 to 5.925 billion tons, continuing a six-year period during which it has remained essentially constant, according to preliminary estimates.[1] (See Figure 1.) Meanwhile, deforestation is thought to have added an additional 1.1–3.6 billion tons of carbon to the atmosphere.[2]

Other greenhouse gases, including chlorofluorocarbons, methane, and nitrous oxide, are also accumulating in the air from human activities. But the warming impact of the climb in carbon dioxide (CO_2) concentrations alone is at least 60 percent higher than those of the other gases combined.[3] And carbon dioxide is by far the longest-lived of these gases; in the long run, its concentration will largely determine the scale of the greenhouse effect.[4]

Rising carbon emissions were once a constant of economic growth. Estimated at 93 million tons in 1860, emissions jumped to 525 million tons by 1900, and to 1.62 billion tons by 1950, still less than a third of today's level. Yet emissions growth has slowed since the oil shocks of the seventies—from an average 4.6 percent annually between 1950 and 1973 to just 1.6 percent between 1973 and 1988.[5] Higher energy prices encouraged people to conserve energy and to develop energy-efficient technologies. At the same time, in western industrial countries, economic growth began to come not from industries such as mining but from less energy-intensive ones, such as education.[6]

Despite the recent plateau, carbon emissions are likely to rise steadily in the next few years. Two short-term causes have maintained this plateau: the economic recession in western industrial countries, and an even deeper contraction in the former Soviet bloc—both of which seem to have largely run their course. Economic growth in western industrial countries climbed to 2.7 percent in 1994, led by strong growth in the energy-intensive U.S. economy.[7] And the contraction in the former Soviet bloc is projected to nearly end during 1995; emissions there can be expected to reach their lowest point around the same time.[8]

The fastest rise in emissions is occurring in the industrializing countries of Asia and Latin America. Though developing countries emit only 0.5 tons of carbon per person (compared with 3.0 tons per person in industrial countries), they already account for a third of the global total, and their contribution is growing fast enough to double every 14 years.[9] (See Figure 2.) Taken together, these trends are expected to result in a global emissions rise of 1–2 percent a year through the year 2000.[10]

Even if emissions remain flat at today's level, however, they will still surpass the rate at which the world's oceans and forests can absorb the chemical, leading to a steady increase in the amount staying in the air. At the end of 1994, the atmosphere contained 4 billion tons more carbon than 12 months earlier.[11] This lifted the overall concentration of carbon dioxide from 357.0 parts per million to 358.9, the biggest jump in six years.[12] (See Figure 3.) In fact, since 1860, people have added about 350 billion tons of carbon to the air; roughly 150 billion tons of it remain there.[13]

Scientists estimate that to stabilize the amount of carbon in the air and avert the risk of climate change, global emissions will have to fall at least 60 percent.[14] From this fact arise the stark geopolitics of the CO_2 problem. One group of countries emits most of the carbon; the other has most of the people, and appears bent on matching the first's profligacy as quickly as it can. It thus seems incumbent upon the rich minority to lead the way in demonstrating how modern societies can reduce carbon emissions through the more efficient use of energy and the use of renewable sources.

The Framework Convention on Climate Change signed at the Earth Summit in 1992 was a step in this direction. It required industrial nations to formulate climate policies with the goal of lowering emissions by the end of the decade.[15] Yet the signs so far are not promising: Almost every industrial country is finding it difficult to muster the political will to confront a problem whose effects are uncertain and lie much farther off than the next election. As a result, many countries, including Japan and the United States, appear to be on a course to overshoot the target.[16]

Carbon Emissions Resume Rise

WORLD CARBON EMISSIONS FROM FOSSIL FUEL BURNING, 1950–94

YEAR	EMISSIONS (mill. tons of carbon)
1950	1,620
1955	2,020
1960	2,543
1961	2,557
1962	2,659
1963	2,804
1964	2,959
1965	3,095
1966	3,251
1967	3,355
1968	3,526
1969	3,735
1970	4,006
1971	4,151
1972	4,314
1973	4,546
1974	4,553
1975	4,527
1976	4,786
1977	4,920
1978	4,960
1979	5,239
1980	5,172
1981	5,000
1982	4,960
1983	4,947
1984	5,109
1985	5,282
1986	5,464
1987	5,584
1988	5,801
1989	5,912
1990	5,941
1991	6,026
1992	5,910
1993 (est)	5,893
1994 (prel)	5,925

SOURCES: Thomas A. Boden et al., eds., *Trends '93: A Compendium of Data on Global Change* (Oak Ridge, Tenn.: Oak Ridge National Laboratory, 1994); 1993 and 1994, Worldwatch estimates based on Marland et al., on OECD, and on BP.

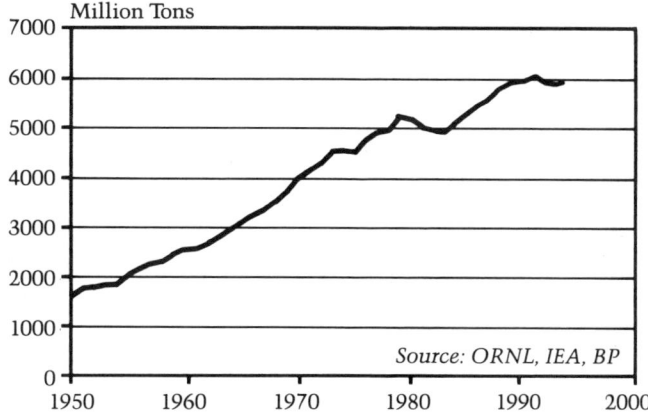

Figure 1: World Carbon Emissions from Fossil Fuel Burning, 1950–94

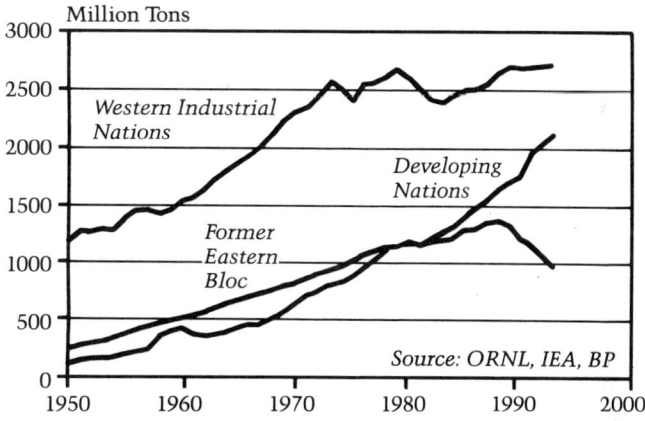

Figure 2: Carbon Emissions from Fossil Fuel Burning, by Economic Region, 1950–93

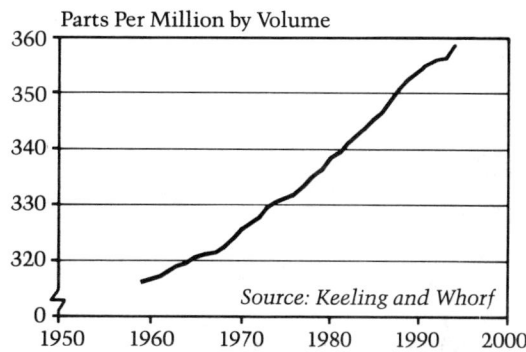

Figure 3: Atmospheric Concentrations of Carbon Dioxide, 1959-94

Economic Trends

World Economy Expanding Faster
Lester R. Brown

In 1994, world economic output expanded 3.1 percent.[1] (See Figure 1.) Following increases of 1.7 percent in 1992 and 2.3 percent in 1993, this indicates that the protracted global economic slowdown of the early nineties has ended.[2] The recent trend of slower growth in industrial countries of roughly 2.5 percent a year, compared with 5–6 percent in developing countries, continues.[3]

For the first time during the nineties, the growth in world output of goods and services per person moved solidly ahead of population. (See Figure 2.) After two consecutive declines in the early nineties, it edged up by 0.7 percent in 1993 and 1.4 percent in 1994.[4] Even with these gains, however, output per person in 1994 barely regained the 1990 level.[5]

For the United States, the 3.7-percent economic expansion in 1994 was the most robust in six years.[6] This, combined with Canada's vigorous 4.1-percent growth, meant that North America was leading the economic recovery in industrial countries.[7]

For Europe, the improved performance in 1994 signalled a recovery after being in the economic doldrums for the last few years. The German economy, which contracted by 1 percent in 1993, grew 2.3 percent in 1994.[8] France had a similar experience, going from a decline of 1 percent in 1993 to an increase of nearly 2 percent in 1994.[9] The 3.3-percent expansion in the United Kingdom in 1994 was the fastest of the large European industrial economies.[10]

The countries of Central and Eastern Europe and the former Soviet Union as a group experienced a fifth consecutive annual decline in the output of goods and services. But some of these nations have largely completed their economic reforms, and their economies are expanding. Poland had its third annual gain, growing at 4.5 percent in 1994.[11] At 8 percent, Albania's expansion was the fastest in the region.[12] Others that have turned the corner include the Czech Republic, Croatia, Slovenia, Armenia, Mongolia, Turkmenistan, and Hungary. The three Baltic states recorded gains in output ranging from 4.1 percent in Latvia to 6.0 percent in Estonia.[13] Yet the Russian economy, the region's largest, shrank by 12 percent in 1994.[14]

With the third consecutive year of 8-percent expansion, the developing countries of Asia set the pace for the Third World. Some of them, including China, Korea, Taiwan, and Thailand, have in the recent past put together two or three consecutive years of double-digit economic expansion.[15]

If China's economy expands at 10 percent in 1995, as projected, it will achieve a remarkable four consecutive years of double-digit growth—13, 13, 11, and 10 percent—leading to an overall expansion during the four-year period of 56 percent.[16] The per capita output of goods and services for 1.2 billion people will have risen by more than half in just four years.[17]

Within Latin America, overall economic growth slowed from 3.4 percent in 1993 to an estimated 2.8 percent in 1994.[18] The leaders were Peru, Argentina, Colombia, and Chile, with respective growth rates of 9, 6, 5, and 4 percent.[19] Moderating the region's expansion were a decline of 3.7 percent in Venezuela and slower growth in Brazil, the region's largest economy.[20]

Africa as a region began to recover in 1994 with an overall expansion of 3.3 percent, marking the first time economic growth had exceeded that of population in several years.[21] South Africa, with a 3-percent rate of economic growth, is clearly showing signs of recovery.[22] North African countries also showed substantial gains in 1994, ranging from 9 percent in Morocco to 3 percent in Algeria.[23]

Africa's expansion was led by strong commodity prices for nearly all the region's export products. Notwithstanding this recovery, the economic fortunes of a number of countries deteriorated. Some are also disintegrating politically, among them Somalia, Rwanda, and Zaire. Zaire has lived through six consecutive years of economic decline, shrinking by 11 percent in 1992 and 17 percent in 1993.[24]

It now seems likely that world economic expansion will continue. International Monetary Fund economists are projecting growth in 1995 of 3.6 percent, compared with 3.1 percent in 1994.[25] If this materializes, it will be the largest annual gain thus far in the nineties.

World Economy Expanding Faster

Gross World Product, Total and Per Person, 1950–94

YEAR	TOTAL (trill. 1987 dollars)	PER PERSON (1987 dollars)
1950	3.8	1,487
1955	4.9	1,763
1960	6.1	2,008
1961	6.4	2,079
1962	6.7	2,137
1963	7.0	2,184
1964	7.5	2,289
1965	7.9	2,362
1966	8.3	2,430
1967	8.6	2,468
1968	9.1	2,560
1969	9.7	2,673
1970	10.1	2,727
1971	10.5	2,776
1972	11.0	2,850
1973	11.7	2,973
1974	11.8	2,941
1975	11.9	2,912
1976	12.5	3,006
1977	13.0	3,073
1978	13.5	3,137
1979	14.0	3,197
1980	14.1	3,165
1981	14.3	3,156
1982	14.4	3,124
1983	14.8	3,156
1984	15.4	3,228
1985	16.0	3,297
1986	16.4	3,321
1987	17.0	3,382
1988	17.8	3,480
1989	18.4	3,534
1990	18.8	3,549
1991	18.7	3,471
1992	19.0	3,448
1993	19.5	3,464
1994 (prel)	20.1	3,577

SOURCES: World Bank and International Monetary Fund tables.

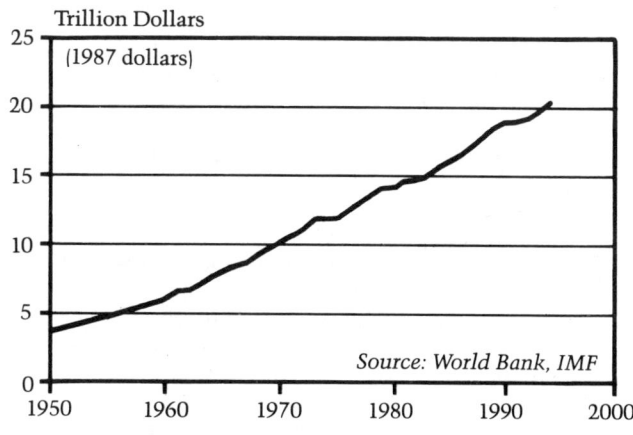

Figure 1: Gross World Product, 1950–94

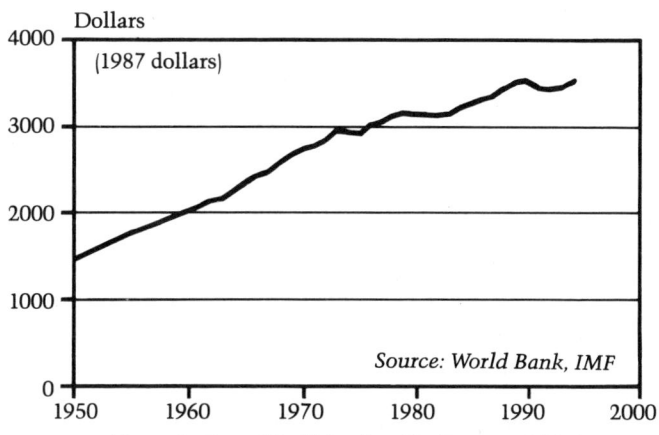

Figure 2: Gross World Product Per Person, 1950–94

Third World Debt Still Growing

Gary Gardner

The external debt of developing countries grew to an estimated $1.9 trillion in 1994, up more than 7 percent over 1993.[1] (See Figure 1.) This debt represents money owed to public and private foreign creditors by developing nations (including China), Eastern Europe, and the republics of the former Soviet Union. In 1994, the greatest growth in debt occurred in East Asia.[2]

During the past decade, a great deal of debt has been renegotiated on terms more favorable to debtor countries; this "restructuring" now covers roughly 80 percent of the funds owed to commercial banks.[3] This has led analysts to declare the debt crisis over, at least for the private banks. But the poorest nations have yet to see much relief. African debt-service payments eat up more than 30 percent of export revenues, about twice as much as before the debt crisis began in 1982.[4] (See Figure 2.)

The worst situation today is that of sub-Saharan Africa, excluding South Africa. Collectively, the region's debt amounts to $180 billion—three times the 1980 total, and 10 percent higher than its annual output of goods and services.[5] Debt-service payments come to $10 billion annually, about four times what the region spends on health and education combined.[6] Economic development is being choked over much of the continent.

Eastern Europe and the countries of the former Soviet Union are also heavily indebted. The region's total debt rose from 161 percent of export earnings in 1986 to an estimated 291 percent in 1993.[7] Russia's debt stands at over $80 billion, and the country is hard-pressed to meet its obligations: interest payments in 1994 were budgeted at less than 15 percent of interest due.[8] Poland had 40 percent of its debt forgiven in 1994; half of Bulgaria's debt was forgiven in 1993.[9]

In Latin America, restructuring has eased the burdens in Mexico, Argentina, and Brazil, but their debts remain high. Peru is the region's last country with a large amount of unrestructured debt, currently amounting to $26 billion.[10]

Restructuring has brought some new actors onto the scene—and changed the roles of established players. After shedding much of the "old," high-risk debt of the eighties, commercial banks are moving aggressively into lucrative East Asian markets and into private-sector lending in Latin America. U.S. banks, for instance, posted a 17-percent increase in developing-country loans over the year ending March 1994 and a 33-percent increase since 1990.[11]

As private lending goes elsewhere, the poorest countries are turning to multilateral institutions such as the World Bank and the International Monetary Fund. Multilateral debt among the lowest-income countries grew from around 15 percent of total debt in 1980 to more than 24 percent in 1992.[12] Multilateral loans typically carry stricter terms than bank debt. Neither the World Bank nor the Fund will directly forgive or restructure debt; this could jeopardize their "preferred status" in capital markets and force them to raise interest rates.[13] Preferred status also means that payments to these institutions take precedence over payments to all other creditors.

The multilaterals do, however, facilitate restructuring by providing most of the financing for what are known as Brady bonds, used to restructure the old debt of middle-income countries such as Brazil, Mexico, and Argentina. But these are not available to the poorest countries.

Organizations not in the business of lending money have become involved in restructuring as well, through swap agreements. Debt-for-nature and debt-for-development swaps are designed to win government commitments to environmental and development projects. In these arrangements, a nongovernmental organization obtains the debtor nation's IOU from a bank at a substantial discount. The group then typically restructures the debt by passing along some of the discount conceded by the bank, accepting payments in local currency, and investing the returns locally—to fund a national park, for instance, or a public health project. Between 1985 and 1992, such swaps accounted for only about 2 percent of debt conversions.[14] But for some countries, they offer welcome relief: Madagascar has cut its $100-million commercial bank debt in half through debt-for-nature swaps.[15]

Third World Debt Still Growing

EXTERNAL DEBT AND DEBT SERVICE OF ALL DEVELOPING COUNTRIES, 1970–94

YEAR	DEBT	DEBT SERVICE
	(bill. 1993 dollars)	
1970	217	33
1971	280	32
1972	315	37
1973	355	46
1974	408	52
1975	512	56
1976	587	62
1977	729	77
1978	848	104
1979	998	135
1980	1,140	171
1981	1,190	181
1982	1,281	195
1983	1,338	178
1984	1,340	187
1985	1,453	193
1986	1,550	201
1987	1,701	208
1988	1,643	215
1989	1,664	202
1990	1,687	195
1991	1,717	187
1992	1,739	184
1993	1,812	192
1994 (prel)	1,945	199

SOURCES: World Bank, *World Debt Tables 1994–95* (Washington, D.C.: 1994); International Monetary Fund, *World Economic Outlook*, October 1994.

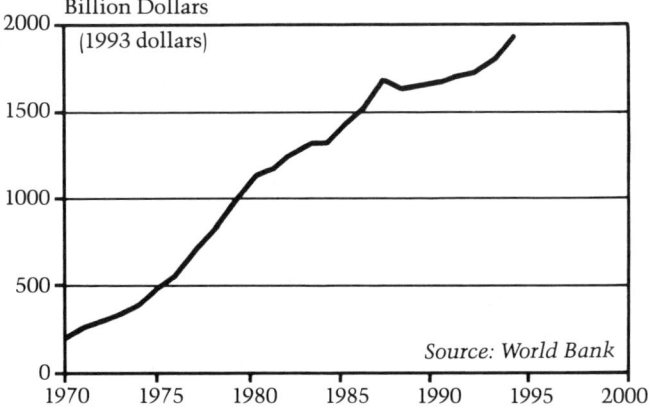

Figure 1: External Debt of Developing Countries, 1970–94

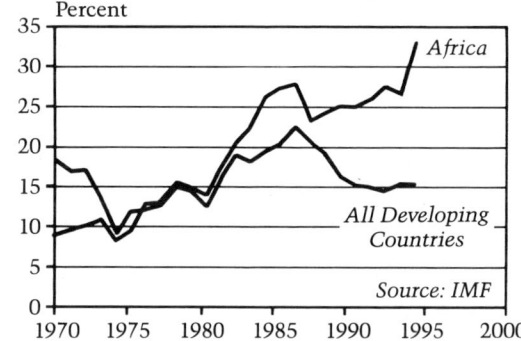

Figure 2: Third World Debt Service as Share of Exports, 1970–94

World Trade Climbing

Gary Gardner

Global exports expanded to an estimated $3.92 trillion in 1994 (in 1990 dollars), a 2.2-percent increase in value over 1993.[1] (See Figure 1.) The increase is a by-product of economic recovery in industrial nations, export-led growth strategies in many developing nations, and lowered barriers to trade in some regions. (See Figure 2.) 1994 saw the first developing country—China—surpass $100 billion in exports, a mark reached by only nine other countries.[2]

Implementation of the North American Free Trade Agreement (NAFTA) in 1994 boosted North American trade significantly. U.S. exports to Mexico and Mexican exports back each rose by better than 20 percent in the first nine months of 1994.[3] U.S.-Canadian trade was up 12–14 percent through October 1994.[4] The surge in North American trade made Mexico the second largest consumer of U.S. products, surpassing Japan.[5] The devaluation of the peso in December 1994 will likely cut into Mexican imports of U.S. goods in 1995.

Prices of some primary products rose sharply in 1994. The International Monetary Fund's index of nonfuel commodity prices jumped more than 14 percent in the year ending August 1994.[6] Coffee prices hit an eight-year high, while copper rose some 30 percent between the first quarter and August.[7] While welcomed by primary-product exporters, rising prices did little to offset a long-standing deterioration in the terms of trade—the value of exported primary products relative to imported manufactures. For commodity-dependent nations, these reached their lowest point in 90 years in 1992.[8]

The Uruguay Round of the General Agreement on Tariffs and Trade, ratified by key member-states in 1994, paved the way for reductions in trade barriers beginning in 1995. Expanded trade is expected to add billions of dollars per year to the global economy—up to $274 billion in the tenth year of the agreement—but the fruits of expansion will not be shared equally.[9] Industrial nations will reap some 65–85 percent of the projected gains, while Africa is projected to lose more than $2 billion as its exports lose preferential access to European markets, and as its agricultural imports rise in price.[10]

Regional initiatives to lower trade barriers were also undertaken in 1994. NAFTA member-states invited Chile to apply for membership; full accession negotiations are to begin in 1995.[11] Leaders from throughout the Americas agreed to establish a Free Trade Area of the Americas—covering 850 million people with $13 trillion in purchasing power—by 2005.[12] In the Pacific Rim region, members of Asia Pacific Economic Cooperation (APEC) agreed to work toward establishment of a free-trade zone by 2020.[13] None of these initiatives will affect trade immediately, but they point to growing sentiment for lower trade barriers and likely continued expansion of trade.

Continued rapid economic growth in some developing countries is altering global trade patterns. Trade among industrial nations grew modestly in the early nineties, typically under 3 percent annually.[14] But exports to developing nations leaped ahead: Japanese exports to developing nations were up by 29 percent per year, U.S. exports by 22 percent, and European exports by 13 percent.[15] The strong demand from developing countries is credited with helping industrial nations out of recession, and indicates the growing economic clout of some of these nations.[16]

Asian developing nations are especially vibrant, averaging more than 8 percent growth between 1992 and 1994, and their effect on trade is clear.[17] Most of the increase in APEC's share of world exports—up from 38 percent in 1983 to 46 percent in 1993—was generated by Asian nations.[18] Indeed, intra-Asian trade is rising four times faster than trade between Asia and the United States.[19]

A clear split emerged in 1994 between developing and industrial nations about the place of environmental issues in trade relations. Developing nations, fearful that environmental standards would be used to keep their products out, want the new World Trade Organization (WTO) to stay clear of such issues.[20] Europe and the United States want the WTO to deal with environmental disputes.[21] WTO's Subcommittee on Trade and the Environment began work in 1994, but its jurisdiction remained unclear.

World Trade Climbing

WORLD EXPORTS, 1950–94

YEAR	EXPORTS (bill. 1990 dollars)
1950	328
1955	451
1960	586
1961	606
1962	633
1963	687
1964	744
1965	799
1966	855
1967	900
1968	1,025
1969	1,143
1970	1,263
1971	1,328
1972	1,451
1973	1,635
1974	1,728
1975	1,640
1976	1,828
1977	1,897
1978	1,994
1979	2,136
1980	2,211
1981	2,230
1982	2,154
1983	2,207
1984	2,400
1985	2,475
1986	2,492
1987	2,643
1988	2,920
1989	3,137
1990	3,337
1991	3,487
1992	3,658
1993	3,839
1994 (prel)	3,924

SOURCE: Worldwatch calculations based on IMF data and deflators.

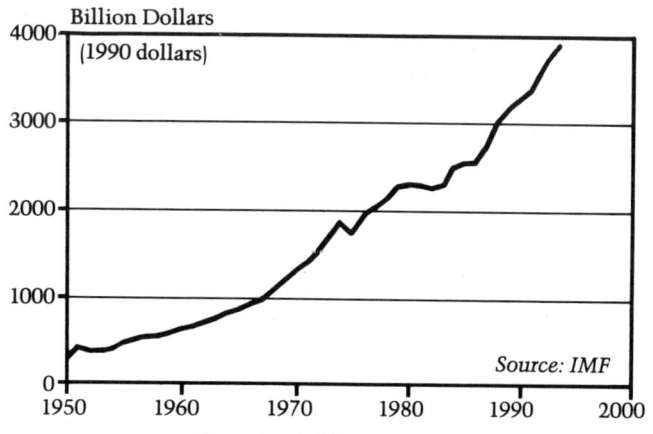

Figure 1: World Exports, 1950–94

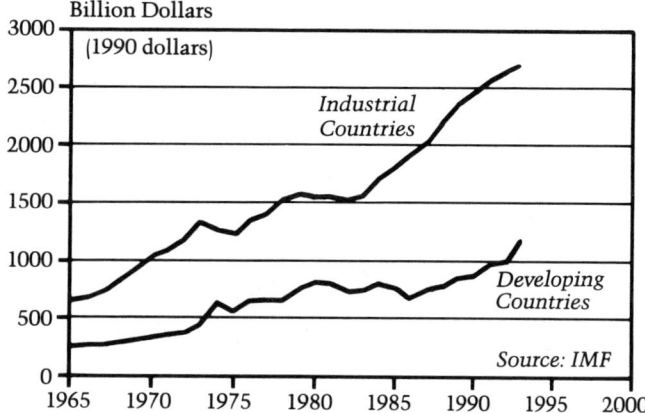

Figure 2: Exports from Industrial and Developing Countries, 1965–93

Television Continues to Spread

David Malin Roodman

In 886 million households, perhaps half of humanity was able to watch television in 1994.[1] The rise of 45 million over the previous year continued the rapid growth seen since 1990.[2] (See Figure 1.)

Invented during the thirties, modern television had to await the postwar economic boom before leaving the laboratory. In 1946, only 8,000 homes had television.[3] But the number reached 180,000 by 1948, 4 million by 1950, and 41 million by 1955.[4] Since then it has risen an average 8 percent annually.[5]

TV took root earliest among World War II victors. The United States had more than 90 percent of the world's televisions in 1951.[6] Most of the rest—about 1.2 million—were in the United Kingdom.[7] West Germany had fewer than 1 million until 1957, as did Japan—with twice the population—until 1958.[8]

In industrial countries today, growth continues, but more slowly.[9] (See Figure 2.) In the United States, the United Kingdom, and Germany, 97 percent or more of all homes have at least one set.[10] Since the seventies, the television explosion has moved to countries that are poorer but rapidly adopting western-style consumerism. Between 1975 and 1994, the number of households with TVs jumped 360 percent in Latin America and 950 percent in Asia.[11] (See Figure 3.) Since the developing world has a rapidly growing population and relatively fewer homes with TVs, growth there could continue for years, pushing the global total toward 2 billion.

As these trends suggest, the count of households with television tracks closely the shifts toward resource-intensive ways of life. But television is not only an indicator of change; it is an agent. With the possible exceptions of the telephone and the automobile, no other technology has so revolutionized how people live, and how they see the world.

Television can entertain, but it can also educate. For example, in the remote Peruvian Andes, one priest has used video tapes to teach villagers about sanitary habits and the treatment of diarrhea, a childhood killer.[12] In some countries, images of freedom beamed in from outside have worked to undermine dictatorships.[13] TV can strengthen democracies by providing a forum for debate, and by bringing people together to witness historic moments.

Yet, one of the clearest impacts has been on how people spend their time. Citizens in every European country watch at least 2 hours a day on average, with the British topping the list at 3.5 hours.[14] Americans surpass that, watching 4 hours each day—more time than they spend on any other activity except working and sleeping.[15] The lost time may most hurt children, for whom every waking moment is an educational experience. More time in front of "the tube" means less spent with family and friends—potentially slowing social development—and less spent learning to read.[16]

Of concern, too, is the experience of watching TV itself. The paramount purpose of almost every television program is to keep the viewer watching. Producers have discovered that the best way to do this is to fill the screen with attention-grabbing stimuli, including constantly changing camera angles, fast action, rapid topic changes, violence, and sexual innuendo.[17]

For a society whose citizens get most of their information about the world from television, the results are worrisome. An emphasis on data over analysis and change over continuity tends to fragment the watcher's worldview, in particular severing any sense of connection to nature or the past.[18] Political and moral discourse gets reduced to sound bites.[19] Television also tends to distort perceptions of reality, particularly for impressionable preadolescent children. Several studies have found a strong link between exposure to television violence as a child and violent behavior as an adult.[20] The average American 14-year-old has witnessed 11,000 murders on TV.[21]

Finally, television is both a consumer good and a vehicle for selling others. As an advertising medium, TV works to persuade its audience that happiness lies in the escalating consumption of material goods. The rising consumption of raw materials and energy that this implies are major environmental threats. On balance, making the best use of television constitutes a major challenge in the creation of a sustainable global society.

Television Continues to Spread

World Households with Television, 1950–94

YEAR	HOUSEHOLDS (million)
1950	4
1951	12
1952	18
1953	24
1954	33
1955	41
1956	49
1957	57
1958	69
1959	80
1960	93
1961	107
1962	120
1963	134
1964	151
1965	164
1970	244
1975	323
1976	349
1977	374
1978	401
1979	427
1980	450
1981	471
1982	491
1983	511
1984	535
1985	557
1986	581
1987	601
1988	619
1989	633
1990	658
1991	718
1992	775
1993	841
1994 (prel)	886

SOURCE: U.S. Bureau of the Census, *Historical Statistics of the United States: Colonial Times to 1970* (Washington, D.C.: 1975); United Nations, *Statistical Yearbook* (New York: various years); *Screen Digest*, March 1993; Screen Digest Ltd., London, private communications and printouts, February 1995.

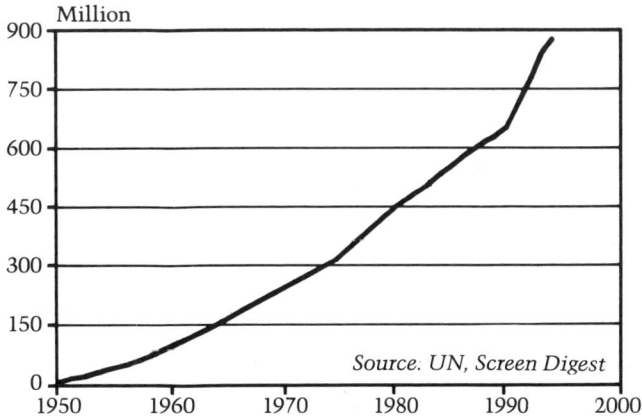

Figure 1: World Households with Television, 1950–94

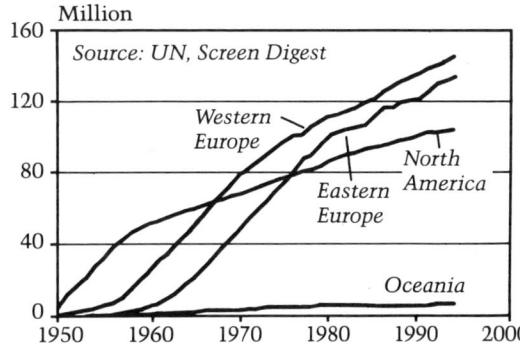

Figure 2: Households with Television in Europe, North America, and Oceania, 1950–94

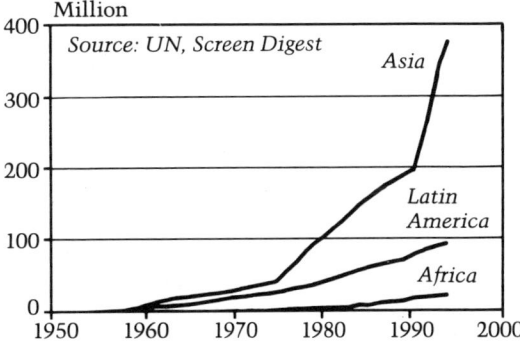

Figure 3: Households with Television in Asia, Latin America, and Africa, 1950–94

Transportation Trends

Bicycle Production Rising — Gary Gardner

World bicycle production increased to more than 110 million units in 1994, even as important bicycle markets in Japan and Europe exhibited sluggish growth.[1] The trend continues the nearly unbroken rise in global bicycle production since 1970. (See Figure 1.)

China, the world's top producer with nearly 40 percent of the global total, built an estimated 43 million bicycles in 1994, up some 4.8 percent over 1993.[2] India, the second largest producer, expected output to rise as much as 10 percent, fueled in part by aggressive exporting: Indian bicycle exports doubled between 1992 and 1993 and were expected to grow another 30 percent in 1994.[3] (See Figure 2.)

Despite steady growth in bicycle production during the past two decades, the potential for further growth is great, especially if several obstacles are overcome. The first barrier is unfriendly attitudes toward bicycles. In 1993, officials in Guangzhou, China, banned bicycles from 11 major thoroughfares, blaming them for growing traffic congestion.[4] Shanghai followed suit in 1994.[5] Around the world, transportation policy is frequently driven by the needs of motor vehicles.

Bicycle production is also restricted by weak demand in some areas. Although the cost is minuscule compared with automobiles, at $100 and up, bicycles can easily require several months' wages in parts of Africa and Latin America.[6] The high cost often results from stiff import tariffs; because most developing countries import some or all of the parts needed to assemble a bicycle, tariffs can raise a bicycle's price—and limit its market—significantly.[7]

Sales are also limited by cultural attitudes surrounding women bikers. In parts of Africa, where women are responsible for most of the movement of goods, a bicycle could be a welcome work tool.[8] Yet men frequently regard female cycling as "unladylike" and associate women's mobility with promiscuity.[9] Changes in attitude, combined with design improvements directed at women—such as smaller frame sizes, elimination of the "male" horizontal crossbar, and addition of sturdy load-carrying equipment—could expand the bicycle market in developing countries.[10]

One source of market expansion is the use of bicycles in the workplace. Developing countries are long familiar with the utilitarian advantages of bikes, but new uses continue to be found. A six-month experiment in San Salvador demonstrated that a trailer-towing cyclist could distribute as much Pepsi-Cola per month as someone driving a five-ton truck.[11] Operating costs for the trailer-bike are only one tenth those of the truck, and Pepsi is considering replacing its truck fleet with bicycles.[12]

Work-related bicycle use is picking up in industrial nations as well. Organizations with extensive worksites often use bicycles as a means of internal transportation. In the United States, universities, theme parks, oil refineries, large manufacturing plants, and even NASA's Kennedy Space Center use bicycles for internal transport.[13]

Urban gridlock makes bicycles increasingly competitive for crosstown work purposes as well. Pizza is delivered in Washington, D.C., by bicycle.[14] Mail carriers in downtown St. Petersburg, Florida, use bikes on their rounds.[15]

Increased demand for couriers in Amsterdam prompted one service to increase its bicycle fleet from 3 to 17 in 1994.[16] A San Francisco courier company added trailer bikes to its fleet, and now uses them for deliveries of all kinds, from groceries to recyclable materials. In New York and Amsterdam, bicycle rickshaws were introduced in 1994 as short-haul taxis.[17] At 50¢ per minute in New York, these "pedicabs" are cheaper and faster than regular taxicabs for trips of under five blocks, and competitive with standard taxis for some longer trips.[18]

Police departments in more than 400 U.S. cities now include bicycles as a permanent part of their patrol fleets.[19] In Phoenix, Arizona, paramedics began to use bikes in 1994 as the most efficient way to reach victims surrounded by large crowds, at parades and sporting events, for example.[20] With developments such as these, bicycles hold promise of becoming recognized as a valuable, environmentally friendly means of transportation.

Bicycle Production Rising

WORLD BICYCLE PRODUCTION, 1950–94

YEAR	PRODUCTION (million)
1950	11
1955	15
1960	20
1961	20
1962	20
1963	20
1964	21
1965	21
1966	22
1967	23
1968	24
1969	25
1970	36
1971	39
1972	46
1973	52
1974	52
1975	43
1976	47
1977	49
1978	51
1979	54
1980	62
1981	65
1982	69
1983	74
1984	76
1985	79
1986	84
1987	98
1988	105
1989	95
1990	90
1991	96
1992	103
1993	108
1994 (prel)	111

SOURCE: *Interbike Directory 1995* (Newport Beach, Calif.: Primedia, Inc. 1995).

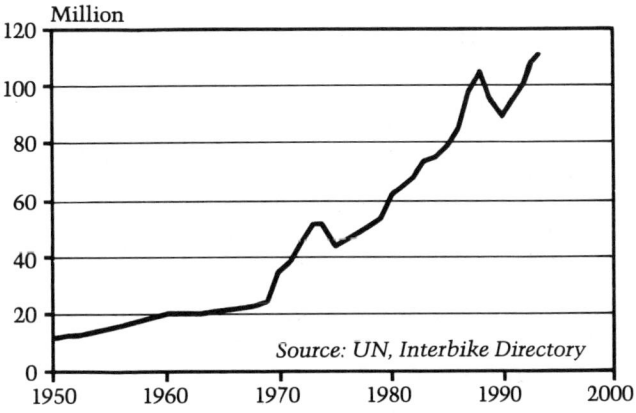

Figure 1: World Bicycle Production, 1950–94

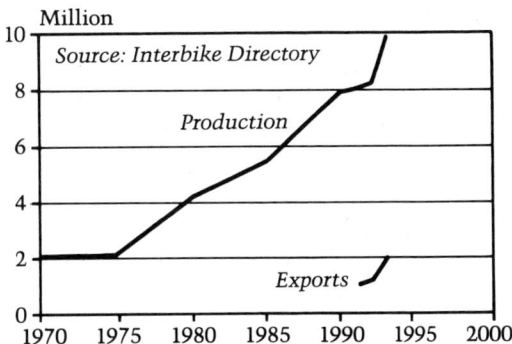

Figure 2: Bicycle Production and Exports in India, 1970–93

Vital Signs 1995

Auto Production on the Rise

Odil Tunali

After four consecutive years of decline, world auto production climbed in 1994. Output reached 34.9 million cars—up 3.3 percent from 1993 levels, but still below the 1990 peak of 35.8 million.[1] (See Figure 1.) The number of people per car remained unchanged, as the expansion in the world auto fleet was offset again by population growth. (See Figures 2 and 3.)

The rise in production was fueled by recovering national economies and accelerating consumer demand in most parts of the world. Total new car sales went up by 5 percent.[2]

The United States recorded a 15-percent growth in production—the highest among the traditional auto markets.[3] In Western Europe, the downturn of the last three years was reversed, and output went up by 3.5 percent.[4] In Japan, on the other hand, the rising demand for new cars was met by existing inventories, and production fell by 3 percent in the fourth successive annual decline.[5]

The most striking upward trends in the auto industry continue to occur outside traditional markets. East European motor vehicle fleets grew at an average rate of 8 percent within a year.[6] Brazil's auto production jumped by nearly 40 percent from 1992 to 1994, peaking at 1.5 million.[7] And output in the Asia/Pacific region grew by 18 percent in 1994, with China's production skyrocketing 28 percent in a year.[8] Noticing the growth potential of these new markets, the largest Japanese, French, and German carmakers, along with the American "Big Three," have launched ambitious investment campaigns, particularly in the fast-growing economies of Asia.[9]

China indisputably has the greatest lure for foreign investors. With a population of 1.2 billion people, the nation has only 1.8 million automobiles, less than 5 percent of which are privately owned.[10] Given China's double-digit economic growth rates and rising personal expectations for better living standards, industry analysts predict that the number of cars on Chinese roads will soar elevenfold by the year 2010; by then, 60 percent are expected to be in private hands.[11] The Chinese government, convinced that an expanding auto industry is vital for rapid economic growth, has decided to subsidize private car purchases and open its doors to foreign car companies.[12]

Many developing nations, including India, Thailand, Indonesia, and Vietnam, are encouraging foreign or joint auto ventures with the hope that these will propel growth by creating jobs and stimulating the economy.[13] Yet the prospect of expanding auto fleets raises certain issues that should not be overlooked. For example, air pollution in many cities has already reached alarming levels, and adding millions of cars to the streets will only exacerbate the health problems associated with it.

In addition, most developing countries have limited energy supplies, and must import their fuel. Faced with the fuel demands of growing auto fleets, governments may be forced to allocate an even larger part of their foreign-exchange reserves to fuel imports. Furthermore, growing fuel demand will increase countries' reliance on the volatile Persian Gulf region for additional oil supplies.[14]

Recent technological developments show that the pollution- and energy-related problems of increased automobile use may be eased through investments in "clean" cars that run on a host of alternative fuels, from natural gas to electricity. As more clean cars are produced, economies of scale and better production know-how will make these vehicles more affordable and widespread in the future.[15]

Nevertheless, clean cars do not offer solutions to other problems arising from expanding auto fleets. The transport infrastructure in most developing countries is not up to sustaining the predicted increases in cars, while the land required to build it must be used for crops in order to feed growing populations. Moreover, city streets are already overtaxed by bicycles, pushcarts, motor scooters, and pedestrians.

In the face of infrastructure and land constraints, as well as growing traffic congestion, societies may have more to gain from alternative means of transport than from personal cars.

Auto Production on the Rise

WORLD AUTOMOBILE
PRODUCTION, 1950–94

YEAR	PRODUCTION (million)
1950	8
1955	11
1960	13
1961	11
1962	14
1963	16
1964	17
1965	19
1966	19
1967	19
1968	22
1969	23
1970	22
1971	26
1972	28
1973	30
1974	26
1975	25
1976	29
1977	30
1978	31
1979	31
1980	29
1981	28
1982	27
1983	30
1984	30
1985	32
1986	33
1987	33
1988	34
1989	36
1990	36
1991	35
1992	35
1993	34
1994 (prel)	35

SOURCES: American Automobile Manufacturers Association; DRI/McGraw-Hill.

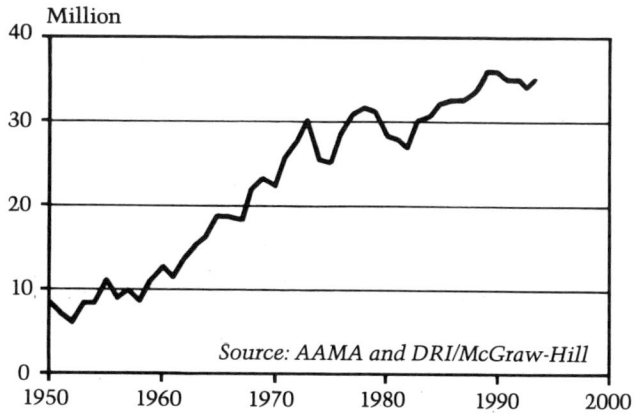

Figure 1: World Automobile Production, 1950–94

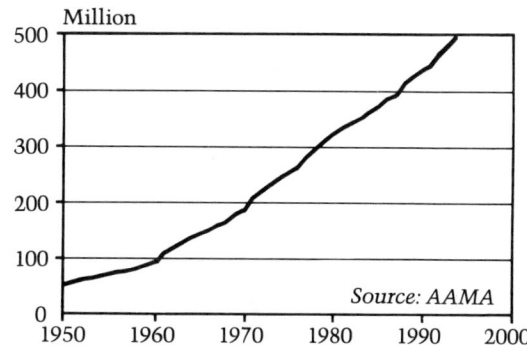

Figure 2: World Automobile Fleet, 1950–94

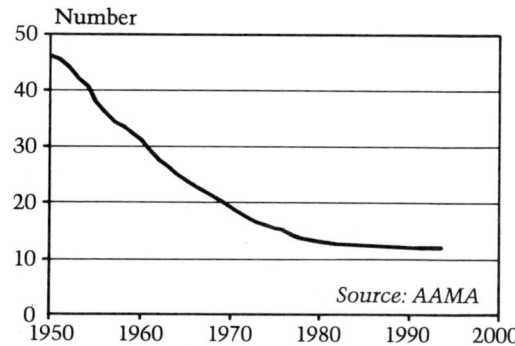

Figure 3: People Per Automobile, 1950–94

Environmental Trends

Sulfur and Nitrogen Emissions Fall Slightly   Hal Kane

World emissions of nitrogen and sulfur from the burning of fossil fuels declined slightly in 1992, the most recent year for which data exist.[1] (See Figures 1 and 2.) This will mean reduced damage to agricultural crops, and less harm to human health caused by these air pollutants. Particular progress was made with sulfur: 1 million fewer tons were emitted.[2] The decline in nitrogen emissions from 26.6 million to 26.5 million tons was so small as to be essentially unchanged.[3]

In addition, another 10 million tons or so of sulfur are released through industrial processes other than the burning of fossil fuels.[4] And some 6–12 million tons of nitrogen are added to the atmosphere through the burning of forests and other biomass.[5] All figures are unofficial estimates because no comprehensive official data gathering system measures international nitrogen or sulfur pollution.

Sulfur is contained in oil, and especially in coal. As these fuels are burned, sulfur dioxide is emitted; but scrubbers and other cleaning technologies have the ability to take most of the sulfur pollution out of waste gases before they reach the atmosphere. Sulfur oxides come mostly from power plants and factories, and also from diesel fuel and fuel oil.[6]

Nitrogen is contained in air (in fact, air is mostly nitrogen), and during the process of burning gasoline in cars and various fuels in industry it is released as nitrogen oxides.[7] Technologies that burn fuel more efficiently and at precise temperatures release considerably less nitrogen into the atmosphere than less well tuned equipment, and catalytic converters can remove nitrogen oxides from emissions.[8] Nitrogen oxides are notorious pollutants from cars and other transportation vehicles.[9]

The most important reasons for the slowdown in nitrogen and sulfur pollution are improvements in industrial technologies and the international treaties and domestic legislation that encourage manufacturers to use better technology. During the eighties, for example, Austria cut its sulfur dioxide emissions by 75 percent, West Germany cut them by 67 percent, Sweden by 60 percent, and Norway by 58 percent.[10]

Much of the improvement came from the commitment of the 1979 Convention on Long-Range Transboundary Air Pollution signed by 33 countries in Europe and North America under the auspices of the U.N. Economic Commission for Europe.[11] Although some of the pollution cuts would have happened even without the treaties, because of technological change, today most of these governments have agreed to go beyond their earlier commitments.[12]

Progress on controlling emissions has been most successful with sulfur because most of its emissions can be controlled by regulating a single activity—power generation. Nitrogen is tougher because its effects are more complicated (and thus less well understood) and because its sources include not only power generation but also transportation. As a result, many countries have failed to achieve their initial goals of a 30-percent reduction in nitrogen oxide emissions.[13]

In 1980, about 62 percent of global sulfur emissions originated in Europe and North America.[14] As developing countries contribute a larger share of the total, however, their choices about energy and transportation technologies will become more important. Thus, future world air pollution trends are likely to be driven in large part by economic growth and choices of energy sources and technologies in China, India, and other developing countries likely to burn increasing quantities of fossil fuels.

Three quarters of China's energy needs are met by burning coal, much of it of low quality and some of it high in sulfur, using a system of nineteenth-century technologies.[15] As its economy and its use of coal grow, China could undercut the progress made in other nations if it does not adopt the pollution reduction strategies that have worked so well elsewhere.

Sulfur and Nitrogen Emissions Fall Slightly

WORLD NITROGEN AND SULFUR EMISSIONS FROM FOSSIL FUEL BURNING, 1950–92

YEAR	NITROGEN	SULFUR
	(mill. tons)	
1950	6.8	30.1
1960	11.8	46.2
1970	18.1	57.0
1971	18.6	56.9
1972	19.5	58.2
1973	20.6	60.9
1974	20.8	60.9
1975	19.9	56.4
1976	21.0	58.6
1977	20.8	60.1
1978	22.3	61.0
1979	22.4	62.6
1980	22.3	62.9
1981	22.1	61.9
1982	22.2	62.1
1983	22.5	63.0
1984	23.3	64.5
1985	23.4	64.2
1986	23.6	65.2
1987	24.3	66.5
1988	25.3	68.4
1989	26.5	70.8
1990	26.3	68.7
1991	26.6	69.7
1992	26.5	68.7

SOURCES: J. Dignon, Lawrence Livermore Laboratory, unpublished data series, private communication, February 1, 1995; Hameed and Dignon, *Journal of the Air & Waste Management Association*, February 1991; Dignon and Hameed, *JAPCA*, February 1989.

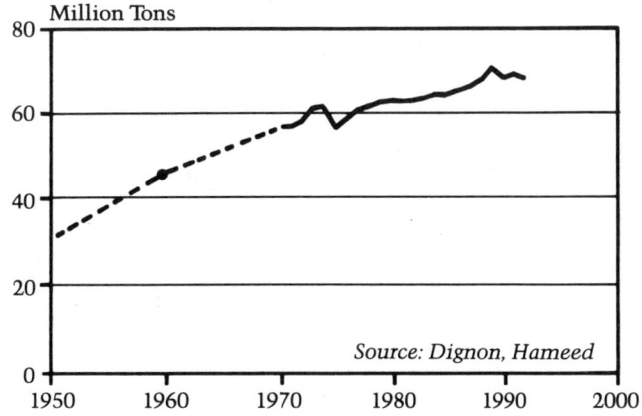

Figure 1: World Sulfur Emissions from Fossil Fuel Burning, 1950–92

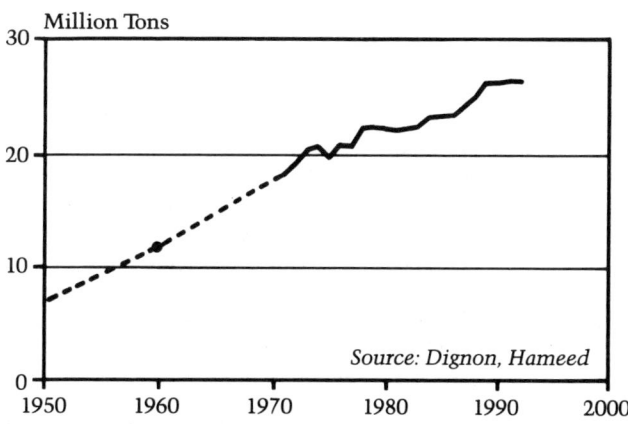

Figure 2: World Nitrogen Emissions from Fossil Fuel Burning, 1950–92

Nuclear Waste Still Accumulating — Nicholas Lenssen

In 1994, the world's 431 commercial nuclear reactors created more than 10,000 tons of irradiated fuel, bringing the total accumulation of used fuel to more than 130,000 tons—more than twice as much as at the end of 1987.[1] (See Figures 1 and 2.) Nearly a quarter of this—some 30,000 tons, with a radioactivity of 26 billion curies—is found in the United States.[2]

Civilian nuclear power has produced roughly 95 percent of the radioactivity emanating from waste in the world, most of it in the form of irradiated or spent fuel that is created by reactors that generate electric power.[3] The world's nuclear industries began accumulating radioactive waste 50 years ago, but no country has yet found a safe, permanent way to dispose of it.[4] And nuclear waste can remain dangerous for hundreds of thousands of years.

Nearly all governments plan to bury radioactive waste hundreds of meters below the earth's crust eventually, though scientists recognize that some of this waste will make its way back to the surface at some point.[5] Given the technical and political difficulties of such an undertaking, no country plans to actually bury long-lived waste before the early part of the next century.[6]

Despite recognition as early as in the fifties that no fail-safe method existed for isolating nuclear waste for millennia, one country after another plunged ahead with building nuclear power plants in the sixties and seventies. Even today some countries, such as Indonesia, still consider tapping atomic power without facing up to the waste problem.[7]

Officials often maintain that the waste issue has been solved elsewhere, but upon inspection, most governments have found their efforts to bury waste moving in reverse. In 1991, the French government decreed that no decision on a final burial place will be made until at least 2006, following widespread opposition to its attempt to site a repository.[8]

U.S. government efforts to force Nevada to take the nation's most dangerous nuclear waste—irradiated fuel from power plants and high-level reprocessing wastes from military activities—continue to face scientific and political difficulties. Exploratory drilling in 1994 found evidence of rapidly flowing groundwater within the proposed Yucca Mountain site, contrary to the previous contention by U.S. Department of Energy (DOE) scientists that one of the site's strongest points was its absence of significant groundwater flows.[9]

Furthermore, the U.S. Nuclear Regulatory Commission warned DOE in October 1994 that it may need to halt its research efforts if it cannot improve its scientific and engineering quality control.[10] Such a move would be popular in Nevada, where despite a multimillion-dollar public relations campaign by dump supporters—mainly electric utilities hoping to unload waste stranded at power plants—residents still oppose a repository at Yucca Mountain by more than a three-to-one margin. Originally scheduled to open in 1998, Yucca Mountain is unlikely to receive waste until after 2010, if ever.[11]

Ten years ago, Germany had hoped to open its deep burial facility at the Gorleben salt dome by 1998; now 2008 is given as the target year.[12] Despite 14 years of drilling and testing, public opposition and technical uncertainties over salt continue to delay work at the site.[13]

Some countries, such as France, Japan, Russia, and the United Kingdom, reprocess irradiated fuel. This was originally developed to extract the fission by-product plutonium for atomic bomb production. But the process involves chemical procedures that also remove the remaining uranium (only about 3 percent of the original uranium is fissionable).[14]

Although reprocessing "disposes" of irradiated fuel, it actually leaves behind 97 percent of the radioactivity of used reactor fuel, some of it very long-lived isotopes.[15] And by separating plutonium, reprocessing continues the production of material that can be used for nuclear weapons. Worldwide, civilian nuclear reactors alone produced some 50 tons of plutonium in 1994, enough to build more than 6,000 atomic bombs.[16]

Above-ground storage seems to be the "temporary" solution for many nations, including the United States, for the next few decades. This at least buys time while the search for a technologically and socially feasible route continues.[17]

Nuclear Waste Still Accumulating

ANNUAL AND CUMULATIVE GENERATION OF IRRADIATED FUEL FROM COMMERCIAL NUCLEAR PLANTS, 1965–94

YEAR	ANNUAL	CUMULATIVE
	(thousand tons)	
1965	0.10	0.27
1966	0.14	0.41
1967	0.17	0.57
1968	0.22	0.79
1969	0.28	1.07
1970	0.37	1.44
1971	0.51	1.96
1972	0.71	2.67
1973	1.07	3.74
1974	1.22	4.96
1975	1.65	6.61
1976	2.04	8.65
1977	2.66	11.31
1978	2.94	14.25
1979	3.12	17.37
1980	3.42	20.80
1981	3.92	24.72
1982	4.11	28.83
1983	4.94	33.77
1984	5.82	39.59
1985	6.91	46.50
1986	7.51	54.02
1987	8.23	62.25
1988	8.92	71.17
1989	9.10	80.27
1990	9.25	89.53
1991	9.86	99.39
1992	9.87	109.25
1993	10.37	119.63
1994 (prel)	10.67	130.30

SOURCE: Worldwatch Institute, based on Pacific Northwest Laboratory, United Nations, British Petroleum, Russian Center of Public Information for Atomic Energy, and U.S. Department of Energy.

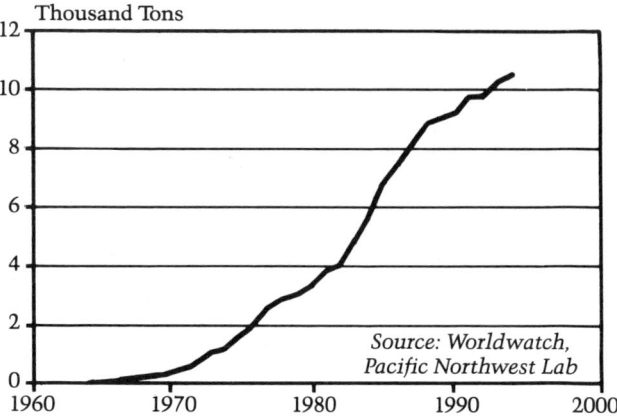

Figure 1: Annual Generation of Irradiated Fuel from Commercial Nuclear Plants, 1965–94

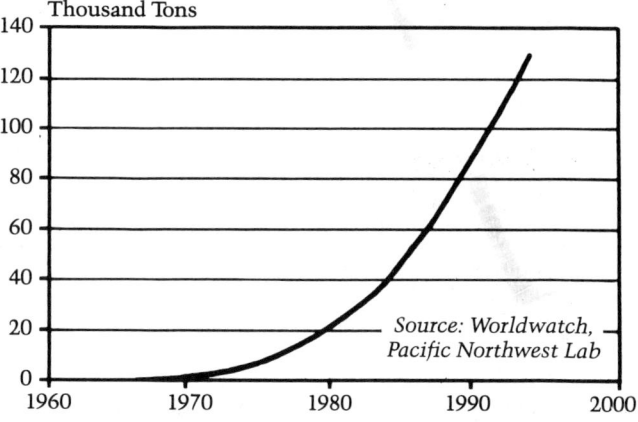

Figure 2: Cumulative Generation of Irradiated Fuel from Commercial Nuclear Plants, 1965–94

Environmental Treaties Grow in Number — Hilary F. French

Two more titles were added to the list of international environmental treaties in 1994, bringing the total to 173.[1] (See Figure 1.) The additions covered desertification worldwide and trade in endangered species in Africa. (The official titles are the United Nations Convention to Combat Desertification in Those Countries Experiencing Serious Drought and/or Desertification, Particularly in Africa, and the Lusaka Agreement on Cooperative Enforcement Operations Directed at Illegal Trade in Wild Fauna and Flora.)[2]

Recent months also saw three landmark accords enter into force after the required number of countries ratified them: The Convention on Biological Diversity and the Framework Convention on Climate Change, both initially opened for signature at the June 1992 Earth Summit, entered into force on December 29, 1993, and in March 1994, respectively.[3] And the 1982 Law of the Sea treaty finally entered into force on November 16, 1994, when it received the necessary 60 ratifications.[4]

The number of international environmental treaties has been growing steadily since 1950, but the trend began to accelerate rapidly in the early seventies. More than two thirds of existing treaties have been negotiated since the beginning of 1972, when the U.N. Conference on the Human Environment first put the environment on the international agenda.[5] If other, less binding types of accords as well as bilateral agreements are included in the total, nearly 900 international environmental instruments are on the books, according to one count.[6]

Some of these agreements have led to measurable gains. The 1987 Montreal Protocol on the Depletion of the Ozone Layer is the most notable success to date. As a result of this accord, global chlorofluorocarbon emissions have already dropped 77 percent from their 1988 peak.[7] Computer models suggest that chlorine concentrations in the lower atmosphere should thus be beginning to level off rather than climbing as high as 12 parts per billion by volume early in the next century, as was originally forecast.[8] (See Figure 2.) Through international cooperation, therefore, millions of skin cancer cases will be averted, and untold damage to agricultural productivity and ecosystems prevented.[9]

Similarly, air pollution in Europe has been reduced dramatically as a result of the 1979 treaty on transboundary air pollution.[10] Mining exploration and development have been forbidden in Antarctica for 50 years under a 1991 accord.[11] And the export of hazardous wastes from industrial to developing countries will be prohibited starting on December 31, 1997, following a March 1994 decision by the parties to the 1989 Basel Convention on trade in hazardous wastes.[12]

Though some treaties have been successes, many more have failed to ignite the needed changes in domestic policies.[13] All too often, environmental accords are written in such vague terms that they commit signatories to little. The Rio treaties on climate and biological diversity are vulnerable to criticism on these grounds.

Monitoring of compliance with agreements is generally cursory at best, with countries often failing even to submit the required reports on efforts to implement the accords. A 1991 U.S. General Accounting Office survey found that only about 60 percent of the parties to the 1972 London Dumping Convention complied with reporting obligations, while only 30 percent of the members of the MARPOL convention on pollution from ships did.[14] Although 80 percent of the parties to the Montreal Protocol submitted some information, much of it was incomplete.[15]

Even when violators are identified, sanctions are rarely imposed. And developing countries often cannot comply with international accords because industrial countries fail to deliver on promises of financial and technological assistance. For instance, the good intentions behind the 1972 World Heritage Convention, intended to preserve important cultural and biological sites, have been largely undermined by a failure of participating countries to contribute the promised funds.[16]

Encouragingly, the broad framework of international agreements needed to protect the global environment is in place. The challenge now is to see that existing agreements are translated into action around the world.

Environmental Treaties Grow in Number

INTERNATIONAL ENVIRONMENTAL
TREATIES, 1950–94

YEAR	CUMULATIVE (number)
1950	7
1956	14
1960	25
1961	27
1962	29
1963	35
1964	37
19651	38
1966	39
1967	41
1968	44
1969	50
1970	52
1971	58
1972	64
1973	71
1974	76
1976	86
1977	88
1978	93
1979	99
1980	104
1981	109
1982	116
1983	122
1984	123
1985	131
1986	140
1987	143
1988	147
1989	153
1990	158
1991	164
1992	171
1994	173

SOURCES: UNEP, *Register of International Treaties and Other Agreements in the Field of the Environment 1993* (Nairobi: 1993); Mark Labelle, Treaty Office, United Nations, New York, private communication, October 17, 1994.

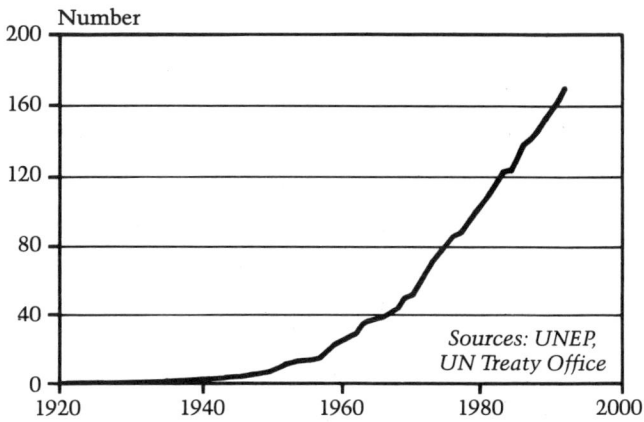

Figure 1: International Environmental Treaties, Cumulative, 1921–94

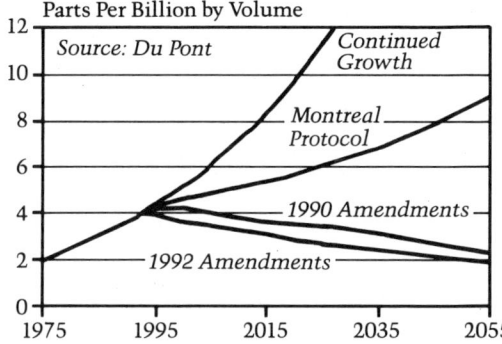

Figure 2: Atmospheric Chlorine, 1975–93, with Projections to 2055 Under Four Scenarios

Social Trends

Population Growth Steady

Aaron Sachs

Population growth remained steady in 1994, as we added another 88 million people—the equivalent of two new South Koreas.[1] The world's population is now just over 5.6 billion.[2] (See Figures 1 and 2.)

Annual population growth seems to have reached a plateau, at least temporarily. The world has added between 86 million and 90 million people every year for the past decade.[3] There was a similar levelling off during the seventies, before the annual addition began to jump upward again in the eighties.

The average annual growth rate—the net population addition expressed as a percentage of the total population—continues to decline very gradually. Since peaking at 2.2 percent in 1963, it has come down to 1.54 percent as of 1994.[4] (See Figure 3.)

Despite this steady decline, the world will not be on its way toward population stabilization until the net annual increase starts coming down as well. Annual population growth may turn out to have reached its peak in 1989, when it was just under 90 million.[5] But demographic forecasters say that it will probably not begin a steady drop from its current plateau until about 2025.[6]

A certain amount of population growth over the next several decades is inevitable. Even if the nearly 1.9 billion people now under the age of 15 were to have only enough children to replace themselves—two each—population growth would continue for at least a few generations.[7] After all, parents are not literally replaced by their children until several decades later, by which time they may already have grandchildren and great grandchildren.

By 2050, according to the most recent U.N. projections, global population will have risen to at least 7.9 billion: at a minimum, the world will have added the equivalent of three new Africas.[8] More likely, total population will be closer to 9.8 billion by then, and it could possibly reach 11.9 billion.[9] Where we fall within this range will depend largely on the level of the international community's commitment to population issues.

At the remarkably successful International Conference on Population and Development (ICPD), held in September 1994 in Cairo, the world's nations renewed that commitment. The conference, third in a series of U.N.-sponsored population meetings, produced a 20-year Programme of Action endorsed by 180 countries.[10] If the world effectively implements the plan's objectives, which address "many of the fundamental population, health, education, and development challenges facing the entire human community," global population as of 2050 should end up below the medium U.N. projection of 9.8 billion.[11]

Previous population policies tended to focus simply on supplying more couples with more contraceptives. But more-recent studies showed that to achieve population stabilization, couples' desired fertility levels must drop: in many parts of the developing world, no matter how accessible family planning services are, many men and women still say that they wish to have six or more children.[12] Large numbers of women, especially, were put off by the old approach, since they came to feel as though they were merely instruments in government efforts to comply with population quotas.[13]

The ICPD approach emphasizes creating conditions under which couples willingly lower their fertility. The most important element in the new Programme of Action is the focus on empowering women.[14] Many women in the developing world—where more than 90 percent of current population growth occurs—choose to have large families simply because they have no other means of achieving social and economic security.[15]

All too often, females in male-dominated societies find themselves deprived of an education and forced to marry at a very young age. Women get paid about 40 percent less than men for the same jobs; they have very limited access to bank credit and land; and they have hardly any opportunities to participate in politics.[16] Clearly, policies designed to improve the well-being of women, to expand access to health care, education, and employment, and to make men more responsible for families would go far in both promoting basic human development and slowing population growth.

Population Growth Steady

WORLD POPULATION, TOTAL AND ANNUAL ADDITION, 1950–94

YEAR	POPULATION (billion)	ANNUAL ADDITION (million)
1950	2.555	37
1955	2.779	53
1960	3.038	41
1961	3.079	56
1962	3.135	70
1963	3.204	71
1964	3.276	69
1965	3.345	70
1966	3.414	69
1967	3.484	71
1968	3.555	74
1969	3.629	75
1970	3.704	78
1971	3.782	77
1972	3.859	77
1973	3.936	76
1974	4.012	74
1975	4.086	73
1976	4.159	73
1977	4.231	73
1978	4.304	76
1979	4.380	77
1980	4.457	77
1981	4.533	81
1982	4.614	81
1983	4.695	80
1984	4.775	81
1985	4.856	83
1986	4.941	87
1987	5.029	88
1988	5.117	88
1989	5.205	90
1990	5.295	86
1991	5.381	88
1992	5.469	88
1993	5.556	88
1994 (prel)	5.644	88

SOURCE: U.S. Bureau of the Census, Center for International Research, private communication, February 6, 1995.

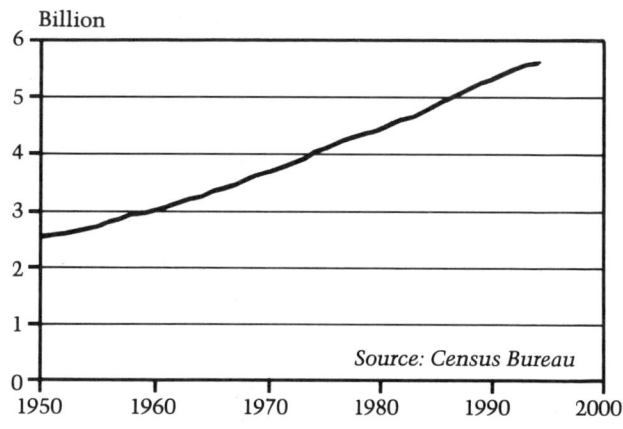

Figure 1: World Population, 1950–94

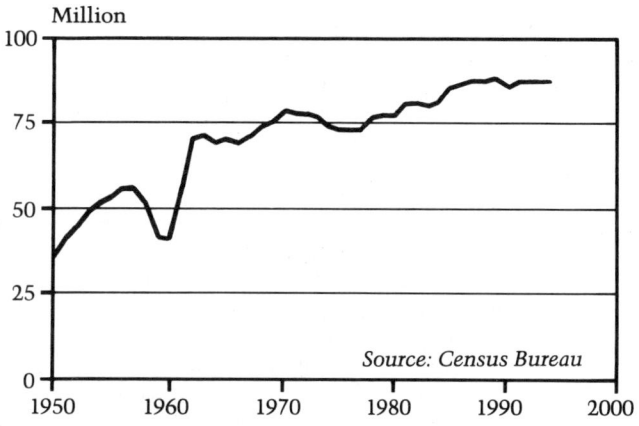

Figure 2: Annual Addition to World Population, 1950–94

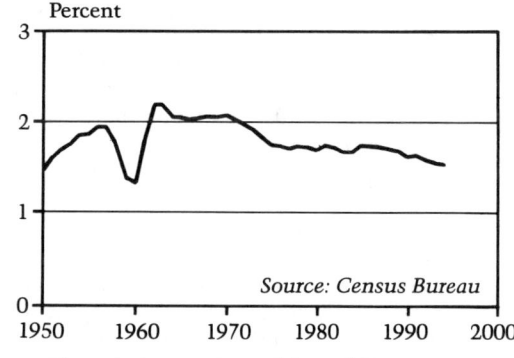

Figure 3: Average Annual Growth Rate, 1950–94

Cigarette Production Up Slightly

Hal Kane

The number of cigarettes produced in the world rose 1 percent in 1994, to 5.34 trillion.[1] (See Figure 1.) World cigarette production per person fell slightly, however, continuing a downward trend under way since 1988.[2] The average number of cigarettes available per person in the world was 946, down 8 percent from the peak of 1,029 in 1988.[3] (See Figure 2.)

The biggest increase in production came in China, where 25 billion more cigarettes were produced in 1994 than in 1993, and fully 100 billion more than in 1991.[4] With 1.7 trillion cigarettes a year, China is the world's largest producer.[5] (See Figure 3.) Other East Asian countries showed smaller changes, with Indonesia's output rising by 2.5 billion, Japan's production dropping by 3.5 billion, and South Korea's falling by more than 3 billion.[6]

The most important drops in production came in Europe and the United States. The U.S. cigarette industry produced 654 billion cigarettes, almost 7 billion fewer than in 1993 and 64 billion fewer than in 1992.[7] France cut almost 3 billion from its output, Germany cut 2 billion, and Spain made about 2.5 billion fewer cigarettes.[8] The United Kingdom raised output by almost 9 billion, though, offsetting other reductions in the area.[9]

Russia boosted cigarette production by 8 billion, as it continues to make up for the sharp drop in output that occurred when the Soviet Union collapsed.[10] Consumers' appetites for tobacco in that part of the world sometimes appear insatiable. The rise in production there also reflects the entrance of western tobacco companies into the Russian market during the early nineties. Their new plants and remodeled facilities are now beginning to operate.[11] Similar situations in other former Soviet lands raised Ukrainian cigarette production by 2 billion pieces, Tajik production by almost 1 billion, Kazakh output by nearly 1 billion, and Uzbek production by 2 billion.[12] Romanian production is up by 1.5 billion pieces.[13]

China is not only the largest producer of cigarettes, it is the largest market—with more than 300 million smokers.[14] Cigarette consumption there grew 5 percent a year during the eighties, and that growth is expected to accelerate as incomes continue their meteoric rise.[15] The *Guangming Daily,* an official newspaper, reports that in China 35 percent of children aged 12 to 15 smoke, as do 10 percent of 9- to 12-year-olds, providing the base for massive cigarette consumption in the future.[16]

Currently, foreign-brand cigarettes get less than 1 percent of China's market, but demand among consumers for foreign tobacco is high, and economic reforms are gradually opening the economy to the outside world.[17] Following their expansions into the former Soviet Union, Philip Morris and RJR Nabisco have signed agreements with the government-run China National Tobacco Corporation to produce in China.[18]

As a result, tobacco production and use will have major effects on China. Farmland planted in tobacco has increased 10 times—to 1.6 million hectares—in the last three decades, despite competition with cotton and grain.[19] And in a country deeply concerned about its air pollution because of excessive reliance on coal, second-hand tobacco smoke will add to the illness rates. A study done for the United States, for example, found that a 2-percent decrease in environmental tobacco smoke would do as much to lower exposure to harmful particulates as eliminating all the coal-fired power plants in the country.[20]

Ever increasing restrictions on smoking in industrial countries are likely to force the tobacco industry to expand into developing nations not just in eastern Asia, but also southern Asia, Latin America, and possibly Africa. In the United States, for instance, bans continue to spread. The U.S. military declared in 1994 that smoking will no longer be permitted in the military workplace, the most comprehensive ban ever imposed by a federal agency or business.[21] City governments, airlines and airports, restaurants, sports facilities, and office buildings have all tightened restrictions on smoking lately.[22]

Cigarette Production Up Slightly

WORLD CIGARETTE PRODUCTION, TOTAL AND PER PERSON, 1950–94

YEAR	PRODUCTION (billion)	PER PERSON (number of cigarettes)
1950	1,686	660
1955	1,921	691
1960	2,150	708
1961	2,140	695
1962	2,191	699
1963	2,300	718
1964	2,402	733
1965	2,564	767
1966	2,678	784
1967	2,689	772
1968	2,790	785
1969	2,924	806
1970	3,112	840
1971	3,165	837
1972	3,295	854
1973	3,481	884
1974	3,590	895
1975	3,742	916
1976	3,852	926
1977	4,019	950
1978	4,072	946
1979	4,214	962
1980	4,388	985
1981	4,541	1,002
1982	4,550	986
1983	4,547	968
1984	4,689	982
1985	4,855	1,000
1986	4,987	1,009
1987	5,128	1,020
1988	5,266	1,029
1989	5,257	1,010
1990	5,417	1,023
1991	5,350	994
1992	5,361	980
1993	5,285	951
1994 (prel)	5,340	946

SOURCE: USDA, FAS, unpublished printouts, various dates; data for 1950–58, estimates based on U.S. data; China from Pete Burr, private communications, December 1993; U.S. from USDA, *Tobacco Situation and Outlook Yearbook*, December 20, 1994.

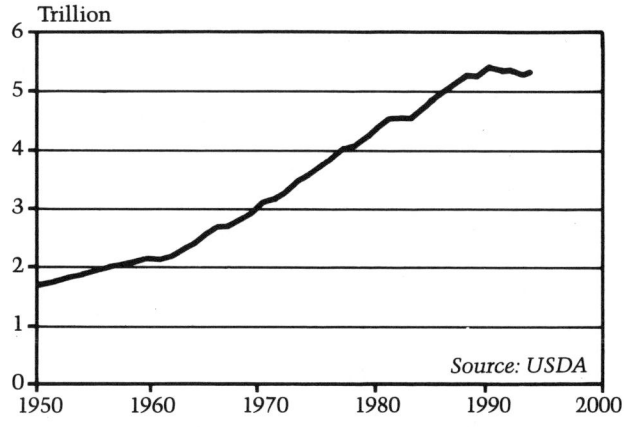

Figure 1: World Cigarette Production, 1950–94

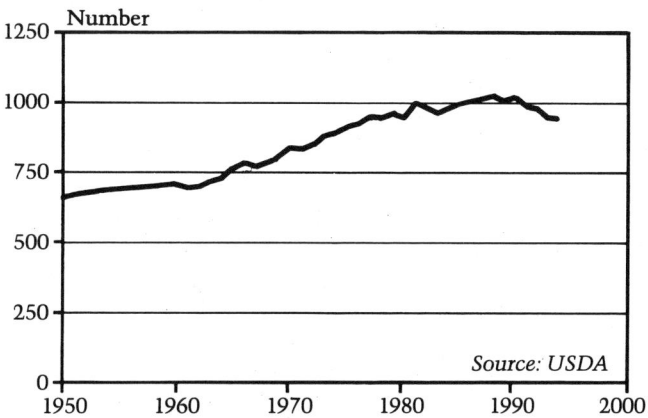

Figure 2: World Cigarette Production Per Person, 1950–94

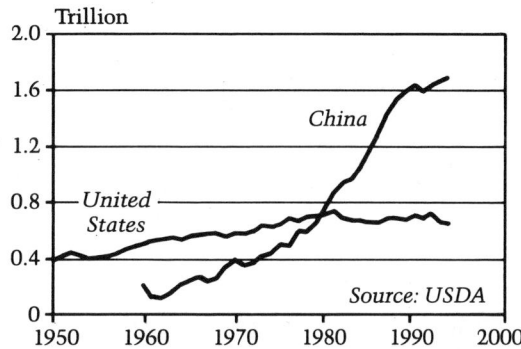

Figure 3: Cigarette Production, United States and China, 1950–94

HIV/AIDS Cases Rise at Record Rates

Aaron Sachs

In 1994, a record number of people—some 4 million—contracted the human immunodeficiency virus (HIV), which causes AIDS.[1] Some 400,000 babies were born with HIV in 1994, and 1.4 million women contracted the virus, representing 39 percent of all newly infected adults.[2] During the same 12 months, an estimated 1.6 million carriers of HIV developed full-blown cases of AIDS, also more than in any previous year.[3] And a record number died of AIDS—1.5 million.[4]

Since the beginning of the HIV/AIDS pandemic, in the late seventies, 20–26 million people have been infected with the deadly virus.[5] (See Figure 1.) Some 5–9 million of these individuals have already developed full-blown AIDS (see Figure 2), and nearly 90 percent of these AIDS patients have died.[6]

Unfortunately, experts are projecting that the spread of HIV will continue at record rates for the next few years. Since the virus is especially active right now in Asia, home to some of the world's most densely populated countries, the number of people carrying the virus could quite easily double by the end of this decade.[7]

Much of the money currently spent on HIV/AIDS goes toward the development of vaccines and drugs. Such research is crucial, but HIV replicates and mutates so frequently that it has so far proved resistant even to the most sophisticated biochemical interventions.[8] Moreover, most of the people who have HIV/AIDS live in impoverished regions of sub-Saharan Africa and Southeast Asia, where they have no access to any drugs whatsoever.[9]

Experts on the pandemic have called for an increase in funding and a redirection of spending toward prevention and affordable care for people in the developing world—but with few results. Only 10 percent of the global HIV/AIDS budget is spent by industrial countries in the comparatively poor developing countries, though as of 1994, 92 percent of all HIV infections had occurred in the developing world.[10]

In 1994, 48 percent of the new HIV infections—1.9 million out of 4 million—occurred in sub-Saharan Africa, the epicenter of the pandemic.[11] But Southeast Asia had 1.7 million new infections, and there will probably be more new annual infections in Asia than in Africa within a few years.[12] Just between 1992 and 1994, the number of HIV infections in India tripled.[13]

In sub-Saharan Africa, where HIV is spread primarily through heterosexual sex, there were more new infections among women than among men.[14] Prevention programs that encourage men to be sexually responsible and that empower women, perhaps through wider distribution of female condoms, merit special attention, since many women in male-dominated societies currently have no way to protect themselves.

One reason HIV/AIDS poses so great a threat is that its extremely long incubation period makes it hard to detect: infected people often end up spreading the virus for several years before realizing they have it themselves. In Asia, this pattern has been especially devastating. Many Asian countries have thriving sex industries, and young adults often have multiple sex partners. In addition, rapid economic transformations in much of Asia have created huge populations of internal migrants, whose unstable lives make them particularly vulnerable to infection.[15]

HIV/AIDS is also destabilizing on a broad scale because it claims mainly the most economically productive members of society. In Zambia, the health ministry estimates that 20–25 percent of women aged 15–49 are HIV-positive.[16] Most beds in many African hospitals go to AIDS patients, and some industries are beginning to experience labor shortages.[17] Although new HIV infections in sub-Saharan Africa seem to have reached a plateau, the region's AIDS caseload will likely triple in the next decade.[18] By 2010, according to current projections, AIDS will have cut the average life expectancy in many African countries by more than 25 years.[19]

We know exactly how to slow the spread of HIV; we lack only the political will. Spending just $1.5 billion a year on Asian prevention programs, for instance, would save at least 5 million people from infection by the end of this decade.[20]

HIV/AIDS Cases Rise at Record Rates

GLOBAL ESTIMATES OF CUMULATIVE HIV/AIDS CASES, 1980–94

YEAR	HIV INFECTIONS (million)
1980	0.2
1981	0.6
1982	1.1
1983	1.8
1984	2.7
1985	3.9
1986	5.3
1987	6.9
1988	8.7
1989	10.7
1990	13.0
1991	15.5
1992	18.5
1993	21.9
1994 (prel)	25.9

YEAR	AIDS CASES (million)
1980	0
1981	<0.1
1982	<0.1
1983	0.1
1984	0.2
1985	0.4
1986	0.7
1987	1.1
1988	1.6
1989	2.3
1990	3.2
1991	4.2
1992	5.5
1993	6.9
1994 (prel)	8.5

SOURCE: Global AIDS Policy Coalition, Harvard School of Public Health, Cambridge, Mass., private communication, January 20, 1995.

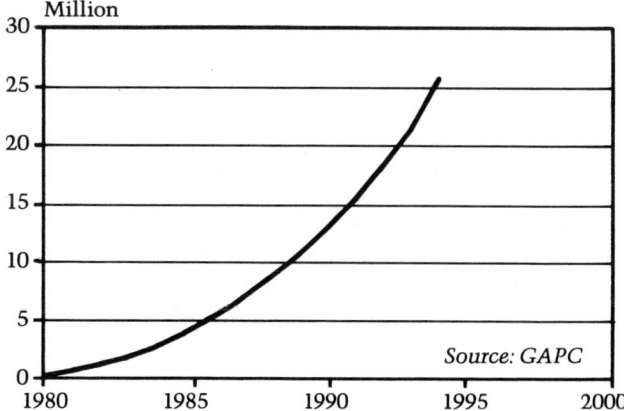

Figure 1: Estimates of HIV Infections Worldwide, 1980–94

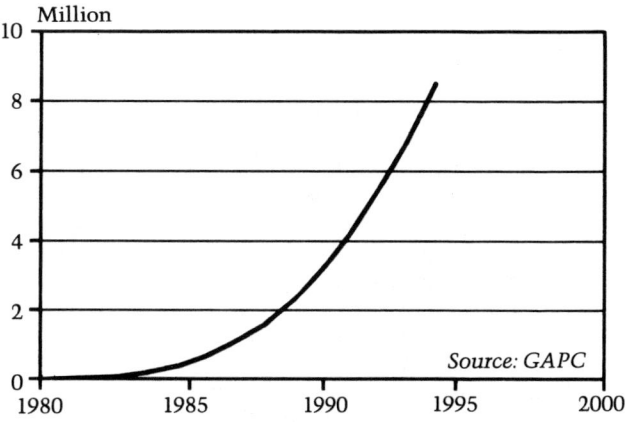

Figure 2: Estimates of AIDS Cases Worldwide, 1980–94

Urbanization Spreading

Elena Wilken

Since 1950, the number of people living in urban areas has jumped from 737 million to 2.6 billion.[1] (See Figure 1.) The urban share of total population increased from 29 to 45 percent. The United Nations estimates that by 2025, 60 percent of the world's population will live in urban areas.[2]

The populations of the industrial regions of North America, Europe, Japan, and Oceania were already more than half urban by 1950, so much of the current trend is due to urbanization in the developing regions of Asia, Africa, and Latin America.[3] The share of urban populations in developing regions more than doubled, from 17 to 37 percent between 1950 and 1995.[4] (See Figure 2.)

Three factors drive urban growth: internal population growth, rural-to-urban migration, and the inclusion of new urban areas.[5] Rural-urban disparities in income and access to services precipitate rural-to-urban migration, but as global estimates fail to distinguish between the types of growth, gauging the contribution of each factor is difficult.[6]

The number of people living in cities of 4 million or more leapt from 88 million to 495 million between 1950 and 1990, making this the fastest growing class of city, with most of the growth in developing regions.[7] (See Figure 3.) In 1950, five cities in developing regions had populations over 4 million. Today there are 43.[8]

Despite the rapid rate of growth in larger urban areas, more than 70 percent of the world's urban population lives in cities with fewer than 2 million people.[9]

These cities suffer many of the same environmental and social ills as the larger urban centers. In a study comparing people's access to services, the Stockholm Environment Institute found that the overall wealth of a city, not its size, determines living conditions.[10] Pollution and resource scarcity affect residents in poorer cities directly, whereas wealthier cities are able to export water and solid waste pollution and to import resources.

In Accra, Ghana, only a third of the people have running water and flush toilets in their houses. The other two thirds rely on street vendors for clean water and use common latrine facilities. Inadequate water supplies and sewage systems contribute to the two most common diseases: diarrhea and malaria.[11] São Paulo, on the other hand, serves two thirds of its population with plumbing. But as most of the city' sewage is untreated, downstream communities and ecosystems bear the brunt of pollution.[12]

Solid waste also contributes to disease. Half of the 2 million people in Surat, India, live in unauthorized colonies with no sewage or garbage collection.[13] Rotting animal carcasses and piles of garbage abetted the epidemic of pneumonic plague that swept the city in the summer of 1994.[14] Although an extreme example of poor waste management, Surat exemplifies the difficulties faced by mid-sized, middle-income cities. Higher levels of consumption and industry generate more waste, yet inadequate funding limits the ability to meet the needs of growing populations.[15] When villages around Chiang Mai, Thailand, refused to accept more waste, 250 tons of garbage a day piled up in the streets while the government sought new dumping sites.[16]

Air pollution contributes to respiratory ailments and declining ecosystems.[17] Scarcely a century ago, Los Angeles was a small city in the most productive U.S. agricultural valley. It is now a 450-square-mile (1,200-square-kilometer) network of roads and development.[18] With little public transportation, residents rely on automobiles: the region has perhaps the highest number of vehicles per person in the world, and daily commutes of 60–80 miles (95–130 kilometers) are not unusual.[19] Despite increasingly stringent control measures, smog continues to plague residents both in the city and in outlying regions. The state standard for ozone was exceeded at all monitoring sites in 1990, and in some areas on more than 100 days in the year.[20]

Urbanization Spreading

WORLD URBAN POPULATION, 1950–95

YEAR	POPULATION (million)
1950	737
1955	862
1960	1,032
1965	1,191
1970	1,353
1975	1,537
1980	1,752
1985	2,000
1990	2,282
1995 (prel)	2,603

SHARE OF POPULATION THAT IS URBAN, INDUSTRIAL COUNTRIES, 1950–95

YEAR	SHARE (percent)
1950	54
1955	57
1960	61
1965	64
1970	67
1975	69
1980	70
1985	72
1990	73
1995 (prel)	74

SHARE OF POPULATION THAT IS URBAN, DEVELOPING COUNTRIES, 1950–95

YEAR	SHARE (percent)
1950	17
1955	19
1960	22
1965	23
1970	25
1975	26
1980	29
1985	32
1990	34
1995 (prel)	37

SOURCE: United Nations, *World Population Prospects: The 1992 Revision* (New York: 1993).

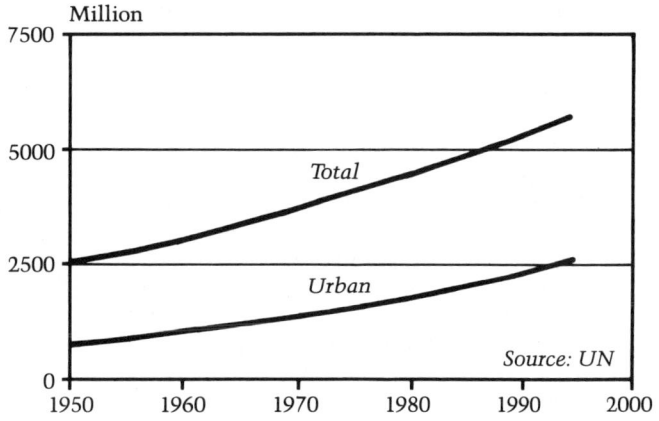

Figure 1: World Population, Total and Urban, 1950–95

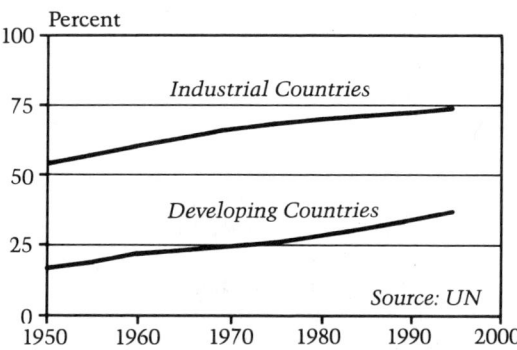

Figure 2: Share of Population That Is Urban, by Region, 1950–95

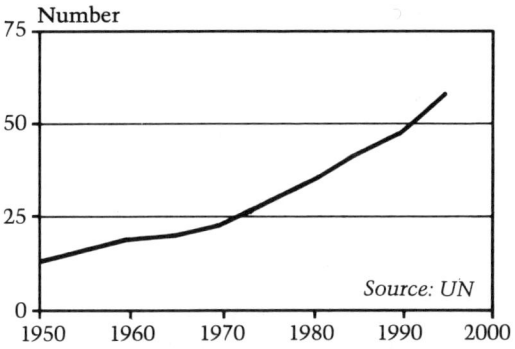

Figure 3: Cities with Populations of 4 Million or More, 1950–95

Refugee Flow Unabated
Hal Kane

The number of official refugees in the world reached 23 million in 1994.[1] (See Figure 1.) These individuals met the criteria written in 1951 and affirmed in 1967 by the United Nations as people who demonstrate "a well-founded fear of being persecuted for reasons of race, religion, nationality, membership of a particular social group or political opinion."[2] The figure reflects rapid and almost continuous growth since the mid-seventies, at an average of 12 percent per year.[3]

Afghanistan was the source of the largest number of refugees—almost 3 million at the end of 1994.[4] But that figure represents a sharp decline from more than 6 million in the early nineties.[5] The second largest source was Bosnia and Herzegovina—more than 2.7 million individuals by year's end—although those displaced people are a somewhat unusual group because many have not crossed a national border.[6] They are internally displaced peoples, but the U.N. High Commissioner for Refugees has included them in the count of the world total because of their urgent need for protection.

Rwanda accounted for the third largest number of refugees, at more than 2.1 million.[7] Liberia was fourth with 848,000, though with migrants from that country added into the figure, almost half of its 2.5 million citizens are in exile (and many of the migrants also left because of fears).[8] It is followed by Mozambique, Azerbaijan, Croatia, and Tajikistan, all of which have refugess who are mainly internally displaced people, reflecting a growing willingness on the part of the United Nations to protect people who have not crossed international borders.[9]

The net increase of 3 million in the number of refugees in 1994—in just one year—is large by historical standards. For example, the figure is more than all the migrants who left Spain (at their leisure) to colonize the Americas during the nineteenth and early twentieth centuries, one of the times of heaviest migration.[10]

Significant repatriations of refugees also took place in 1994. Some 2.8 million Afghanis have returned home since 1990.[11] A million and a half Iraqis have returned since 1991.[12] Almost all of Mozambique's 1.5 million refugees have repatriated since 1992.[13] Some 600,000 people repatriated to Ethiopia since 1991 out of 1 million at the peak of flight in 1989.[14] About a half-million refugees from Rwanda have recently returned, though fears of continued fighting keep most refugees away.[15] Almost a half-million have returned to Burundi, and 400,000 to Somalia.[16]

Europe passed Asia in 1993 as having the second highest number of refugees of any continent.[17] But Africa also passed Asia in 1993 to take first.[18] (See Figure 2.) The effects are being felt there of such slow growth that the gross domestic product per person is no higher than it was in 1980.[19] Rapid population growth in countries with limited cropland and few jobs has contributed to volatile circumstances, from Rwanda to Somalia, Liberia, Kenya, and elsewhere.

Many countries in Africa and around the world have been living off their capital—consuming their foreign reserves, their forests, soils, and underground aquifers, and the patience of their citizens in order to survive in the short term. As these reserves are diminished, pressures and conflicts mount and some people are forced to flee.

While crisis-driven expenditures are rising out of necessity, efforts to foster the development that could enable people to stay home are decreasing. Official development assistance from the world's 25 wealthiest countries fell by 8 percent in 1993.[20] In 1994, the United Nations expected to spend at least $1 billion more on refugees and peacekeeping than on economic development.[21] The budget of the U.N. Development Programme is now not much larger than that of the U.N. High Commissioner for Refugees.[22]

If this trend endures, the rapid current and historical growth in the number of refugees is likely to continue. Indeed, new countries appear poised to join the list of nations that refugees have fled. Most recently, violence between fundamentalist Muslims and the military government in Algeria has killed 28,000.[23] Other countries that appear likely sources of refugees in the future include Iraq, Myanmar (formerly Burma), Sudan, and Zaire.

Refugee Flow Unabated

WORLD REFUGEES, 1960–94

YEAR	TOTAL (million)
1960	1.4
1961	1.3
1962	1.3
1963	1.3
1964	1.5
1965	1.6
1966	1.8
1967	2.0
1968	2.2
1969	2.3
1970	2.5
1971	2.5
1972	2.4
1973	2.4
1974	2.4
1975	2.6
1976	2.8
1977	3.3
1978	4.6
1979	5.7
1980	8.2
1981	9.8
1982	10.4
1983	10.9
1984	10.5
1985	11.6
1986	12.4
1987	13.3
1988	14.8
1989	14.9
1990	17.2
1991	17.0
1992	18.2
1993	20.0
1994 (prel)	23.0

SOURCE: U.N. High Commissioner for Refugees, *The State of the World's Refugees* (New York: Penguin Books, 1993); UNHCR, private communications, February 1995.

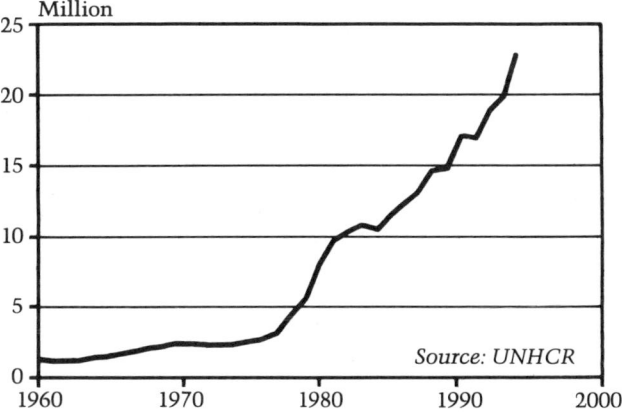

Figure 1: World Official Refugees, 1960–94

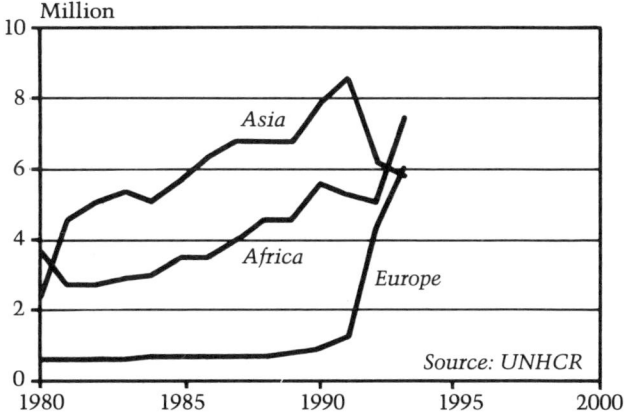

Figure 2: Official Refugees, Asia, Africa, and Europe, 1980–93

Military Trends

Nuclear Arsenals Decline Again — Michael Renner

The number of nuclear warheads worldwide declined by 3 percent in 1994, from 49,910 in 1993 to 45,100.[1] (See Figure 1.) Together, they contain the destructive equivalent of 9,700,000,000 tons of TNT.[2]

Since the 1986 peak of 69,480 warheads, the global nuclear arsenal has dropped by 35 percent. Yet today's numbers are still substantially above the roughly 41,000 deployed in 1968—the year the Nuclear Non-Proliferation Treaty (NPT) was signed and the nuclear weapons states pledged to move toward disarmament.[3]

Five governments have acknowledged possession of nuclear arms—the United States, the former Soviet Union (Russia being the sole successor state that is to retain its arsenal), China, France, and the United Kingdom. They manufactured a total of 128,000 nuclear warheads since 1945.[4] And they have spent more than $5 trillion on warheads and the bombers, missiles, and submarines to deliver them.[5]

The United States and Russia together control more than 97 perent of all nuclear warheads worldwide. In 1994, the two countries together had 16,900 strategic and 27,000 nonstrategic warheads, down from peak levels of 23,797 strategic warheads in 1989 and 45,906 tactical warheads in 1986.[6] (See Figure 2.) Once the two Strategic Arms Reductions Treaties (START I and II) are fully implemented by 2003, each of these countries will retain 3,000–3,500 strategic warheads.[7]

Even before START I became effective on December 1, 1994, the United States and Russia started to deactivate some of their strategic weapons. By the end of 1994, the United States had removed all 3,906 ballistic missile warheads that are to be eliminated from launchers, and had eliminated 34 percent of the launchers themselves.[8] Russia had gotten rid of approximately 50 percent of the ballistic missile launchers that it is required to destroy under START.[9] Presidents Clinton and Yeltsin agreed to seek ratification of the START II Treaty by the spring of 1995 and to accelerate deactivation and dismantlement of systems slated for elimination.[10]

Proliferation has emerged as a major concern—both from the possibility of other countries developing nuclear capabilities and from the smuggling of nuclear-weapons materials out of the Soviet successor states. Israel, India, and Pakistan are thought to either have small nuclear arsenals or be able to assemble them, and additional countries are believed to be pursuing nuclear status.[11] On the other hand, South Africa announced in 1993 that it had dismantled its arsenal of six warheads.[12]

Belarus, Kazakhstan, and Ukraine committed themselves in May 1992 to relinquish the atomic arsenals inherited from the Soviet Union. But Ukraine subsequently displayed great reluctance to follow through on this, and so held up Russian ratification of the START treaties.[13]

It was only in November 1994 that the Ukrainian parliament ratified START I and agreed to join the NPT as a nonnuclear party.[14] However, Kiev had already begun moving its strategic weapons to Russia for dismantlement. By the end of 1994, 700 out of a total of 1,734 Ukrainian warheads had been taken out of deployment, and half of those were already back in Russia.[15] Kazakhstan had deactivated 810 out of its 1,410 warheads and shipped about 500 to Russia. Belarus, with a smaller nuclear force of 54 waheads, had already come very close to denuclearization.[16]

The number of nuclear test explosions has declined sharply in recent years. (See Figure 3.) Russia and France have observed moratoria on testing since 1991; the United States joined them in October 1992 (meaning that the United Kingdom, which relies on the U.S. test ground in Nevada, had to suspend testing as well).[17] However, China, intent on modernizing its arsenal, has continued testing, detonating one bomb in 1993 and two in 1994.[18]

Comprehensive nuclear test ban talks began in January 1994. Progress toward outlawing all nuclear explosions is one critical issue for the April 1995 international conference that is to decide whether and under what conditions the NPT should be renewed. (Another is a ban on the production of fissile materials for weapons purposes.) The nuclear weapons states want unconditional extension, but many other countries want to see more evidence that these nations are disarming as required by the NPT.[19]

Nuclear Arsenals Decline Again

WORLD NUCLEAR ARSENALS, 1945–94

YEAR	NUCLEAR WARHEADS (number)
1945	2
1950	304
1955	2,632
1960	20,368
1961	24,729
1962	30,405
1963	34,080
1964	37,015
1965	39,050
1966	40,330
1967	41,685
1968	41,055
1969	39,600
1970	39,695
1971	41,365
1972	44,020
1973	47,745
1974	50,840
1975	52,325
1976	53,255
1977	54,980
1978	56,805
1979	59,120
1980	61,480
1981	63,055
1982	64,770
1983	66,980
1984	67,865
1985	68,590
1986	69,480
1987	68,835
1988	67,040
1989	63,650
1990	60,240
1991	55,775
1992	52,875
1993	49,910
1994 (prel)	45,100

SOURCES: *Bulletin of the Atomic Scientists,* December 1993 and November/December 1994; *New York Times,* October 26, 1994.

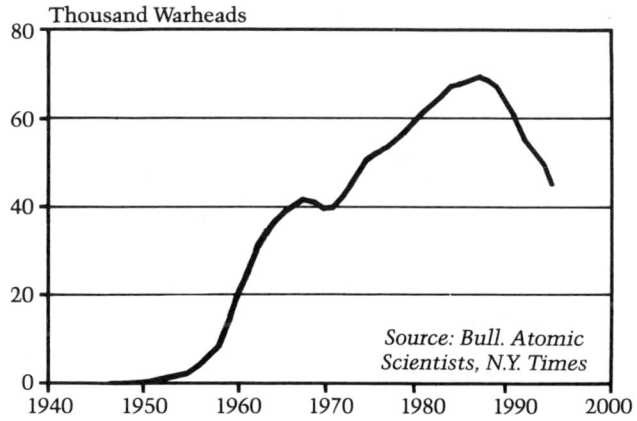

Figure 1: Global Nuclear Arsenal, 1945–94

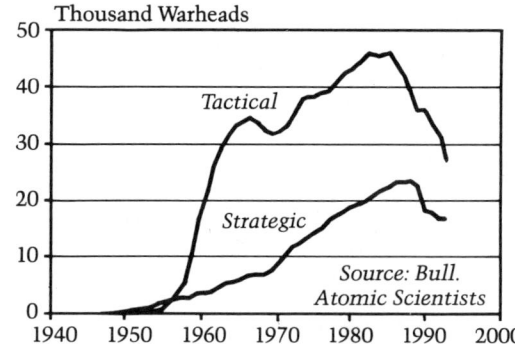

Figure 2: U.S. and Soviet Strategic and Tactical Nuclear Warheads, 1945–94

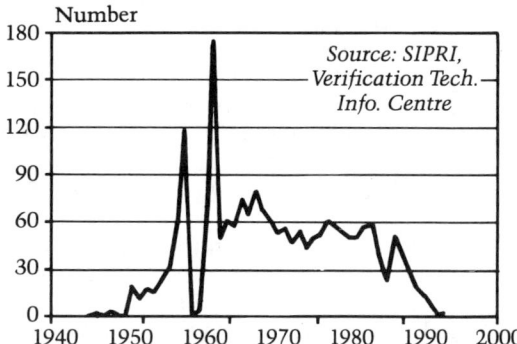

Figure 3: Nuclear Warhead Tests, 1945–94

Peacekeeping Expenses Reach New High — Michael Renner

Expenditures for United Nations peacekeeping operations reached an estimated $3.7 billion in 1994, an increase of 22 percent in one year.[1] Since 1987, the rising number, size, and complexity of such missions caused spending to increase more than fourteenfold. (See Figure 1.)

More than half the nearly $14 billion in outlays from 1947 to 1994 were made in just three years—during 1992–94.[2] By 1994, the U.N. had 17 ongoing peacekeeping operations, and was engaged in peace efforts in nine additional conflicts; some 76 countries contributed 77,783 military and civilian personnel, up from 26 countries and 11,121 individuals in 1988.[3]

Peacekeeping expenditures represent the largest single item in the broader category of peace expenditures, which includes spending for nuclear, chemical, and conventional disarmament; demobilization of soldiers and ex-combatants; land mine clearance; repatriation of refugees; military base closures; and defense conversion.

Combined global expenditures for all peace-related endeavors grew from $2.5 billion in 1989 to $15.8 billion in 1994.[4] (See Figure 2.) Even after this sixfold growth, however, the world's governments still spend about $50 on the military for every $1 devoted to peace and disarmament.[5]

U.N. peacekeeping has suffered from having to shoulder a mushrooming number of difficult tasks without receiving anywhere near adequate financial support. Many governments continue to pay their share of assessed costs late, or only a portion of what they owe. Member-governments' collective arrears ballooned just as rapidly as the U.N.'s peacekeeping expenditures: from $19 million in 1975 to $993 million at the end of 1993.[6] They reached a record $2.5 billion in July 1994, before belated contributions by several member-states reduced them to $1.3 billion at the end of the year.[7] (See Figure 3.)

The United States and Russia are by far the biggest debtors. In July 1994, U.S. peacekeeping debts peaked at $956 million. They were reduced to $221 million by the year's end, but are certain to balloon again, particularly given rising congressional hostility toward the United Nations.[8] Russia, in dire economic straits, owes the U.N. $496 million.[9]

To avoid financial collapse, the U.N. has had to resort to internal borrowing—juggling money among different accounts—and to delay reimbursing governments that contribute personnel and equipment to peacekeeping operations. At the end of 1993, the organization owed some $335 million to these countries.[10] But by the fall of 1994, the reimbursement backlog reached more than $1 billion. At least 20 countries have indicated that they consider this an obstacle to their participation in ongoing or future peacekeeping missions.[11]

Just two operations—in the former Yugoslavia and in Somalia—accounted for 70 percent of total peacekeeping costs in 1994.[12] (The third of the three most expensive operations—in Cambodia—came to a successful end in 1993.) The U.N. Security Council voted to terminate the mission in Somalia, widely considered to be a failure, by March 1995.[13] Prospects for the operation in the former Yugoslavia are clouded. U.N. personnel are stationed in both Croatia and Bosnia. But the U.N. might terminate the mission in Bosnia if a peace agreement is not reached soon, and Croatian President Tudjman announced in January 1995 that he would not agree to an extension beyond March 1995 of the mandate for U.N. troops in his country.[14]

Following the experiences in Bosnia and Somalia, it is extremely doubtful that the Security Council will embark on any large new missions in situations where there is no peace to keep. The refusal of governments to contribute to a proposed U.N. force that might have halted the genocide in Rwanda early in 1994 is symptomatic of the new attitude.[15]

Overall, the peacekeeping boom may have peaked. Operations ending in early 1995—in Somalia, Mozambique, and El Salvador—accounted for one third of the 1994 expenditures and personnel.[16] New missions in Angola and Haiti will only partly offset this reduction.[17] At the political level, U.N. peacekeeping had already begun to enter a period of retrenchment during 1993; expenditure and personnel statistics continued to grow during 1994 but will likely reflect this lack of political support during 1995.

Peacekeeping Expenses Reach New High

U.N. Peacekeeping Operation Expenditures, 1986–94

YEAR	EXPENDITURE (mill. dollars)
1986	242
1987	240
1988	261
1989	626
1990	455
1991	490
1992	1,767
1993	3,059
1994 (prel)	3,719

SOURCE: Field Operations Division, Department of Peace-Keeping Operations, United Nations, New York, private communication, September 15, 1994.

Global Peace and Demilitarization Expenditures, 1989–94

YEAR	EXPENDITURE (mill. dollars)
1989	2,486
1990	3,111
1991	6,314
1992	9,507
1993	13,229
1994 (prel)	15,770

SOURCE: Michael Renner, *Budgeting for Disarmament: The Costs of War and Peace,* Worldwatch Paper No. 122 (Washington, D.C.: Worldwatch Institute, 1994).

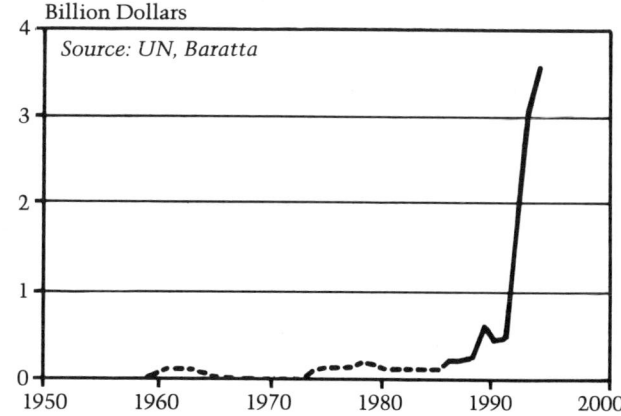

Note: Dotted line indicates rough estimates.

Figure 1: U.N. Peacekeeping Expenditures, 1950–94

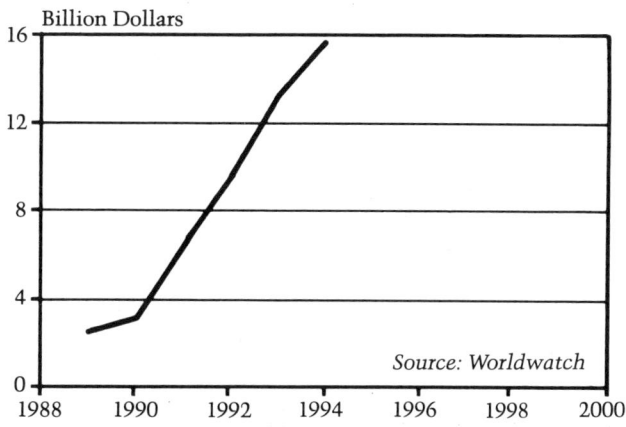

Figure 2: Global Peace and Demilitarization Expenditures, 1989–94

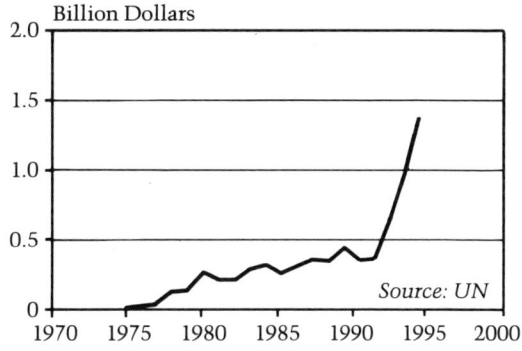

Figure 3: Arrears of U.N. Members for Peacekeeping Expenses, 1975–94

Wars Reach a Plateau

Hal Kane

After rising dramatically from the late seventies until the mid-eighties, the number of major wars raging in the world appears to have plateaued.[1] (See Figure 1.) Armed conflicts that claimed at least 1,000 lives rose slightly during 1994, but several of these have now been resolved, raising the hope for a decline in warfare in 1995.[2]

Nevertheless, almost three times as many wars raged during 1994 as took place at any one time during the fifties, and twice as many as during the sixties.[3] Looking just at conflicts that have taken more than 100,000 lives, the deadliest wars dropped from 11 in 1991 to 7 in 1994.[4] (See Figure 2.)

Africa has the most armed conflict, but several of its wars have recently ended. A conflict in Mozambique that dates back to 1976 and may have taken a million lives stopped with a ceasefire that has more or less held since 1993.[5] Ethiopia is peaceful, at least for the time being, and Eritrea today is full of optimism as a new country with much national unity that has taken steps toward land redistribution and gender equality, which could strengthen the chance for long-term peace.[6] Angola and Chad both have encouraging prospects for peace.[7] And apartheid in South Africa has ended, after taking more than 18,000 lives in the nineties.[8]

Four Latin American conflicts are among those that appear to have come to an end during the nineties. Peru's Shining Path guerrillas were brought under control in 1994.[9] With U.S. peacekeepers in place, Haiti attained stability, at least for the moment.[10] And two long-standing wars have ended as peace has been negotiated in El Salvador and Nicaragua, though both situations remain fragile.[11]

The British government and the Irish Republican Army have had their most promising talks ever aimed at resolving that historical conflict.[12] Israel and Jordan have signed peace agreements.[13] Asia's best prospect for peace rests in Cambodia, a country much in need of relief from warfare, but fighting there continues.[14]

Of course, countries emerging from wars are at least partially offset by new ones where war has erupted. The Chechnyan region of Russia, for example, blazed into war in 1994.[15]

Few of the armed conflicts taking place today are between states. (See Figure 3.) Rather, almost all are civil wars.[16] Even the rare examples of conflicts that cross state borders are more cases of internal conflicts spilling over a boundary than of aggression between two nations. The war over Nagorno-Karabakh in Azerbaijan, for instance, involves two countries but is essentially an internal secessionist struggle.[17] The Israeli occupation of south Lebanon is an extension of Israel's and Lebanon's internal conflicts.[18]

The most recent war that clearly could be categorized as one of aggression between two countries was Iraq's 1990–91 invasion of Kuwait, and the Gulf War that followed.[19] This provided evidence that wars to take foreign territory or to protect against external enemy aggression still do occur, though rarely.

Since 1945, there have been at least 130 wars.[20] Counting only people killed directly in the fighting, more than 23 million have perished.[21] Including those affected by war-related famine or illness, some 40 million died.[22] By one analysis, more than twice as many people have been killed in wars in this supposed postwar period than in the entire nineteenth century, and seven times as many as in the eighteenth century.[23]

Civilians accounted for half of all war-related deaths in the fifties. But by the eighties, they accounted for three quarters. And in 1990, some 90 percent of deaths were civilian.[24] Unicef claims that during the last decade, 2 million children have died in civil wars, which are now killing more children than soldiers.[25] This situation is made even more tragic by the fact that in some wars, such as in Liberia, many of the soldiers are themselves children—in their early teens or younger.[26]

This half-century has been marked by a concentration of hostilities in the Third World. Developing countries bear the burden of well over 90 percent of both the conflicts and the casualties.[27] Only in the latest years—beginning in 1989 in the Soviet Union and 1991 in Yugoslavia—have industrial countries suffered a serious escalation of this kind of violence.

Wars Reach a Plateau

NUMBER OF WARS, 1945–94

YEAR	WARS WITH MORE THAN 1,000 DEAD	WARS WITH MORE THAN 100,000 DEAD
	(number)	
1950	11	6
1955	10	4
1960	12	7
1961	11	8
1962	16	10
1963	13	8
1964	12	8
1965	17	10
1966	15	9
1967	16	9
1968	15	8
1969	17	8
1970	17	8
1971	18	9
1972	18	9
1973	19	7
1974	18	7
1975	20	8
1976	16	6
1977	16	6
1978	20	8
1979	21	5
1980	26	7
1981	30	10
1982	30	10
1983	33	11
1984	34	11
1985	33	11
1986	33	10
1987	33	10
1988	31	11
1989	33	10
1990	33	9
1991	33	11
1992	32	8
1993	32	7
1994	34	7

SOURCE: Worldwatch, based on Leitenberg and Ball, and on Wallensteen and Axell.

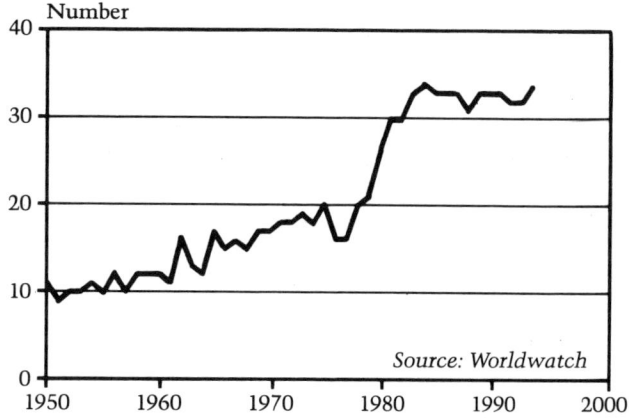

Figure 1: Armed Conflicts With More Than 1,000 Deaths, 1950–94

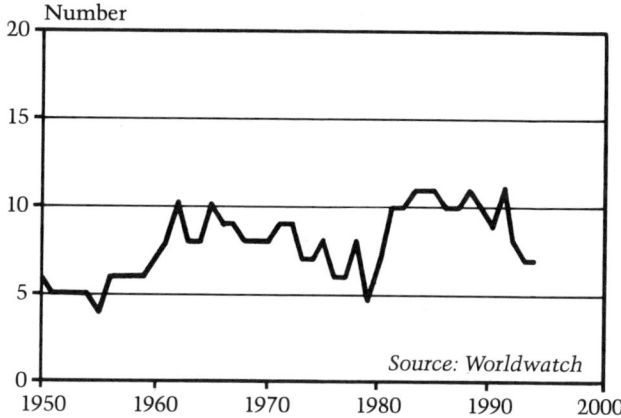

Figure 2: Armed Conflicts With More Than 100,000 Deaths, 1950–94

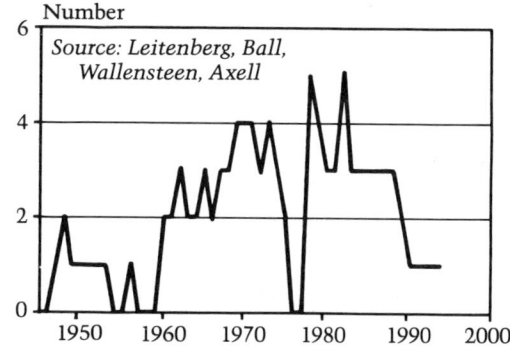

Figure 3: Wars Between States, 1945–94*

* Wars with more than 1,000 deaths between two recognized countries. Does not include foreign interventions in domestic struggles; independence struggles; or conflict in the former Yugoslovia.

Part TWO
Special Features

Environmental Features

Tropical Forests Vanishing

Anjali Acharya

Over the years, tropical forests have been extensively cleared to extract timber, build cattle ranches, grow crops, and construct dams and highways. During the eighties alone, the world lost about 8 percent of its tropical forests—a decline from 1,910 million hectares in 1980 to 1,756 million hectares in 1990.[1] This widespread deforestation is driving countless species to extinction, threatening indigenous cultures and the livelihoods of millions of people, and affecting local and global climate.

Tropical forests account for a third of the world's forests and contain about four fifths of the world's land vegetation—ranging from constantly wet rain forests to dry thorn woodlands.[2] Covering less than 12 percent of the earth's land surface, these forests provide habitat for 50–90 percent of the world's species, and are home to millions of communities that depend on them.[3] They play a vital role in climate regulation by storing carbon that would have otherwise been released to the atmosphere. Tropical forests provide about a fifth of all wood used worldwide in industry.[4] A quarter of the world's pharmaceutical drugs use rain forest plant extracts as ingredients.[5]

Rain forests, in particular, support an incredible diversity of species—providing habitat to more than 60 percent of all known species of plants, 40 percent of birds of prey, and as many as 80 percent of all known insects.[6] The profusion of species in these forests, many of which are found nowhere else, is unequaled by any other biome. Ecuador, for example, is roughly the same size as the United Kingdom but has almost seven times the number of bird species—1,435 species compared with 219.[7]

In the eighties, tropical forests were cleared at an average annual rate of 15.4 million hectares, almost twice the size of Austria.[8] The Asia and Pacific region had the highest average annual deforestation rate (1.2 percent), followed by Latin America and the Caribbean (0.8 percent) and Africa (0.7 percent).[9] (See Table 1.)

TABLE 1. FOREST COVER BY REGION, 1990, AND ANNUAL DEFORESTATION, 1981–90

REGION	FOREST COVER 1990 (mill. hectares)	ANNUAL DEFORESTATION, 1981–90	(percent)
Asia and the Pacific	310.6	3.9	1.2
Latin America and Caribbean	918.1	7.4	0.8
Africa	527.6	4.1	0.7
Total	1,756.3	15.4	0.8

SOURCE: U.N. Food and Agriculture Organization, *Forest Resources Assessment 1990: Tropical Countries*, Forestry Paper 112 (Rome: 1993).

The primary causes of deforestation vary. Asian forests are threatened by commercial logging and agricultural expansion, while the main pressures in Africa include fuelwood collection, overgrazing of cattle, and logging. In Latin America, forest clearance is usually associated with cattle ranching, population resettlement schemes, and major development projects, with some commercial logging.[10]

Logging remains one of the major driving forces behind the loss of tropical forest. Timber harvesting usually involves building a dense network of roads, which exposes forests to exotic pests and diseases, increases soil erosion, and opens up previously inaccessible forests to miners, ranchers, and poor farmers.[11]

To feed the world's growing timber demand, there has been a consistent rise in both total area logged as well as volume of wood produced each year from tropical forests. (See Figure 1.) Globally, 5.9 million hectares are logged annually in the tropics, including 4.9 million hectares in primary forests.[12] Today, tropical forests supply about 30 percent of the world's log exports, 12 percent of sawnwood

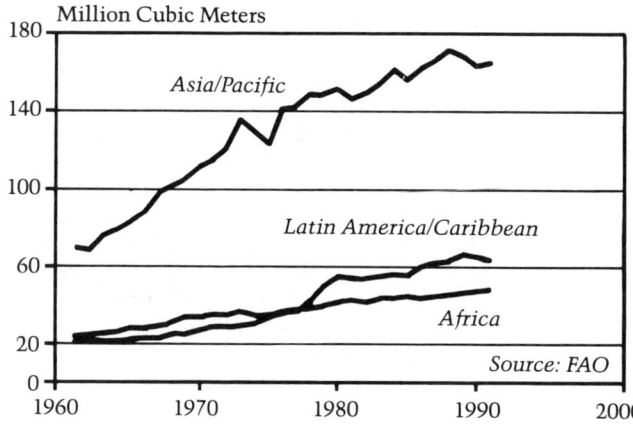

Figure 1: Production of Nonconiferous Industrial Roundwood in the Tropics, 1961–91

exports, and 60 percent of plywood and veneer exports. Nearly half comes from Southeast Asia.[13]

Megadevelopment projects, such as hydroelectric dams and highways, are also opening up previously impenetrable areas of forests to settlers. In the Amazonian state of Rondônia, the construction of the BR-364 road, accompanied by the chaotic infusion of settlers, led to a drop in forest cover from 97 percent in 1980 to 76 percent in 1990.[14]

Shifting cultivation, which involves burning and cutting down forests to grow crops, becomes unsustainable under conditions of poverty, population pressure, and unequal landownership. Population resettlement schemes in Indonesia and Brazil have encouraged people to settle on forestland, which has subsequently been converted to cropland. As much as 5 million hectares of tropical forests are destroyed every year by poor landless peasants.[15] Today, Indonesia's rain forests are being cleared for cultivation at a rate of around 200,000 hectares each year.[16]

During the last two decades, cattle ranches have replaced tropical forests on more than 20 million hectares in Latin America.[17] Two thirds of forest destruction in Costa Rica is attributed to cattle ranching.[18] In Central and South America, about 2 million hectares of forest land is cleared every year to create cattle pasture.[19]

Such deforestation, along with fragmentation and degradation of tropical forests, is leading to devastating losses of plant and animal species. In particular, species-rich rain forests are being reduced by 4.6 million hectares annually.[20] Harvard biologist E.O. Wilson estimates that in tropical rain forests alone, roughly 50,000 species a year—nearly 140 each day—are either extinguished or condemned to eventual extinction by the destruction of their habitat.[21] At current deforestation rates, the earth may lose about 25 percent of its species by the middle of the next century.[22]

The millions of indigenous people who live within tropical rain forests are threatened as well. Africa's last rain forest people, the Pygmies, are threatened by rapidly shrinking forests, and logging activities in Malaysia's Sarawak state endanger the livelihood and culture of the Penans living there.[23]

The burning and destruction of tropical forests has serious implications for both local and global climate. Extensive forest loss results locally in higher temperatures and lower rainfall, leading to more frequent and serious droughts.[24] Global loss of carbon from deforestation in tropical countries is estimated at 1.1–3.6 billion tons—about 30 percent of total carbon emissions.[25]

In the past, international forestry initiatives such as the Tropical Forestry Action Plan, the International Tropical Timber Agreement, and the U.N. Statement of Forest Principles have failed to check forest loss.[26] New and strengthened efforts are now needed to arrest tropical deforestation. These should include improved protection and conservation measures, restricted trade in threatened timber species, and widespread adoption of sustainable forestry practices. Institutional reforms in the forestry sector, accompanied by restructured tenure and forest product pricing policies, are also needed to help save the world's remaining tropical forests.

Soil Erosion's Toll Continues
Elena Wilken

The United States is one of the few countries that closely monitors loss of topsoil. Every five years the Natural Resources Service (NRS, formerly the Soil Conservation Service) measures the rate of wind and water erosion at more than 800,000 sites and, using land use areas from satellite photographs, estimates annual soil loss. Erosion is concentrated in two regions: the humid midwestern grain belt, where soil swept from cropland by water accounts for most of the problem; and the Great Plains and western states, where the dry climate, cropping, and excessive livestock grazing contribute to high rates of wind erosion.[1]

In response to data on increasing losses to water erosion, the U.S. Congress passed the Conservation Reserve Program (CRP) in 1985. Its first phase established 10-year contracts with farmers to convert highly erodible cropland to less intense forms of production, such as trees and permanent grasses.[2] Since 1982, the registered amount of soil lost to water erosion dropped from 1,700 million to 1,150 million tons. The amount of land vulnerable to wind erosion increased slightly, but the average rate has fallen from 12 to 11 tons per hectare a year.[3] The program seeks to reduce the loss below a tolerable rate ranging from 12 tons per hectare a year for deep soils to 2 tons for shallow soils.

The second phase of the CRP, designed to encourage implementation of conservation techniques on highly erodible land still under cultivation, is more difficult to enforce and monitor. Farmers receiving price support payments must have a conservation plan for their land approved by the NRS. This creates conflict between the agency's advisory and enforcing roles, hampering the program's effectiveness.[4]

Although similar monitoring systems could guide conservation policy in other agricultural regions of the world, not many countries are able to withhold sizable amounts of land from production. As populations increase and farmers abandon depleted cropland, new land is brought under cultivation. In regions where most of the prime farmland is already producing crops, farmers often expand onto highly erodible soils, either by clearing forests or by plowing sloped land.[5]

Many governments lack the financial and technical resources to create an accurate database on soil erosion. Satellite mapping can document gully formation and changes in land use over large areas, but it is expensive and too broad for planning purposes. Monitoring the sediment load of major rivers indicates the amount of soil lost in a watershed (see Table 1), but does not indicate its source. Field-level measurements are often inadequate; one severe rain or windstorm can remove more than 6 tons of soil from a hectare of land, but this is only 1 millimeter less topsoil.[6] Variations in vegetative cover and

TABLE 1. ANNUAL SEDIMENT LOADS OF SELECTED RIVERS

RIVER	BASIN AREA[1] (thousand square kilometers)	SEDIMENT LOAD[2] (million tons per year)
Huang He (Yellow)	752	1,866
Ganges/Brahmaputra	1,480	1,669
Amazon	4,640	928
Indus (Pakistan)	305	750
Yangtze	180	506
Orinoco (Venezuela)	938	389
Irrawaddy (Myanmar)	367	331
Magdalena (Colombia)	240	220
Mississippi	327	210
MacKenzie (Canada)	1,800	187

[1]Area drained by the river and its tributaries upstream of the measurement station. [2]Annual average weight of solid and dissolved materials.
SOURCES: World Resources Institute, *World Resources 1992–93* (New York: Oxford University Press, 1992); J.D. Milliman and R.H. Meade, "Worldwide Delivery of River Sediment to the Oceans," *Journal of Geology*, January 1983.

Soil Erosion's Toll Continues

weather can also skew annual rate measurements.

Erosion does not affect all parts of the soil equally. The smallest, lightest particles and clay are washed or blown away first, carrying off nutrients. Soils consisting of the remaining larger particles are less able to absorb and retain water. The combined effects of lower nutrient levels and water-holding capacity reduce crop yields.[7]

Yields from croplands in the semihumid grassland region in Argentina have fallen by up to 30 percent on highly eroded fields.[8] The soils, once anchored by deep, matted grass roots, erode quickly when exposed to the elements. Annual rates of erosion range as high as 300 tons per hectare.[9]

Maintaining a vegetative cover on fields during fallow periods and rotating grasses and legumes such as alfalfa or clover with grain crops reduces erosion to acceptable rates.[10]

Nutrients lost to erosion can be replaced by fertilizers, but at additional cost to farmers. China loses 27 million tons of organic matter, 5.5 million tons of nitrogen, and 500,000 tons of available potassium each year to soil erosion. This accounts for 29 percent of the nitrogen and 27 percent of the potassium in nonorganic fertilizers applied annually.[11] As continuous applications decrease the inherent fertility of the soil, additions to noneroded soils are more effective than those to severely eroded soils.[12]

Wind erosion lowers the inherent productivity in dry, flat areas with strong winds. In Kazakhstan, known for its broad fields, three quarters of the nonirrigated cropland is subject to wind erosion.[13] Researchers have recorded annual average losses of 58 tons per hectare on a large state farm.[14] Farmers are aware of the problem, but due to economic pressures and lack of technical advice, many of them to continue farming with methods that expose their land to erosion.

In rangeland areas, concentrated livestock populations weaken the vegetative cover and expose soils to wind and water erosion. A study in eastern Kenya found soil erosion exceeded tolerable levels when the ground cover was less than 20 percent.[15] Since the land is communally owned, individual farmers are often unwilling to adopt conservation practices. Controlled herding does alleviate damage from grazing, but livestock populations, which have increased by as much has half in the last 30 years, will continue to adversely affect soil stability.[16]

Vegetative cover is the most important defense against erosion. Agriculturally induced erosion was traditionally limited when 7-to-15-year fallow periods allowed vegetation to grow back. As populations increase and land becomes scarcer, fallow times are reduced or disappear altogether, limiting the soils' ability to replenish nutrients and rebuild structure.

Sediment deposited downstream causes further damage to water supplies, irrigation systems, and hydroelectric plants. Only 40 percent of China's eroded sediment makes it to the ocean; the rest, a total of 3,500 million tons each year, is deposited in riverbeds, lakes, and reservoirs.[17] All told, China loses about 390 million cubic meters of water storage capacity each year, or about 1 percent from its 20 largest storage areas.[18] Dams are built with an assumed sedimentation rate; higher rates of erosion shorten the dams' lives by as much as half.[19]

Although soil forms from eroding bedrock and surface material, the rate of formation—between 200 and 1,000 years to form 1 inch (2.5 centimeters) of topsoil—is so slow that the resource is essentially nonrenewable in human life spans.[20] Without substantial investment in both monitoring and conservation, soil erosion will continue to undermine water storage capacity and global food security.

Amphibian Populations Take a Dive
Howard Youth

Until very recently, amphibians mainly captured the attention of children or people looking for fishing bait. In contrast to the attention lavished on birds and mammals, this animal group has received scant notice except from a handful of dedicated scientists. The distribution and life histories of the world's estimated 4,500–5,130 species of frogs, toads, salamanders, and caecilians (chiefly tropical burrowing amphibians that superficially resemble worms) remain, in most cases, poorly understood.[1]

Today, many scientists and environmentalists consider declining amphibians (see Table 1) to be valued environmental indicators—small creatures whose diminishing abundance likely reflects a weakening of the natural fabric of the earth's ecosystems.

Concern for amphibians is also growing as studies reveal the vital roles these creatures play within their ecosystems. In Appalachian forests, for example, the biomass, or total weight, of salamanders rivals or surpasses that of birds or mammals.[2] These salamanders and other amphibians are important prey species, but they are also hunters themselves, consuming large numbers of insects and other invertebrates.

Many frogs, toads, and salamanders lead double lives, starting out as aquatic larvae and later having a terrestrial adulthood. Their porous skin and need for moisture leaves them vulnerable to chemical threats and weather changes. Many populations are not self-perpetuating, and rely on immigration from other breeding colonies, a situation altered when habitats are fragmented by deforestation or are bisected by roadways, where roadkills can mean the death of at least 40 percent of migrating frogs.[3]

Destruction of wetlands continues to obliterate the breeding pools and riparian habitats vital to many amphibian populations.[4] And chemical dangers, including fertilizers, pesticides, and heavy metals, threaten the aquatic ecosystems that remain. A laboratory study in 1994 of a treefrog species found that increased levels of nitrates, which often rise in wetlands due to the runoff from farm fertilizers, slowed growth and increased mortality. And the treefrogs seemed more sensitive to nitrate levels than fish did.[5]

The thinning ozone layer may contribute to the decline of some species. A 1994 study in Oregon concluded that natural levels of ultraviolet radiation killed eggs of the declining western toad and Cascades frog but not those of the non-declining Pacific treefrog, a species that apparently produces more of an enzyme that enables it to heal from ultraviolet radiation-caused damage.[6]

Global warming is a concern also, as many areas are predicted to become drier, which would be particularly difficult for moisture-dependent amphibians.[7]

Studies on acid rain's effects on young amphibians show that increased acidity caused stunted growth or death in young eggs or larvae of some species. The virtual disappearance of the natterjack toad in southeastern England has been attributed to acidification of the species' breeding pools.[8] And a study of terrestrial redback salamanders in northeastern United States in the early eighties suggested that this species can sense and avoid soils that are highly acidic.[9]

In the western United States, China, the former Soviet Union, and other countries, game fish and bullfrogs that are introduced to an area prey on and outcompete native frogs, toads, and salamanders.[10] Introduced fish may also indirectly endanger amphibians by spreading a fungal disease, *Saprolegnia*, that is prevalent in fish hatcheries.[11]

The human taste for frog meat further stresses some amphibians. In France alone, 3,000–4,000 tons of frog legs are consumed each year.[12] Such heavy demand has decimated populations of two commonly exported bullfrog species in India and Bangladesh, leading to bans on export in India.[13] Indonesia, Romania, Greece, and other countries have since stepped in to supply the French market.[14]

Additional harvesting of wild amphibians for their skins (in South America and Asia), for use in schools, and for the international pet trade have further stressed once-common species.[15]

Amphibian Populations Take a Dive

Mysterious rapid die-offs in some North American frog species are occurring. Although no conclusions can be drawn until definitive studies are complete, many scientists speculate that the widespread illnesses affecting the dying frogs, such as "redleg" disease, might result from other stresses, such as those just mentioned.[16] The die-offs could also be due to a pox-like virus, like one reported in British frogs in 1992.[17]

The disappearance in 1987 of the golden toad and local populations of the harlequin frog in the Monteverde Cloud Forest Preserve in Costa Rica drew attention to many mysterious amphibian declines in seemingly pristine mountainous habitats, where effects of atmospheric changes or vaporized pesticides could be magnified.[18] El Niño, a periodic climatic disturbance, caused unusually dry conditions in the area in 1987, but scientists do not think that alone could have caused the extinctions.[19]

Although areas of diversity in birds and mammals have been charted, many likely amphibian "hotspots" remain uncensused because a large number of amphibians live in the tropics, where there are fewer scientists.[20]

Historical data on amphibian populations is scant. Many long-term studies that will put the causes of declines into sharper focus have just begun using standardized procedures, such as those just published by the Smithsonian in 1994.[21] As with other animals, many amphibians in fragmented habitats will need protected core areas and habitat corridors linking breeding populations in order to survive.

Efforts to assess the needs of amphibians and the reasons for their declines will help paint a clearer picture of just what is happening to these unobtrusive creatures, and what it means for the future of the planet.

TABLE 1. THREATENED OR DECLINING AMPHIBIAN SPECIES, SELECTED COUNTRIES

COUNTRY	TOTAL SPECIES (number)	THREATENED OR DECLINING SPECIES (number)	THREATENED OR DECLINING SPECIES (percent)	SUSPECTED SOURCE OF THREAT
Australia	194	57	29	H,E
Canada	42	14	33	H,C,I
Chile	41	30	73	H,E
Greece	16	10	63	E,H
Honduras	85	18	21	H
India, Western Ghats	117	ca. 58	ca. 50	H
New Zealand	6	3	50	
Puerto Rico	18	11	61	H,C
Taiwan	30	6	20	
Ukraine	16	8	50	H,C,I
Un. Kingdom	6	2	33	H,C
United States				
Calif., Nev.	64	47	73	H,I
Northeast	43	26	60	H,C
Western Europe (Belgium, France, Netherlands, Portugal, Spain)	33	21	64	H

[1]C = chemical contamination; E = collection for export (froglegs industry, pet trade, scientific specimens); H = habitat destruction, including deforestation, drainage of wetlands; I = introduced fish or frogs.
SOURCES: James L. Vial and Loralei Saylor, *The Status of Amphibian Populations: A Compilation and Analysis* (Milton Keynes, U.K.: Declining Amphibian Populations Task Force, World Conservation Union, 1993); information on Argentina from *Froglog*, August 1994; information on Greece from Alegra Filio and Asimakopoulos Byron, "On the Legal Status Concerning the Protection of Amphibians and Reptiles in Greece," *Herpetological Review*, Vol. 21, No. 2, 1990. The compilers stress that in absence of long-term studies and uniform monitoring, these figures are only short-term, anecdotal observations.

Water Tables Falling

Gary Gardner

Water tables are falling in many areas as groundwater consumption exceeds the rate at which aquifers are replenished. More and more cities and farms overdraw aquifers to keep expanding economies afloat and to quench the thirst of growing populations. But regions that depend on aquifers are subject to disruption as they are depleted.

In most of the world, comprehensive information on groundwater stocks is unavailable, yet national and local data reveal clear trends. Ten countries—all in the Middle East or North Africa—currently overdraw their national renewable water account and borrow from groundwater stocks to help make up the difference.[1] (See Table 1.)

Six others consume more than 50 percent of their renewable water resources.[2] Most of these have high rates of population growth; their water use will soon surpass their renewable supply if population projections materialize (assuming no change in consumption patterns). In Egypt's case, this could happen in the next year or two; in Uzbekistan, in some 10 years; in Afghanistan, 24 years; in Azerbaijan, 30 years; and in Tunisia, renewable water supplies could run out in 34 years.[3] The resulting deficits will be met in part through aquifer depletion, although desalinated water and reclaimed wastewater help to meet water demand in some areas.

The Middle East and North Africa are severely water-stressed. Between 1990 and 2025, average renewable supplies per person in these areas are expected to fall from 1,436 cubic meters to 667 cubic meters.[4] Much of the region depends on groundwater: more than 80 percent of Saudi Arabia's water comes from aquifers, while the rate is 60 percent in Jordan, Israel, and the West Bank.[5]

Seawater has invaded Israel's overpumped coastal aquifer, one of the country's three principal freshwater sources. Ten percent of wells are too salty for use in agriculture; the level is expected to jump to 50 percent within 25 years.[6] In Libya and Saudi Arabia, groundwater is mined in part to support an unsustainable agricultural expansion.[7]

National data can hide serious water depletion problems at the local level; many water-surplus nations have regions that lack an adequate supply. In northern China, for example, 10 percent of the cultivated area is irrigated by overdrafting groundwater, but the most serious shortages are found in urban areas.[8] Two thirds of China's cities are short of water.[9]

In Beijing, groundwater levels decline steadily; wells that drew water from a depth of some 5 meters in the fifties now pump from around 50 meters on average.[10] So serious is the water scarcity that restrictions on migration to the city are in effect, and the government is considering moving the capital to the south. Thirty-six cities experience subsidence—the

TABLE 1. NATIONS CONSUMING MORE THAN HALF OF RENEWABLE WATER SUPPLY

COUNTRY	SHARE OF RENEWABLE WATER SUPPLY USED ANNUALLY[1] (percent)
Libya	374
United Arab Emirates	299
Qatar	174
Saudi Arabia	164
Yemen	136
Bahrain	more than 100
Israel	more than 100
Jordan	more than 100
Kuwait	more than 100
Oman	more than 100

[1]Renewable water supply includes river inflows from other countries.
SOURCES: World Resources Institute, *World Resources 1994–95* (New York: Oxford University Press, 1994); World Bank, "Forging a Partnership for Environmental Action," Washington, D.C., December 1994.

sinking of land as aquifers are depleted—or have seen coastal aquifers invaded with seawater, which leads to the abandonment of drinking and irrigation wells.[11]

India also shows signs of serious groundwater stress. In the northwest state of Gujarat, 90 percent of wells monitored showed water level declines in the eighties, some of more than 9 meters.[12] Groundwater extraction exceeds recharge in 24 taluks (subprovincial administrative units) and is approaching total recharge in another 36.[13] In parts of Maharashtra, the water table has dropped nearly 8 meters and an estimated 25 percent of wells—the shallowest ones—have dried up.[14]

Falling water tables in India have caused an increase in salinization: roughly 65 percent of the water under Haryana state is saline.[15] In extensive coastal areas of Gujarat and Tamil Nadu, salinity has made water unfit for domestic or agricultural purposes; nearly half of the handpumps in coastal Gujarat were reported in 1986 to be yielding saline water.[16]

In the western United States, California gets about 12 percent of its water from aquifers, and Californians overdraw aquifers by about 1.36 billion cubic meters per year, mostly in the agriculture-rich San Joaquin Valley and in a few coastal areas.[17] The southern Central Valley has suffered severe subsidence—more than 8 meters in some locations—as a result of groundwater extraction.[18]

Population growth is stressing water supplies in the region. Arid Las Vegas grew 62 percent in the eighties, to nearly 1 million inhabitants, and now adds some 4,000 newcomers a month.[19] The city has applied for annual rights to more than a billion cubic meters of water from nonrenewable aquifers hundreds of miles to the north.[20] Besides being unsustainable, aquifer drawdown in northern Nevada would dry up natural springs that support the habitat of species, from mountain sheep to eagles and badgers.

Falling water tables in Thailand are a direct consequence of deforestation. As forest coverage shrank by half since the sixties, Thailand's vegetation-depleted soil lost much of its capacity to hold water.[21] Rainfall that once percolated into aquifers now washes into the country's rivers and out to sea.

Thai industries get nearly all their water from the ground, and consume the resource at double the rate of replenishment. As a result, parts of Bangkok are sinking several centimeters per year.[22] Government water policy does not encourage conservation. Industry pays for water at regressive rates, farmers pay nothing, and the government for years encouraged cultivation of a second crop of rice during the dry season.[23] While the Thai government now prompts farmers to switch to less water-intensive crops, its chief response to the water shortage has been to look for new sources of supply.[24]

Among cities, Mexico's capital stands out in terms of water scarcity. Groundwater supplies 70 percent of the water consumed there.[25] The resource is overdrawn by anywhere from 50–80 percent annually.[26] This extreme overdrafting caused subsidence of up to 30 centimeters a year in the eighties: downtown Mexico City once sat 1.2 meters above neighboring Lake Texcoco, but now rests 2 meters below the lake.[27] As depletion proceeds, remaining groundwater grows ever saltier and must be treated before it can be drunk or even used for industrial purposes.

At 300 liters per day, 1992 per capita consumption rivaled that in the profligate United States and was twice the level in Western Europe or Japan.[28] Authorities encourage conservation by raising water tariffs: industrial rates jumped 50 percent in 1992 for base usage and quadrupled for heavy users. Residential rates rose even more, to more than 18 times the previous level for an average household.[29] Management capacity, however, is still weak: in 1992, only 40 percent of households in Mexico City were metered, and only 30 percent of water levies were actually collected.[30]

Population growth and economic expansion will continue to tempt water-scarce areas to overdraw easily accessible groundwater. But chronic overpumping of aquifer water is unsustainable, and will eventually affect the economy and environment of regions supplied by overdrafted aquifers.

Dam Starts Up

Gary Gardner and Jim Perry

Dam construction is up, and average dam size is increasing, according to available data on global construction trends for the early nineties.[1] The number of dams under construction in 1993 rose 9.2 percent, to 1,242, after a much smaller increase in 1992.[2] The increases follow a general decline in the eighties, when construction worldwide averaged less than half that of the preceding 25 years.[3]

Data for the early nineties, though incomplete, indicate a shift toward larger dams. In 1992, 60 percent of the dams being built were more than 30 meters high, compared with only 21 percent of existing dams in 1986.[4] Construction of dams higher than 100 meters rose by some 27 percent between 1991 and 1993; half of these large structures were built by just three countries—Japan, China, and Turkey.[5]

Modern dam construction began in the twenties, when some of the world's largest structures were started in the Soviet Union and the United States. Construction surged after 1950, raising the global total from more than 5,000 in 1950 to roughly 38,000 today.[6] Industrial nations led the way, but by the sixties, developing countries were also heavily involved.[7] In 1993, developing countries accounted for nearly three quarters of construction activity; China, Turkey, and South Korea alone claimed half of the global total.[8] (See Table 1.)

Dams have generally been regarded as a symbol of modernity and a source of national prestige, partly because they are seen as a multipurpose tool of development. Dams and their reservoirs are a source of electric power, a means of flood control, a consistent supply of water for irrigation, and a recreational outlet. They generated more than 18 percent of the world's electricity in 1992, for example.[9] In some regions, the rate was far higher: nearly 80 percent in South America.[10]

Reservoir water irrigates millions of hectares of land around the world, raising agricultural yields two to three times over those of dryland farming, and in many cases bringing agriculture to regions that could not otherwise support it.[11] Areas with a high percentage of irrigated agriculture, such as China, India, and the western United States, rely heavily on reservoirs for irrigation water.[12] Irrigation is increasingly listed as the primary purpose of new dams, possibly reflecting growing food needs and water scarcity in many developing countries.[13]

Dams are also a valuable hedge against drought. By holding water that would normally run to the sea, reservoirs provide insurance in times of scarce rainfall. Water in the world's reservoirs effectively increases the normal supply from rivers by some 30 percent.[14] This insurance can be invaluable: Egyptians maintain that the Aswan Dam paid for itself within two years of its construction because of its spur to economic growth, and, more important, that it saved Egypt from catastrophe during the drought of 1979–88.[15]

But in the past two decades, with the emerging understanding that dam costs are measured not only in investment dollars but also in

TABLE 1: LEADING DAM-BUILDING COUNTRIES, 1993[1]

COUNTRY	NEW STARTS (number)	TOTAL UNDER CONSTRUCTION (number)
China	85	311
Turkey	84	190
Japan	11	140
South Korea	2	125
India	48	76
United States	30	55
Spain	16	53
Romania	0	39
Italy	0	37
Tunisia	16	28
Algeria	6	27
Iran	1	76
Thailand	7	17
Greece	3	14
France	8	12
Brazil	4	12

[1]Dams higher than 10 meters.
SOURCE: International Commission on Large Dams, Paris.

environmental and social terms, dam construction began to decline. These structures change their surroundings in major ways. Large tracts of riverside land are permanently inundated when reservoirs are created; losses from the flooding can be significant. The Narmada Sagar Project in India is expected to drive 31 species of plant to extinction because of habitat changes caused by reservoir creation.[16] Moreover, decomposing plant life at reservoir bottoms can release as much methane and carbon dioxide—both greenhouse gases—as a coal-fired plant with the same electricity-generating capacity, according to the Freshwater Institute in Canada.[17]

In disrupting stream flows, dams have other, unintended consequences. Fish migrations have been seriously impaired, as on the Columbia River in the United States, where salmon migrations have been nearly eliminated.[18] Temperature and water quality are often changed in the reservoir as well as downstream, altering habitats of fish and other wildlife.[19] Nutrient-rich sediment that would normally enrich floodplain soils along the length of a river gets trapped instead in the dam's reservoir. This last problem, known as siltation, can shorten a dam's useful life: in an extreme case, the turbines of China's Sanmenxia Dam were shut down in 1964 after only four years of operation when the dam's reservoir filled with sediment.[20]

Dams exact a high toll on humans as well. Millions of people were resettled in the past half-century to make room for reservoirs created by dams.[21] China's Three Gorges Dam alone is expected to displace more than 1 million people.[22] Those affected have had little say in determining whether and how resettlement is done, and most resettlement leaves displaced citizens in a worse situation than before their move.[23]

People living near dams often have increased health risks. Waterborne diseases, including malaria and river blindness, have been introduced and spread as reservoirs are created.[24] Large-scale water projects were a major contributor to the 75-percent global increase in cases of schistosomiasis, a sometimes fatal disease, between 1947 and the early eighties.[25]

Advocates of dams acknowledge many of the technology's shortcomings, but argue that its negative effects can be mitigated, or that the alternatives to dams would be worse. Others argue that evaluation of dams requires a project-by-project analysis; the widely differing environmental, social, and political contexts of proposed dams prevents any general judgment of them.

Ecologist Robert Goodland of the World Bank has developed criteria by which to judge a proposed dam: A dam should yield as much power as possible per hectare inundated; should retain water for days or weeks, not months, in order to preserve water quality in the reservoir and downstream; and should be located above undammed tributaries, to minimize the effect on the tributary.[26] At the same time, dams should not displace people, unless this would make their lives "promptly better"; should not be likely to promote water-related diseases; and should not be sited in centers of species endemism or rich biodiversity.[27]

Recognition of the many costs of dams has changed the way they are viewed by many. The World Bank—long a strong supporter—appears to have slowed its involvement, at least with major dams. The Bank was involved with an average of 18 dam projects a year between 1980 and 1985, but with only 6 a year between 1986 and 1993.[28]

Sensitive about this aspect of its work, the Bank established a commission in 1994 to hear complaints from parties affected by proposed dam projects. The first applicants were residents affected by the Arun III dam in Nepal.

The future of dams is unclear. Dam enthusiasts point out that only a fraction of the technically usable hydropower potential in developing countries has been harnessed to date.[29] But the discussion has moved well beyond technical considerations. Whether proposed dams can meet the increasingly stringent environmental and social standards expected of them remains to be seen.

Lead in Gasoline Slowly Phased Out
Odil Tunali

Between 1970 and 1993, the total amount of lead added to gasoline worldwide dropped by 75 percent—from more than 375,000 tons to less than 100,000.[1] Several industrial and developing countries eliminated leaded gasoline from their markets, while many others reduced the lead content and introduced unleaded gasoline. But for numerous developing nations, leaded gasoline continues to be the predominant automobile fuel. (See Table 1.)

The health impacts of lead in gasoline were evaluated as early as in the twenties. Despite warnings from toxicity experts, however, adding lead to gasoline to boost performance became standard practice. Current data show that leaded fuel use for the past seven decades produced significant environmental contamination worldwide, and increased average blood-lead levels in the population.[2]

Burning leaded gasoline emits microscopic particles of lead into the atmosphere, which can remain there for weeks before settling out. When inhaled, the particles that reach the deepest part of the lungs are absorbed into the blood with almost 100-percent efficiency.[3] Epidemiological studies found that such exposure to lead can result in mental retardation in children, and in high blood pressure and an increased risk of heart attacks and strokes in adults.[4]

In response to growing concerns about lead's health effects, a few countries started phasing it out of gasoline in the early seventies, and saw clear benefits. In the United States, for example, blood-lead levels dropped 78 percent between 1976 and 1994, in parallel with the reduction in the lead content of gasoline from 0.78 grams per liter to the current allowable level of 0.026.[5]

Japan was among the first to begin the phaseout in the seventies, a process completed in 1993.[6] Canada had already prohibited the use of leaded gasoline in automobiles in 1990; Austria followed by banning its import and production in 1993.[7] In Sweden, a national ban on lead in gasoline took effect in March 1995.[8]

In the developing world, Brazil, Colombia, and South Korea have phased out leaded gasoline.[9] Several others, including Thailand, are planning to do so soon.[10] At the 1994 Summit of the Americas, Latin American governments agreed that leaded gasoline would be eliminated from their hemisphere by the end of this decade.[11]

The U.S. phaseout is also near completion:

TABLE 1. USE OF LEADED GASOLINE, SELECTED COUNTRIES, 1993

COUNTRY	MARKET SHARE (percent)	LEAD CONTENT (grams per liter)
Japan	0	—
Brazil	0	—
South Korea	0	—
United States	1	0.026
Germany	11	0.15
Australia	53	0.30
Mexico	70	0.07
China[1]	70	0.25
Thailand	79	0.15
Poland	88	0.15
Venezuela	90	0.37
Spain[1]	94	0.15
Russia	95	0.20
India[2]	100	0.15
Saudi Arabia	100	0.40
Nigeria	100	0.66

[1]1992 data. [2]Introducing unleaded gasoline in 1995.
SOURCE: Valerie Thomas, "The Elimination of Lead in Gasoline," *Annual Review of Energy and Environment* (Palo Alto, Calif.: Annual Reviews, Inc., forthcoming).

Lead in Gasoline Slowly Phased Out

leaded gasoline accounts for less than 1 percent of all motor gasoline used, and a ban will take effect on January 1, 1996, as dictated by the 1990 amendments to the Clean Air Act.[12]

In the meantime, many countries have reduced the lead content of gasoline and introduced unleaded gasoline. The European Union (EU), for example, has limited lead in gasoline to 0.15 grams per liter.[13] Unleaded gasoline became available in 1989, when all new cars were required to use catalytic converters, which work only with lead-free fuel.[14] As a result, leaded gasoline use within the EU has been declining steadily: in 1993, its share in total gasoline consumption fell below 47 percent, whereas in 1986, it constituted 99 percent of the market there.[15]

Several East European countries—Poland, Bulgaria, the Czech Republic, and Hungary—capped the lead content of gasoline at the EU standard of 0.15 grams per liter.[16] Mexico, where lead exposure is thought to contribute to one fifth of all hypertension cases, reduced the lead content of gasoline by 88 percent between 1980 and 1992.[17] Unleaded gasoline became available in 1990, and as of 1993, it must be used in all new cars.[18] India, too, acting to curb severe lead exposure, will introduce unleaded gasoline this year, accompanied by a gradual reduction of lead levels in gasoline, and the requirement of catalytic converters for all new cars in major cities.[19]

On the other hand, a number of countries, particularly in the developing world and in the former Eastern bloc, have yet to address the problem of lead in gasoline. In Russia, for example, unleaded gasoline is not available outside Moscow and a few other cities, while the lead content of gasoline can be as high as 0.38 grams per liter.[20] China has a rapidly growing motor vehicle fleet that uses huge quantities of gasoline with a lead content varying from 0.4 to 0.15 grams per liter.[21] Some sources say the government intends to phase out lead by the year 2000, but unleaded gasoline is still hard to find, except in parts of Beijing, Shanghai, and Guangzhou.[22]

Unleaded gasoline may not be available in certain countries because their refineries so far lack the capacity to produce it. Yet some, including China, Venezuela, and Trinidad and Tobago, are technically capable of producing unleaded gasoline but export most of it, and supply the domestic market with leaded gasoline instead.[23]

Meanwhile, faced with shrinking markets in the industrial world, Octel, Ltd., the principal manufacturer of lead additive for gasoline, and Ethyl Corp., which no longer produces lead additive but buys it from Octel, market heavily in developing countries and the former Soviet Union.[24] About half of all lead added to gasoline in 1993 was used in the former Soviet Union, Asia, and Eastern Europe; the rest, in roughly equal amounts in Latin America, the Middle East, Africa, and Western Europe.[25]

The need to phase out leaded gasoline cuts across the North-South divide. Fortunately, switching to unleaded gasoline is not a substantial expense, according to estimates by the World Bank—on average about 0.5–1¢ a liter per year.[26]

During the phaseout process, some governments offer economic incentives to accelerate the use of unleaded gasoline. The United Kingdom, Denmark, and Australia are among the countries where tax on leaded fuel is higher than on unleaded.[27] Malaysia also made unleaded gasoline 2.7 percent cheaper than leaded, which increased the former's share to 60 percent of the total market.[28] Similarly, South Africa offers a 3¢ discount per liter of unleaded fuel.[29]

The countries that have phased out lead in gasoline or are in the process of doing so have seen not only enormous public health benefits and reductions in environmental contamination, but also monetary returns. The U.S. Environmental Protection Agency reports that by eliminating leaded gasoline, the United States saves more than $400 million a year in children's health care costs alone.[30]

Experiences around the world indicate that it is technically and economically feasible to phase out lead in gasoline. And inexpensive alternatives to lead as an octane enhancer are available. Given the health, environmental, and budgetary benefits, eliminating lead from gasoline is a worthwhile investment for every country.

Steel Recycling Rising

Gary Gardner

Steel recycling continues to rise as producers invest in furnaces fed largely by scrap metal, and as used steel products are collected more efficiently. Scrap accounts for roughly 42 percent of steel produced globally, if scrap from steel mills, industry, and used products is taken into account.[1] The figure in the early eighties was some 25 percent, but that did not include scrap from steel mills.[2] In the United States, the recycled content of new steel was estimated in 1994 as more than 58 percent, again without counting mill scrap.[3] (See Table 1.)

Recycling reduces the flow of materials and energy in an economy. Each ton of recycled steel saves 2,500 pounds of iron ore, 1,000 pounds of coal, and 40 pounds of limestone.[4] Only one third as much energy is needed to produce steel from scrap as from virgin materials.[5] Materials savings, in turn, mean a reduced environmental toll: over half a ton of earthen material is left undisturbed, for example, for each ton of iron ore not mined.[6]

A surge in global use of the electric arc furnace (EAF) is key to the growth in steel recycling. These furnaces use up to 100 percent scrap to make heavy steel products such as structural beams and reinforcing bars.[7] By contrast, the basic oxygen furnace (BOF), used to make "flat-rolled" products such as steel cans or car fenders, is fed primarily with virgin materials—iron ore, limestone, and coked coal—along with an element of scrap.

In the United States, scrap steel makes up 25–30 percent of input to a basic oxygen furnace.[8] The level drops to 18–20 percent in European BOFs and to 8–15 percent in Japanese BOFs.[9] Technological advances in furnace design, including electric furnaces that produce flat-rolled products and basic oxygen furnaces that accept higher levels of scrap input, could increase the level of steel recycling.

A third technology, the air polluting and energy-intensive open hearth furnace, is nearly phased out in the western world and contributes only 16 percent of production in China, but it is still heavily used in the former Soviet Union.[10] Open hearth furnaces use scrap in varying amounts, often around 40–45 percent of total furnace input.[11]

Steel produced in EAFs is projected to increase by nearly 25 percent between 1993 and 2003 while overall steel production rises only 10 percent.[12] In 1993, EAF steel accounted for about 31 percent of global steel production; the figure was some 39 percent in the United States and 22 percent in China.[13] Only 14 percent of steel in the former Soviet Union was produced in electric furnaces in 1991.[14] EAF steel could account for 35–45 percent of global steel output by early in the next century.[15]

The percentage of recycled steel could continue to rise, but two factors currently limit this. First, some products require steel of high purity, which may require the use of virgin material inputs.[16] Recycled steel input can bring higher-than-desired levels of contaminants such as copper, lead, and zinc to the steel mix; the problem has increased with the rise in steel recycling.[17] But more-efficient scrap sorting methods may hold the solution to this problem.

A greater constraint on recycled steel production is the limited supply of scrap in markets around the world, even as many worn-out steel products go uncollected. A tight scrap market in the United States drove prices up by nearly 53 percent in the year ending December 1993, and prices continued to rise through most of 1994.[18] Faced with tight supplies of scrap, steelmakers turned to substitutes such as pig iron, a product made from virgin materials.[19]

Scrap steel comes from three sources. Mill scrap is generated by steel mills in the steelmaking process. Industrial scrap includes trimmings from manufacturers who cut steel materials to fabricate new products. Obsolete scrap is steel from worn-out products. Of the three, obsolete scrap is the least thoroughly reclaimed.

Scrap supply is determined in part by economic cycles. As economic activity quickens and consumers buy new steel products, old goods are sent to scrap dealers. In addition, steel plants and manufacturers generate more scrap when mills and factories are running at high capacity. Thus the supply of mill, indus-

TABLE 1. RECYCLED CONTENT OF U.S. STEEL

YEAR	NET DOMESTIC SCRAP CONSUMPTION[1] (thousand tons)	RAW STEEL PRODUCTION	RECYCLED CONTENT OF NEW STEEL (percent)
1984	36,060	92,528	38.9
1985	38,818	88,259	44.0
1986	38,004	81,606	46.6
1987	44,808	89,151	50.3
1988	49,613	99,924	49.7
1989	50,247	97,943	51.3
1990	51,475	98,906	52.0
1991	46,345	87,896	52.7
1992	45,996	92,949	49.4
1993	50,805	96,077	52.8
1994 (prel.)	57,200	98,100	58.3

[1]Does not include scrap from steel mills.
SOURCE: Consumption and production from Institute of Scrap Recycling Industries, Washington, D.C., personal communication, January 25, 1995; recycled content is a Worldwatch calculation.

trial, and obsolete scrap tends to rise in an expanding economy.

The supply of obsolete scrap is further influenced by a country's developmental level. Developing countries, with few worn-out steel products, generate little obsolete scrap relative to their demand for new steel.[20] In these countries, the increase in scrap output resulting from rapid economic growth in the decades ahead is projected to fall short of the demand for steel. Partly as a result, global supplies of scrap are expected to tighten during the next decade.

Scrap supply is also influenced by changes in technology. Between 1980 and 1993, mill scrap was reduced by more than half with the widespread adoption of an efficient steelmaking process known as continuous casting.[21] Likewise, increased manufacturing efficiency lowers the amount of industrial scrap. Losses of preconsumer scrap, however, are offset by reduced materials inputs to the steelmaking process; the net effect on materials flows is negligible.[22]

Because the supply of mill scrap is projected to decline between 1993 and 2003 while industrial scrap grows marginally, major increases in scrap supply will need to come from worn-out products.[23] Indeed, obsolete scrap will need to increase by more than 30 percent to meet scrap demand through 2003.[24] At present, large products such as automobiles and demolition materials are easy and economical to collect: in the United States, automobile recycling reached 94 percent in 1993 and appliance recycling hit 62 percent.[25] But smaller items such as bedsprings and hinges are dispersed and difficult to isolate from other materials.[26]

One exception to this is the collection of steel cans. In the United States, widespread municipal recycling campaigns have raised steel can recycling from 15 percent in 1988 to a reported 48 percent in 1993.[27] In Europe, some 30 percent of steel cans are recycled.[28] Expansion of recycling infrastructure globally will be needed if the last plentiful source of scrap is to be fully exploited.

Continued adoption of scrap-fed furnaces and increased collection of scrap steel will provide upward pressure on steel recycling rates. But if high steel demand in scrap-scarce developing nations outstrips the global supply of recycled steel, production from virgin materials will rise.

Social Features

Computers Multiplying Rapidly

John E. Young

Rapidly increasing capabilities and plummeting prices are continuing to fuel explosive growth in the number of computers. In 1993, 25 million new computers came into use, bringing the 1994 estimated world total to 173 million.[1] By comparison, only about 4 million computers existed worldwide in 1981.[2] (See Figure 1.)

Personal computers (PCs) have accounted for most of the growth in computers since 1981, when a large share of the total consisted of mainframes or somewhat smaller multiuser minicomputers. By 1994, there were 166 million PCs, accounting for 96 percent of world computers.[3]

Because each generation of new machines has been orders of magnitude more powerful than the last, growth in global processing power has been even more rapid than that in the number of computers. Measured in MIPS (million instructions per second—a standard measure of processing power), the total power of the world's computers has risen fifteenfold in the last seven years.[4] The amount of computing power that can be purchased for a given price has been doubling every two years or less for three decades, making the computer easily available to many individuals and most institutions.[5]

Computer use is unevenly distributed, however, with most of the machines concentrated in western industrial nations. There are 287 computers per 1,000 people in the United States in 1993, 97 per 1,000 in Japan, and only 1 per 1,000 in China and India.[6] (See Table 1.) The United States—where both the microprocessor and the personal computer were invented—has two fifths of the world's computers, but only a twentieth of the world's people.[7] Computers may soon be more numerous there than cars, which have been perhaps the most dominant U.S. cultural artifact to date.

Parallelling the growth in computers has been an extraordinary expansion of the number of machines connected to one another through computer networks. Though the exact number is impossible to know, perhaps as many as 40 million people are now connected to the Internet, the world's largest collection of computer networks, through which people share electronic mail and other information.[8] Most of the Internet's users are found in industrial nations.

Computers have historically been a tool for governments, corporations, the military, and other large institutions. Nonetheless, environment, development, peace, labor, human rights, and other progressive activists around the world have benefited from the proliferation of these machines, and from the rapid evolution of computer networking. For example, more than 25,000 such groups and individuals in at least 130 countries now belong to the 19 closely linked networks of the Association for Progressive Communications.[9] The systems operate on common software, and support hundreds of computer conferences that are truly global in scope. The group has also helped foster the development of more than 50 partner networks in developing countries, many of which are likely to become full members of the system.[10]

These machines are also helping environmental scientists, industrial managers, community activists, and government officials sort through the interconnected

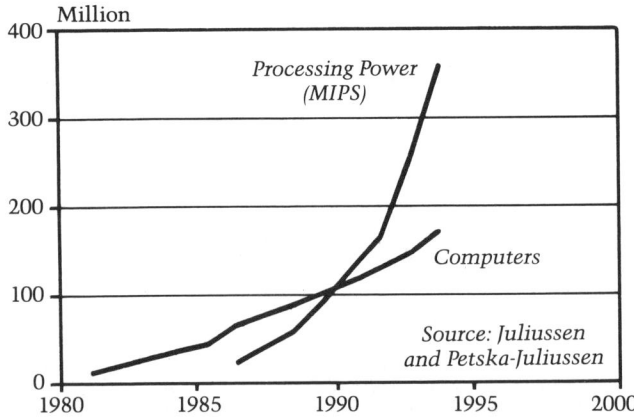

Figure 1: World Computers and Processing Power, 1981–94

TABLE 1. COMPUTERS IN SELECTED COUNTRIES, 1993

COUNTRY	COMPUTERS (per 1,000 people)
United States	287
Australia	192
Canada	188
United Kingdom	162
France	129
Japan	97
Spain	79
Taiwan	74
Hungary	27
Mexico	17
South Africa	10
Russia	8
Brazil	6
Indonesia	2
China	1
India	1
World	31

SOURCE: Egil Juliussen and Karen Petska-Juliussen, *Computer Industry Almanac 1994-95* (Lake Tahoe, Nev.: Computer Industry Almanac, Inc., 1994).

workings of a wide variety of complex systems—from factories to forests—to identify what is going wrong and develop corrective strategies. And they are providing a way to test theories about such systems without conducting dangerous, often unintentional, experiments in the real world, such as those now under way involving the addition of large amounts of pollutants to the atmosphere and biosphere.

Rapid growth in computers has also had its environmental dark side. Instead of creating the "paperless office" so optimistically predicted a decade ago, computers have contributed to an ever-growing demand for paper. And simply turning on a computer contributes to environmental problems, since electric power plants are major contributors to a variety of environmental problems, including global warming, acid rain, and destruction of natural habitats. Computers have become a major electricity consumer in industrial countries, and overall now use about as much electricity each year as Brazil.[11] Machines that need less power are now widely available, however, thanks to the Energy Star efficiency-certification program launched by the U.S. Environmental Protection Agency in 1992. The agency estimates that the program should save up to $1 billion worth of electricity in the United States each year.[12]

Computer manufacturing, which has quickly grown into one of the world's largest, most powerful industries, also has environmental impacts that, until recent years, have largely gone unrecognized. Few Americans realize, for example, that the "clean" or "sunrise" industry that arose in Silicon Valley has also created in its California birthplace the highest concentration of hazardous-waste cleanup sites in the United States.[13] Though electronics makers have begun to address problems created by the host of toxic substances they use—and have been notably successful in reducing the use of ozone-depleting chlorofluorocarbons—the industry still has a long way to go in developing cleaner production processes that avoid both environmental damage and toxic risks to workers.

Women Slowly Accepted as Politicians Anjali Acharya

During the past 50 years, the number of women politicians has slowly increased. In a few countries, there has been a steady rise; in most, the trend has been erratic, fluctuating with changes in government and electoral systems. Despite the small improvements, women today hold only about 10 percent of the seats in national parliaments.[1] In 1990, just 3.5 percent of the world's cabinet ministers were women, and women held no ministerial positions in 93 countries.[2] On the whole, women are better represented at the state and local levels than at the national level.

The steady increase in women's participation in the formal labor force has not been matched in political life. In many countries, women were traditionally discouraged and even prohibited from participating in the political process. Even today, as women push to overcome illiteracy, apathy, and society's expectations, they remain marginalized.

At the beginning of this century, New Zealand was the only country that had granted women the right to vote; by 1940, about 38 countries had done so.[3] Today, women's suffrage is nearly universal, with only Bahrain, Kuwait, and the United Arab Emirates continuing to deny women the right to vote or stand for election.[4]

Yet even when women can vote, it is often some time before a woman is actually elected to a national seat. Australia has the longest gap of this sort, with the first female being elected to parliament 65 years after women were permitted to stand for elections.[5]

In 1960, Sirimavo Bandaranaike became Prime Minister of Sri Lanka, earning her place in history as the first woman elected to a country's highest executive office. Since then, some 20 countries have had a woman as a head of state or government, with South Asia having more female heads of state than any other region.[6] Some of these individuals have come to power through family ties, while others have risen through political ranks to reach the highest office. As of early 1995, women head the governments of Bangladesh, Dominica, Iceland, Ireland, Nicaragua, Norway, Pakistan, Sri Lanka, and Turkey.[7]

On average, the number of women in national legislative bodies has increased slowly over the years, but the proportion remains low.[8] (See Table 1.) According to the Inter-Parliamentary Union, in only 21 nations are more than 20 percent of these seats held by women.[9] Furthermore, in more than 60 countries less than 5 percent of the parliament is female, including eight countries where there are no women in this national body.[10]

Between 1988 and 1993, there was a sharp drop in the proportion of women in parliaments globally—from 14.6 percent to 10.1 percent.[11] The decline was especially pronounced in East European countries, which faced changes in their economic and electoral systems. Then in 1994, the proportion of women in parliament increased marginally. In some countries, such as Estonia and Hungary, recent political and institutional changes have resulted in more women being elected to fill national seats. In the first multiracial elections in South Africa, women won a quarter of the seats in the National Assembly.[12]

There are even fewer women at the ministerial level of governments. Often, women who are appointed to the cabinet are given what are traditionally seen as less powerful portfolios, such as education, health, family affairs, and social welfare.[13] Very rarely has a woman served as the minister of defense, foreign affairs, planning, or finance.

The Nordic countries and Cuba provide the exception to these rules, with more than 30 percent of their parliamentarians being women.[14] In September 1994 elections, Sweden voted women into 41 percent of its parliamentary seats—currently the world's highest. And the incoming government appointed women to 7 out of 17 cabinet positions.[15]

Despite poor representation in elected and appointed office, women play an active role in the political parties of many countries—especially in campaigning, organizing rallies, and lobbying the government. They have also been among the founders of political parties. There is, however, a gap between a woman's entry into a political party and her acceptance as its leader. Few countries have a woman

Women Slowly Accepted as Politicians

leading a major political party.

Women usually have better success in state and local government elections, having greater access to these posts. The proportion of women in local government has often increased at a faster rate than at the national level. In the United States, for example, 21 percent of state legislators are women—a fivefold increase since 1969—compared with only 11 percent of the Members of Congress.[16] Elsewhere, inclusion remains low in both national and local posts: women in Japan, for instance, account for only 4.4 percent of city assemblies, 1.3 percent of town and village assemblies, and 2.7 percent of the parliament.[17]

To remedy the continuing low involvement of women in the political arena, some governments have advocated the use of a quota system, reservation of seats, or some other form of affirmative action. In the Nordic countries, the introduction of gender quotas in most political parties has helped promote women's participation. Bangladesh, which has 30 national seats reserved for women, has the highest percentage of women parliamentarians in South Asia.[18]

Quotas are sometimes removed with a change of government, however. Formerly supported by such systems, women in many East European countries saw the percentage of seats they held in federal and republic legislatures decrease sharply after the fall of communism.[19] In Albania, for example, parliamentary seats held by women dropped from 29 percent in 1986 to 3.6 percent in 1991 when the quota system was removed.[20]

Women's participation in politics and in the exercise of political responsibilities should be encouraged by governments, political parties, and other organizations. Education may be the most effective means of promoting political awareness among women as well as changing the traditional bias against their involvement in politics. A system of quotas can provide an interim measure to expand opportunities for women to participate in political decision making. With an increased role in public life, women will be able to better express their opinions, voice their concerns, and defend their interests—as well as make a contribution to the development of society.

TABLE 1: WOMEN IN NATIONAL LEGISLATURES, SELECTED COUNTRIES, 1955–94[1]

COUNTRY	1955	1975	1985	1994
		(percent)		
Sweden	—	21	31	41
Cuba	—	—	23	34
Iceland	0	5	15	24
New Zealand	5	5	13	21
China	12	23	21	21
Argentina	16	8	5	16
United States	3	4	5	11
Iraq	—	—	13	11
Bangladesh	—	5	9	10
Soviet Un./Russia	28	32	34	10
United Kingdom	4	4	4	9
India	4	4	8	7
Tunisia	—	2	5	7
Brazil	0	0	1	6
Albania	12	33	30	6
France	4	2	5	6
Zaire	—	11	4	4
Japan	2	1	2	3
Egypt	—	2	8	2
Turkey	—	8	3	2

[1]Percent who are members of single-chamber Parliaments or in the lower chamber of two-chamber systems. Dashes indicate that elections had not yet been held.
SOURCE: Inter-Parliamentary Union.

Breast and Prostate Cancer Rising

Anne E. Platt

Cancer of the breast is the most common tumor in women worldwide, and prostate cancer ranks as the fifth most common cancer among men.[1] Since 1930, the incidence of breast cancer in industrial countries has increased steadily by 1–2 percent annually.[2] The incidence in developing countries is also rising.[3]

As with other types of cancer, the frequency varies widely from place to place and is changing with time, especially as populations age.[4] Prostate and breast cancers are diseases of old age. The incidence is much more common in men and women over the age of 50, and the risks increase with age. According to the American Cancer Society, 97 percent of prostate cancer cases reported from 1984 to 1994 were in men older than 60.[5]

From 1969 to 1986, cancer mortality in people 45 or older increased in the United States, Eastern and Western Europe, East Asia, New Zealand, Australia, and the Nordic countries by average annual rates of 0.7 percent for breast cancer and 1.0 percent for prostate cancer.[6] Worldwide, breast cancer is expected to kill 1 million women annually by the year 2000.[7] In industrial countries alone, prostate cancer accounts for 110,000 deaths.[8]

In the United States, the lifetime risk of breast cancer has increased from 1 in 20 in 1960 to 1 in 8 today.[9] Some 182,000 cases of breast cancer are now reported every year to the National Cancer Institute, resulting in at least 46,000 deaths.[10] Reports of prostate cancer among American men have almost tripled—from 73,000 in 1982 to an estimated 200,000 in 1994—primarily because of the use of the prostate-specific antigen (PSA) blood test, which aids in the detection of tumors.[11]

Many countries do not have comprehensive cancer data or cancer registries.[12] There are no national registries in Africa, India, or China and very few in Asia or Latin America. Bombay, Singapore, Hong Kong, and Shanghai have had city-wide registries for at least 15 years, so those data are used to estimate national trends over time.[13] Although mortality data are available for most industrial countries and selected countries in Latin America and Asia, incidence data are much scarcer.

To compare data from countries with different age structures, epidemiologists from the International Agency for Research on Cancer use truncated rates.[14] These are a ratio of age-standardized data as compared with a universal age range—in this case, ages 30 to 74.

TABLE 1. RATES OF BREAST AND PROSTATE CANCERS, 1970–85[1]

CITY OR COUNTRY	BREAST CANCER RATES		PROSTATE CANCER RATES	
	1970	1985	1970	1985
Finland	74	113	34	49
County Vas, Hungary	55	93	26	33
Israel				
All Jews	117	137	20	27
Non-Jews	21	36	6	11
Varese, Italy	109	138	17	37
Shanghai, China	38	43	neg.	2
Bombay, India	41	51	8	9
Miyagi, Japan	28	61	4	10
New Zealand[2]	105	140	33	60
São Paulo, Brazil	96	149	16	45
Detroit, Michigan				
Blacks	100	145	115	158
Whites	137	188	52	93

[1]Truncated rates per 100,000 per year (30–74 years old). [2]Maori people.
SOURCE: M.P. Coleman et al., eds., *Trends in Cancer Incidence and Mortality* (Lyon, France: World Health Organization's International Agency for Research on Cancer, International Union Against Cancer, and the International Association of Cancer Registries, 1993).

Breast and Prostate Cancer Rising

Truncated rates of prostate cancer have been rising steadily since 1960.[15] Italy, China, Japan, and Brazil registered increases in rates of prostate cancer of more than 100 percent from 1970 to 1985. (See Table 1.) African-American men suffer from higher rates of prostate cancer (114–58 per 100,000, compared with 80–93 per 100,000 for white men), but the rates for white Americans are increasing much faster.[16]

Rates of breast cancer registered rapid increases from 1970 to 1985 in Scandinavia, Hungary, Japan, and Brazil, while rates in Italy, China, India, and among Maori women in New Zealand increased as well, but at a much slower rate.[17] Women in North America and Western Europe are at greatest risk due to their reproductive histories, use of oral contraceptives, dietary factors, and family history. In Asia, increasing rates of breast cancer have been attributed to more western life-styles, such as changes in diet from plant-based sources of protein to animal-based ones, which have higher concentrations of fat.[18]

The risk factors and possible causes of breast cancer are well known: age at first menstruation, menopause, and first child; obesity; and the intake of fiber and alcohol. Yet these factors combined account for only 20–30 percent of all cases of breast cancer.[19] Exercise and diet are also variables, and studies have shown that reducing the intake of fat and increasing exercise can lower the chances of breast cancer.[20]

Recently, research and media attention have focused on pollutants and chemicals that duplicate or interfere with the effects of estrogen, the female hormone, as a possible cause for the upswing in cancers of the reproductive system.[21]

Breast cancer mortality in premenopausal Israeli women declined by 30 percent following regulations to reduce levels of DDT and carcinogenic pesticides in dietary fat.[22]

Currently, the efficacy of diagnosis and early detection is being debated. In particular, the discovery of a blood test that can detect levels of prostate-specific antigen corresponding to chances of a prostate tumor has made it economically feasible to screen for tumors in the prostate gland.[23] The PSA test is able to detect the cancerous tumor in its earliest stage, often before it is detected by a routine exam.

The down side is that prostate cancer can live for years without causing its host any harmful effects, and the PSA test does not distinguish between a benign or a malignant tumor.[24] Because prostate gland cells grow so slowly, it takes four years or more for a tumor to double in size; the vast majority of prostate tumors never become large enough to be noticed.[25] According to one report, only 1 percent of the cells ever develop into full-blown prostate cancer, and only 3 in 1,000 tumors have been shown to cause death.[26] The treatment for prostate cancer—surgical removal of the prostate—is a costly endeavor that runs the risk of incontinence, impotence, and even death in rare cases.[27]

In contrast, breast carcinomas can double in less than three months, so early detection is important to improve treatment and chances of survival.[28] However, mammograms are not as effective for women under 50, the average age of menopause, because the breast tissue is denser. A mammogram must distinguish between blood vessels, glands, fatty tissues, and breast tissue, while allowing a doctor to detect a tumor that may appear on film as no larger than a grain of sand.[29] In a 1992 Canadian study, mammograms missed 40 percent of breast cancers that developed among 25,000 women aged 40–49.[30] Regular annual screening is currently not recommended until age 50.[31]

Early detection does not always mean better treatment. Often the mental anguish of knowing that something could go wrong or that a tumor exists that would otherwise go unnoticed until autopsy is an issue that must be addressed by health providers and the patient together.

Cigarette Taxes Show Ups and Downs

Hal Kane

Based on their proven ability to reduce smoking and disease, cigarette taxes rose in many countries in 1994.[1] Data from the eighties and early nineties showing massive savings to health care bills and increased worker productivity fueled the increases. Also during 1994, however, one of the world's highest cigarette taxes was cut, and one promising increase stalled following political changes.

The sudden reduction in taxation came in Canada in February 1994. Citing smuggling of cigarettes from the United States, which has low tobacco taxes, the government pulled back from their highly successful tax program.[2] Smoking in Canada had fallen every step of the way as the tax had risen. Within months of the tax cut, Canadian data showed a rise in cigarette consumption, one that was expected to continue through 1994 and 1995.[3] Few other cases of cutting cigarette taxes exist.

An increase to the U.S. tax would have stopped smuggling as successfully as a reduction in Canada's successful tax. The differential in tax rates between the two neighbors was about $2.50 per pack of 20 cigarettes before the Canadian announcement. Now it is $1.40.[4] (See Table 1.) In 1993 and 1994, the Clinton administration sought large increases, with the most frequent proposal for a 75¢ increase per pack—enough to lengthen the lives of 900,000 Americans alive today by discouraging children and others from smoking, according to former President Jimmy Carter.[5] That increase might also have been enough to have the Canadians leave their tax in place.

By the time of the November 1994 elections in the United States, no federal increase had been passed—the tobacco industry had lobbied successfully against it—and key elements of the push for higher cigarette taxes were lost.[6] Chairmanship of the House of Representative's Subcommittee on Health and the Environment passed from a staunch proponent of cigarette taxes to an active foe.[7] And a Congress that had been home to a subcommittee that voted to increase the cigarette tax far more than the administration requested was replaced by one that appeared poised to fight even a small rise.[8]

Much pressure to raise cigarette taxes is still in force, however. The Institute of Medicine, the health policy advisory arm of the National Academy of Sciences, for example, is advocating a $2.00 per pack tax on cigarettes in the United States.[9] More important, several states raised their cigarette taxes substantially in 1994. In Michigan, for example, a 50¢ boost in the tax caused sales to drop about 30 percent.[10]

In Scandinavia, a bastion of levies targetted at promoting health, cigarette taxes remained strong despite a political climate favoring lower taxation and government spending. With Sweden and Finland voting in December 1994 to join the European Union (EU), taxes in

TABLE 1. SELECTED NATIONAL CIGARETTE TAXES AND PRICES PER PACK, JANUARY 1995

COUNTRY	TAX PER PACK	PACK PRICE
	(dollars)	
Denmark	3.88	4.58
Norway	3.44	5.04
United Kingdom	3.27	4.23
Ireland	2.96	3.82
Sweden	2.80	4.04
Finland	2.73	3.69
Germany	2.25	3.15
New Zealand	2.22	3.29
France	1.94	2.58
Canada[1]	1.96	3.05
Hong Kong	1.50	2.78
Greece	1.35	1.88
Japan	1.32	2.21
Italy	1.31	1.80
Argentina	0.96	1.37
Taiwan	0.63	1.33
Spain	0.59	0.84
United States[1]	0.56	1.89
South Korea	0.45	0.76

[1]Average for provinces or states.
SOURCE: Luc Martial, Non-Smokers' Rights Association of Canada, Ottawa, private communication, January 17, 1995.

Cigarette Taxes Show Ups and Downs

these countries will now be influenced somewhat by the general effort to make economic policies compatible among the nations of that bloc. That may discourage the two governments from rising taxes too far above those of other EU countries.[11] The constraint is not likely to overcome the wills of the Swedes and Finns to protect their health, however, as evidenced by their neighbor Denmark, already a member of the EU and atop the world's list of tobacco taxes.

Elsewhere in Europe, the United Kingdom raised its tobacco tax by 10 pence in 1994 and has committed itself to increase the tax 3 percent more than each year's inflation rate in the future.[12] France's tax has been going up, and smoking there has been dropping.[13] Greece climbed out of the basement by raising its cigarette tax, leaving Spain at the bottom in Europe.[14]

Post-apartheid South Africa has raised cigarette taxes.[15] But many other African countries are in disarray, with high inflation and corruption. Cigarette taxes there are low or sometimes non-existent.[16]

In China, where almost a third of the world's cigarettes are smoked, the government is torn between safeguarding public health and maintaining its own source of tax revenues. If the China National Tobacco Corporation, which is a monopoly, raises prices too far, the resulting drops in smoking will cut its tax base. The tobacco industry is China's largest single source of tax revenue and provides almost 10 percent of the total tax intake.[17] A 1991 study by the Chinese Academy of Preventative Medicine, however, found that China pays out far more to meet tobacco-related medical costs than it takes in from taxes on cigarette sales.[18]

The Centers for Disease Control (CDC) of the U.S. government updated its research in 1994 on the economic costs of smoking. It found that smoking cost the U.S. health care system $50 billion in 1993—about $2.06 for each of the 24 billion packs sold.[19] The largest costs were $26.9 billion for hospitalization, $15.5 billion for physicians' fees, and $4.9 billion for nursing home care.[20] Some $21.7 billion (more than 43 percent) came from public funding such as Medicare and Medicaid.[21]

Beyond those costs, CDC estimated the indirect effect of smoking—lost time from work and the economic burden of premature death of smokers—at about $47.2 billion in 1990 (more recent data for this were not available).[22] Of course, those figures do not include the costs of suffering or the loss of family members. If such intangibles could be included, the costs would rise much higher. The report recommended that the United States boost its cigarette tax sharply.

An international report prepared by a team of scientists from the World Health Organization, the American Cancer Society, and the Imperial Cancer Research Fund in Oxford, England, found that 3 million people worldwide die of illness caused by smoking every year—one person every 10 seconds.[23] By the year 2020, they report, the deaths will reach 10 million a year if current smoking trends continue, making it "the biggest epidemic of fatal disease in the world."[24]

During 1994 new research reported that children of smoking mothers have nicotine and cancer-causing compounds in their blood; that they have more ear and lung infections, worsened asthma, and more visits to the hospital; and that those in preschool whose mothers smoked heavily during pregnancy scored lower on standardized intelligence tests than those whose mothers did not smoke.[25]

Access to Safe Water Expands
Nancy Chege

Although efforts have been made to provide every person with access to safe water, about a fifth of humanity—more than 1 billion people—still have no option but to drink water that is not safe to consume.[1] This is the source of water-related diseases, such as cholera, malaria, and schistosomiasis, that kill millions of people.

More than 3 million people, primarily children, die from diarrheal diseases annually, and at any one time, about 900 million people are afflicted with roundworm infections.[2] In fact, it is estimated that 80 percent of all illness in developing countries can be traced to inadequate water and sanitation supplies, and that half the hospital beds are occupied by patients suffering from water-related diseases.[3]

By the middle of this century, most industrial countries had succeeded in providing their residents with safe water.[4] By contrast, people in most developing countries did not have access to clean and safe water. To draw attention to this situation, the World Health Organization (WHO) carried out its first international survey in 1962, covering 75 developing countries. Comprehensive surveys were also done in 1970 and 1975; by 1975, 38 percent of the developing world's population had access to potable water—9 percent more than five years earlier.[5]

During a U.N. Water Conference held in 1977 in Mar del Plata, Argentina, WHO highlighted the need to intensify efforts initiated during the sixties. The decade 1981–90 was therefore declared the International Drinking Water Supply and Sanitation Decade.[6] During this period, governments of developing nations made an accelerated and concerted effort to expand water supply and sanitation services to underserved populations.

Throughout the eighties, considerable progress was accomplished on all continents. Total water coverage increased from 75 percent in 1981 to 85 percent in 1990 in urban areas, and from 46 percent to 68 percent in rural areas during the same period, offering an additional 1.2 billion people an adequate and safe water supply.[7] The percentage of people having access to safe water increased almost everywhere during the decade, and some countries made exceptional progress. The share went from 30 to 68 percent in Burkina Faso, from 21 to 74 percent in Myanmar (formerly Burma), and from 14 to 46 percent in Oman.[8] (See Table 1.) Although these figures are impressive, they fall short of the decade's goals, one of which was to supply every person with clean and safe water by 1990. The target date has now been extended to the year 2000.[9]

Providing adequate water and sanitation services reaps substantial gains in health benefits and time savings. In French cities, for example, people lived to be roughly 32 years old in 1850, but by 1900 life expectancy had increased to 45 years.[10] This increase corresponds closely to improvements in water supply and wastewater disposal. Today, diarrheal-related deaths of children are 60 percent higher in households lacking adequate service facilities.[11] A change in hygiene habits, encouraged through education and better health programs, would maximize the benefits.

Obtaining water in rural areas can be a costly experience. Women often have to cover long distances on foot, and on their way back home they carry a heavy container either on their heads or on their backs. A study done in Mueda Plateau, a village in Mozambique, found that the time it took a woman to fetch water dropped from 125 minutes to 25 minutes a day when water services were installed.[12] The reduction translates into a time gain that can be used to cultivate crops, trade in the market, care for children, or simply rest.

During the last four decades, the proportion of the global population living in Third World cities has more than doubled—from 17 to 37 percent.[13] Approximately 1.4 billion people live in these urban centers, and by 2025, this figure is expected to reach 4 billion.[14] During the same period, rural populations will grow minimally. Poor migrants moving from rural areas settle on the fringes of large cities in unplanned communities that lack a basic infrastructure of public services. Many are forced to buy drinking water from vendors, often for about 35 times as much as the city charges for its public systems.[15] In Ontisha, Nigeria, for in-

Access to Safe Water Expands

TABLE 1. ACCESS TO SAFE DRINKING WATER, 1980–90

COUNTRY	1980	1990
	(share of population)	
Denmark	100	100
United States	100	100
Barbados	99	100
Canada	98	100
Italy	90	100
Trinidad	97	96
Mexico	73	89
Zimbabwe	52	84
Philippines	45	81
Bangladesh	39	78
Myanmar	21	74
India	42	73
Suriname	88	68
Burkina Faso	30	68
Sri Lanka	28	60
Pakistan	35	55
Oman	14	46
Nepal	11	37

SOURCE: World Bank, *World Development Report 1994* (New York: Oxford University Press, 1994).

stance, buying water accounts for 18 percent of the household's expenses; in Port-au-Prince, Haiti, the figure is 20 percent.[16]

To correct for poor water quality, many households boil their drinking water; this is effective in protecting the family's health, but inadvertently incurs huge energy costs. In Jakarta, for example, boiling water for domestic consumption costs $50 million annually, equivalent to about 1 percent of the city's gross domestic product.[17] Moreover, because of the large quantities of fuelwood, coal, and coke used this way, inadequate water supply indirectly contributes to deforestation and urban air pollution.

The underlying principle at an international water and sanitation conference held in France in February 1994 was that "all human beings, whatever their living conditions or their resources, have the inalienable right to fresh water."[18] To accomplish this, all sectors involved will have to bolster their efforts severalfold—and that will just maintain current coverage levels, not surpass them. Although an estimated $130 billion was invested in water projects during the eighties by governments and donor agencies, significant money and water resources were wasted on costly and ineffective large projects.[19] A shift from high-cost to low-cost technologies by governments and donor agencies would facilitate the process.

An increased role of the private sector is also called for. In industrial countries, engineering works are performed by private firms, which strive to maintain their reputation of providing high-quality, cost-effective services. In developing countries, however, similar works are carried out by the public sector, in which an atmosphere of lethargy exists because job security is guaranteed and superior work is not rewarded. The resulting product is often costly and of poor quality.[20]

Responsibilities for planning, financing, and managing Third World water systems should be expanded to include non-governmental organizations and local communities. The participation of women, in particular, should be sought; after all, it is women who fetch the water, store it, and decide how it shall be used. Moreover, they know exactly what they want.

Homelessness Remains a Problem
Nancy Chege

The fundamental human right to housing has been inscribed in several international documents, including the Universal Declaration on Human Rights.[1] Yet today more than 1 billion people, a fifth of humanity, do not have adequate shelter.[2] Of these, 100 million do not have any shelter whatsoever.[3]

Definitions of homelessness vary from study to study, but there are two main ones that are frequently used. The narrower definition refers to the percentage of a population that sleeps outside dwelling units (on streets, in parks, in railroad stations, or under bridges, for example) or in temporary shelters in charitable organizations.[4] A broader definition includes all persons whose shelter is inadequate—that is, constructed of flimsy material, overcrowded, and lacking in basic services, such as water and sanitation.[5]

The problem of inadequate housing largely occurs in the developing world, often along the fringes of big cities, where slum and squatter areas spring up overnight. But in industrial countries, where illegal occupation of land is rare, those unable to afford conventional housing end up living on the streets. (See Table 1.)

A U.S. study done in 1988 (the latest year for which data are available) found that in any given week, approximately 500,000–600,000 Americans were in shelters, eating at soup kitchens, or living on the street.[6] Of these, 45 percent of the sheltered homeless were unaccompanied men, 23 percent were children and young people (under 18), and 30 percent were single parents with children.[7] Approximately half of the homeless mothers and their children are victims of domestic abuse.[8] The primary causes of homelessness in the United States are an increase in the number of poor people, unemployment and low wages, a significant rise in the cost of housing, a shortage of community facilities for the chronically mentally ill, and reductions in federal and state housing assistance programs.[9]

Among the poor in many European countries, the availability and accessibility of some sort of a national health care system lessens the burden of choosing between medical treatment and shelter.[10] Yet there are still thousands who have no permanent accommodation. Although no official statistics are available, the best estimates suggest that ap-

TABLE 1. SQUATTER HOUSING AND HOMELESSNESS, SELECTED CITIES

CITY	SQUATTER HOUSING[1] (percent)	HOMELESSNESS[2] (per thousand population)
Dar es Salaam, Tanzania	51	0.0
Lilongwe, Malawi	71	0.0
Kingston, Jamaica	33	3.6
Dhaka, Bangladesh	10	11.5
New Delhi, India	17	4.2
Quito, Ecuador	40	0.6
Istanbul, Turkey	51	0.1
Bogota, Colombia	8	3.0
Cairo, Egypt	3	0.1
Beijing, China	3	0.0
Madrid, Spain	0	1.7
London, United Kingdom	0	3.0
Paris, France	0	5.6
Washington, D.C., United States	0	3.6
Stockholm, Sweden	0	0.3
Tokyo, Japan	0	0.2
Helsinki, Finland	0	7.7

[1]The percentage of the total housing stock in the urban area that is occupying land illegally. [2]Number per thousand of the urban area population who sleep outside dwelling units or in temporary shelter in charitable organizations.
SOURCE: "The Housing Indicators Program," Preliminary Results of the Extensive Survey of Housing Indicators 1990, U.N. Centre for Human Settlements and World Bank, Nairobi, April 1993.

Homelessness Remains a Problem

proximately 3 million Europeans are homeless—1 percent of the population.[11] In Germany, single homeless people number about 150,000, while in France, the number is between 200,000 and 400,000, of whom 10,000 are in Paris.[12] A 1991 census in Britain revealed that some 200,000–500,000 residents had no permanent address.[13] Referred to as the "hidden homeless," this group of young people—aged primarily between 18 and 35—sleep on floors or sofas of friends and relatives for short periods of time.

Rapid rates of urbanization have come to symbolize Third World cities. Just four decades ago, 17 percent of residents in these countries lived in urban areas. Today, the figure stands at 37, and is expected to rise to 57 by the year 2025.[14] Accompanying this growth is a mushrooming of slums and squatter settlements on the outskirts of cities, to accommodate those who are too poor to afford regular housing. During the last 20 years, for example, Bombay, India, has grown by 100 percent while the number of squatters there has increased by 1,100 percent.[15]

Clearly, squatter settlements are growing at an unprecedented rate. Features common to such housing include the use of unconventional construction material, such as cardboard and flattened tins; overcrowding due to multiple occupancy; and the acquisition of land without the permission of the owner. The proportion of the urban population occupying land illegally in cities varies widely: 17 percent in New Delhi, 32 percent in São Paulo, and 85 percent in Addis Ababa.[16]

Conditions in squatter settlements are unsafe, unhealthy, and demoralizing. There is little or no public provision of water, sanitation, garbage disposal, storm drainage, or public transport. Not surprisingly, the incidence of disease under such conditions is high. For instance, a study in a small squatter settlement in Allahabad, India, found that half of those tested were suffering from intestinal worms, while dysentery was endemic.[17]

Not recognized by federal and city officials as legal residents of the municipality, slum dwellers live in constant fear of eviction. Lacking power and wealth, and having no tenure to the land they live on, squatters are in no position to protest or stop the evictions that often occur unannounced. Governments justify evictions in several ways: to "beautify" a city, as in Seoul, South Korea, where 720,000 people were evicted in preparation for the Olympic games; to create space for commercial development, as happened to 300,000 people in Lagos, Nigeria, in 1990; or simply to chase away those who have settled illegally on private or public lands, as 10,000 people in São Paulo, Brazil, found out.[18]

No warning is usually given of the arrival of the bulldozer that razes to the ground the fragile houses. The slum residents lose not only their homes but also their most basic belongings. They flee to wherever they can find shelter, breaking up the complex, interdependent relationships that formed a safety net of protection against ill health, income decline, and loss of a job, however menial.

Refugees fleeing political or religious persecution, famine, floods, or ethnic clashes frequently end up homeless.[19] Their numbers are growing too. Rising from 2.5 million in the mid-seventies, the world's population of official refugees is now about 23 million.[20] Those who have been "internally displaced"—forced from their homes but still within the borders of their country—number an additional 27 million at least.[21]

The causes of homelessness, which stem from political activities, economic trends, societal changes, and natural disasters, vary in nature from continent to continent, and therefore require solutions that are region-specific.[22] In June 1996, the United Nations will hold an international Conference on Human Settlements in Istanbul, Turkey—20 years after the first one was held in Vancouver, Canada. The meeting will focus on the world's cities. It will highlight the problems and challenges experienced by the poor in their living environments, and draw up action plans to improve conditions of shelter through the collaborative effort of local and national governments, international agencies, nongovernmetnal groups, and the business community.[23]

Income Gap Widens

Hal Kane

The gap in income among the people of the world has been widening. In 1960, the richest 20 percent received 30 times more income than the poorest 20 percent. By 1991, this group received 61 times more money.[1] While the poorest one fifth in 1960 received a meager 2.3 percent of world income, by 1991 that revenue share had fallen to 1.4 percent. The income share of the richest fifth, on the other hand, rose from 70 percent to 85 percent.[2]

These disparities prevail both among countries and within them, and the large gap between individuals worldwide reflects the combination of both those splits. Almost four fifths of all people live in the Third World, where incomes are only a fraction of those in industrial countries.[3] In turn, within countries in both those groups, gaps in income between citizens can be even wider.

The widest income gap within a country reported by U.N. statisticians is in Botswana, where during the eighties the richest 20 percent of society received over 47 times more income than the poorest 20 percent.[4] (See Table 1.) Brazil was second, with a ratio of 32 to 1, and in Guatemala and Panama, the ratio stood at 30 to 1.

The quickly growing economies of East Asia have had income patterns similar to those of Western Europe and North America, with the richest one fifth often earning 5–10 times more than the poorest fifth. In South Asia, India, Bangladesh, and Pakistan had relatively even distributions of income, with the richest 20 percent getting only four to five times more than the poorest quintile. Some countries that have had military conflicts apparently based in part on inequities among citizens nevertheless have relatively even income distributions—such as Rwanda and Ethiopia.

The split between countries and people can be seen in the marketplace. The value of luxury goods sales worldwide—high-fashion clothing and top-of-the-line autos, for example—exceeds the gross national products of two thirds of the world's countries.[5] The world's average income, roughly $4,000 (current dollars) a year, is well below the U.S. poverty line.[6]

TABLE 1. INCOME DISTRIBUTION, SELECTED COUNTRIES, LATE EIGHTIES

COUNTRY	RATIO OF RICHEST ONE FIFTH TO POOREST
Industrial Countries	
United States	9
Switzerland	9
Israel	7
Italy	6
Germany	6
Sweden	5
Japan	4
Poland	4
Hungary	3
Developing Countries	
Botswana	47
Brazil	32
Guatemala	30
Panama	30
Kenya	23
Chile	17
Mexico	14
Malaysia	12
Peru	10
Thailand	8
Philippines	7
China	6
Ghana	6
Ethiopia	5
Indonesia	5
Pakistan	5
India	5
Bangladesh	4
Rwanda	4

SOURCE: U.N. Development Programme, *Human Development Report 1994* (New York: Oxford University Press, 1994).

The poorest fifth of the world accounted for 0.9 percent of world trade, 1.1 percent of global domestic investment, 0.9 percent of global domestic savings, and just 0.2 percent of global commercial credit at the beginning of the nineties. Each of those shares declined between 1960 and 1990.[7]

These disparities are reflected in the consumption of many resources. At the start of this decade, industrial countries, home to roughly a fifth of the world, used about 86 percent of world aluminum and chemicals, 81 percent of the paper, 80 percent of the iron and steel, and three quarters of the timber and energy.[8] Since then, economic growth in developing countries has probably reduced these percentages. China's economy, for example, is more than 50 percent larger now than it was in 1990, and developing countries have passed industrial ones in fertilizer consumption.[9]

Uneven income distribution is behind some of the most important trends in the world today. It raises crime rates, for example. And it drives migration. People have long responded to economic disparities by following a path from poor regions to richer ones, as tens of millions of workers chase higher wages and better opportunities. Hence, some 1.6 million Asians and Middle Easterners were working in Kuwait and Saudi Arabia before they fled war in 1991, and at least 2.5 million Mexicans live in the United States.[10]

The same is true within countries: rising disparities of income are adding to the growth of cities through rural-to-urban migration. Latin America, with some of the highest disparities of income among its citizens, is also the most urbanized region of the developing world—not entirely by coincidence. From 1950 to today, city dwellers there have risen from 42 percent of the population to 73 percent.[11]

For many years China had one of the most equal distributions of income in the world. But now that is changing as incomes in its southern provinces and special economic zones soar while those in rural areas rise much more slowly. Also not coincidentally, the Chinese National Academy of Social Sciences says that by 2010, half the population will live in cities, compared with 28 percent today and only 10 percent in the early eighties.[12]

In the early nineties, economies in the Third World, and especially in East Asia, have grown faster than they did in industrial countries.[13]

This has the potential to shrink disparities of income, as poorer countries might close part of the gap with richer ones. Yet the divergence may not contract because the economic growth is distributed so unevenly within nations. Despite the recent restoration of economic growth in Latin America, for example, U.N. economists say that no progress is expected in reducing poverty, which is even likely to increase slightly.[14]

Meanwhile, in some regions almost no one has been getting richer. The per capita income of most sub-Saharan African nations actually fell during the eighties. After the latest negotiations of the General Agreement on Tariffs and Trade (GATT) were completed, the *Wall Street Journal* reported that "even GATT's most energetic backers say that in one part of the world, the trade accord may do more harm than good: sub-Saharan Africa," the poorest geographic region.[15] There, an estimated one third of all college graduates have left the continent.[16] That loss of talented people, due in large part to poverty and a lack of opportunities in Africa, will make it even more difficult for the continent to advance.

The economic growth in the Third World that has the potential to close income gaps among peoples is instead becoming a splitting off, with some parts of societies joining the industrial world while others remain behind. Singapore, Hong Kong, and Taiwan have begun to look like wealthy industrial countries, for example.[17] Now parts of China are following, as are the wealthier segments of Latin American society and of Southeast Asian countries.[18] This is good news for members of the middle-income countries and for the world. But it may do little to help the poorest fifth of humanity.

Hunger Still Widespread

Hal Kane

Almost 800 million people in the developing world are undernourished—consuming too few calories to sustain more than light physical activity. That 20 percent of the Third World is fewer than the approximately 1 billion people who were underfed in 1975. Nevertheless, today one third of all children in the developing world are still underweight for their age, more than 40 percent of women are underweight or anaemic, and both human and economic potential worldwide is constrained by lack of food.[1]

One of the most reliable measures of malnutrition is the number of children who get too little food to grow to their expected body size. (See Table 1.) The number of underweight children fell from around 42 percent in 1975 to 38 percent in 1980 and then to 34 percent in 1990.[2] This means the actual number fell from 168 million children in 1975 to 164 million in 1980, but it then rose to 184 million in 1990.[3]

Only in Southeast Asia was the number of children suffering from malnutrition reduced significantly during the eighties. The number remained about even in the Middle East, North Africa, South Asia, and Latin America. But the number of underweight children rose by over 10 percent in China, and went up by almost 40 percent in sub-Saharan Africa during that decade.[4]

Nutrition affects the intellectual development, learning capacity, and school performance of children. Those who suffer from growth retardation have reduced motor and mental functions, and those who have severe undernutrition have less brain growth and lower activity levels. Results of 20-year follow-up testing of malnourished children from the seventies indicate early irreversible damage to intellectual development.[5]

Among adults, malnutrition reduces physical activity, work capacity, muscle strength, and endurance. It also impairs immune systems: disease and illness tend to be more frequent, more severe, and prolonged in poorly nourished people. Nutritional requirements are higher during and following infectious episodes, and fevers in particular increase energy requirements, so the malnourished are often caught in a cycle of hunger and illness.[6]

Malnutrition is also widespread in some of the world's wealthiest countries. The United States has wider disparities of income than most other wealthy countries, and in part as a result some 30 million Americans—more than 10 percent of the population—suffer chronic malnutrition.[7] Almost half the hungry there are children.[8] U.S. hunger also has a racial dimension—76 percent of the hungry are people of color.[9]

Malnutrition can harm people who eat enough calories but get too much of certain foods. Some 24 percent of all deaths worldwide come from cardiovascular diseases that are related to obesity and the amount of saturated fat in the diet (as well as other aspects of life-style, such as smoking and lack of exercise).[10] In industrial countries, almost half the deaths are from cardiovascular disease, often among people whose diets were too high in animal fats and too low in vegetables and fruits.[11]

High rates of these diseases even occur in some of the poorer countries—in Chile and Jamaica, which have relatively few underweight children, more than 10 percent of preschool children are overweight.[12] It is ironic that in countries where people die of underconsumption of food, others become ill from eating too much of certain foods.

Poor diets also contribute to cancer in people who eat too few fruits and vegetables or too much fat. Diets high in plant foods, especially green and yellow vegetables and citrus fruits, are associated with a lower occurrence of cancers of the lung, colon, esophagus, and stomach.[13] A diet is adequate when it provides sufficient energy, protein, fat, carbohydrate, vitamins and minerals, and fiber.

Dietary deficiencies of vitamins and minerals cause learning disabilities, mental retardation, poor health, low work capacity, blindness, and premature death. About 1 billion people, almost all in developing countries, are suffering from these deficiencies, and another billion are at risk.[14]

Deficiency of vitamin A blinds up to a half-million preschool children each year.[15] It also causes the deaths of a smaller number of chil-

TABLE 1. SHARE OF CHILDREN UNDERWEIGHT, SELECTED COUNTRIES, CIRCA 1990

COUNTRY	SHARE (percent)
Bangladesh	66
India	63
Vietnam	42
Pakistan	40
Nigeria	36
Philippines	34
Myanmar	32
Tanzania	25
Zambia	25
China	21
Cameroon	14
Thailand	13
Peru	11
Egypt	10
Colombia	10
Algeria	9
Brazil	7
Jordan	6
Paraguay	4

SOURCE: U.N. Administrative Committee on Coordination, Subcommittee on Nutrition, *Second Report on the World Nutrition Situation, Vol. I: Global and Regional Results* (Geneva: 1992).

dren. In some parts of South Asia and Eastern and Southern Africa, vitamin A supply is so low that almost everyone suffers from deficiency. Fortunately, most regions have recently been able to get more vitamin A into the diets of their people. Parts of Africa, especially East Africa, however, have been less successful in this regard.[16]

Iron deficiency, one result of which is anemia, is the only nutrition problem that is worsening in most parts of the world. Only the Middle East and North Africa have increased people's intake of dietary iron. Deficiencies of iron are especially severe in South Asia, where more than 60 percent of women are anemic.[17] Meanwhile, iodine deficiency remains the most common preventable cause of mental retardation worldwide.

These micronutrients can be delivered easily and at low cost through the fortification of food with nutrients, by dietary change, and with capsules, tablets, or other supplements. In Indonesia and the Philippines, for example, it costs about 25¢ per person a year to deliver vitamin A in capsules; in India in the late eighties, 5¢ per person fortified salt with iodine each year; in Guatemala, it cost 12¢ per person to add iron to sugar.[18] Such protection costs far less than dealing with illnesses, even without considering productivity losses and suffering.

Fortification has wiped out most vitamin and mineral deficiencies in industrial countries. Adding vitamin D to margarine is thought to have eliminated rickets from Britain and Northern Europe earlier this century. Fortification of refined flour with iron in the United States and Sweden is credited with a dramatic reduction of anemia.[19]

One of the keys to reducing infant malnutrition is breast-feeding. During the first four to six months of life, no food or liquid other than breast milk, not even water, is required to meet the normal infant's nutritional requirements. Breast milk also provides protection against infection. Mothers are advised to continue breast-feeding their children up to two years of age, or beyond.[20]

NOTES

GRAIN PRODUCTION REBOUNDS (pages 26–27)

1. U.S. Department of Agriculture (USDA), Foreign Agricultural Service, *Grain: World Markets and Trade*, Washington, D.C., January 1995; USDA, "Production, Supply, and Demand View" (electronic database), Washington, D.C., November 1994.
2. USDA, *Grain: World Markets and Trade*, op. cit. note 1; USDA (electronic database), op. cit. note 1.
3. USDA (electronic database), op. cit. note 1; population from U.S. Bureau of the Census, Center for International Research, Suitland, Md., private communication, February 6, 1995.
4. USDA (electronic database), op. cit. note 1; Bureau of the Census, op. cit. note 3.
5. USDA, *Grain: World Markets and Trade*, op. cit. note 1.
6. Ibid.
7. Ibid.
8. Ibid.
9. USDA (electronic database), op. cit. note 1.
10. Ibid.
11. Ibid.
12. Sun Shangwu, "Building Eats up Farmland as More Mouths Need More Food," *China Daily*, July 18, 1994; India and Indonesia area estimates from USDA (electronic database), op. cit. note 1.
13. USDA, *Grain: World Markets and Trade*, op. cit. note 1.
14. Ibid.
15. USDA (electronic database), op. cit. note 1.
16. USDA, *Grain: Markets and Trade*, op. cit. note 1.
17. USDA (electronic database), op. cit. note 1.
18. Ibid.
19. Ibid.; K. F. Isherwood and K.G. Soh, "The Agricultural Situation and Fertilizer Demand," presented at 62nd Annual Conference, International Fertilizer Industry Association, Istanbul, May 9, 1994.
20. Sandra Postel, *Last Oasis: Facing Water Scarcity* (New York: W.W. Norton & Company, 1992).

SOYBEAN PRODUCTION JUMPS (pages 28–29)

1. U.S. Department of Agriculture (USDA), "World Oilseed Database" (unpublished printout), Washington, D.C., 1992; USDA, "Production, Supply, and Demand View" (electronic database), Washington, D.C., November 1994, with updates from USDA, "Oilseeds: World Markets and Trade," Washington, D.C., January 1995.
2. Ibid.; U.S. Bureau of the Census, Center for International Research, Suitland, Md., private communication, February 6, 1995.
3. USDA (electronic database), op. cit. note 1; Bureau of the Census, op. cit. note 2.
4. USDA (electronic database), op. cit. note 1.
5. Ibid.
6. USDA, "Oilseeds: World Markets and Trade," op. cit. note 1.
7. Ibid.
8. Ibid.
9. USDA (electronic database), op. cit. note 1.
10. Ibid.
11. Ibid.
12. Ibid.; historical data from USDA, "World Oilseed Database," op. cit. note 1.
13. U.N Food and Agriculture Organization (FAO), *Yearbook of Fishery Statistics: Catches and Landings* (Rome: various years); 1993 and 1994 data from Maurizio Perotti, fishery statistician, Fishery Information, Data and Statistics Service, Fisheries Depart-

ment, FAO, Rome, private communications, January 19 and February 1, 1995.
14. USDA (electronic database), op. cit. note 1.
15. USDA, "Oilseeds: World Markets and Trade," op. cit. note 1.
16. Ibid.

MEAT PRODUCTION TAKES A LEAP (pages 30–31)

1. U.S. Department of Agriculture, (USDA), Foreign Agricultural Service (FAS), *Livestock and Poultry: World Markets and Trade*, Washington, D.C., October 1994.
2. Ibid.; U.S. Bureau of the Census, Center for International Research, Suitland, Md., private communication, February 6, 1995.
3. USDA, op. cit. note 1.
4. USDA, FAS, *World Agricultural Production*, Washington, D.C., January 1995.
5. USDA, op. cit. note 1.
6. Ibid.
7. Ibid.
8. U.N. Food and Agriculture Organization (FAO), *Food Outlook*, Rome, September 1994.
9. USDA, op. cit. note 1.
10. Ibid.
11. Ibid.
12. Ibid.
13. Ibid.
14. Ibid.
15. Ibid.
16. USDA, op. cit. note 4.
17. Ibid.
18. Ibid.
19. Ibid.
20. Ibid.
21. Ibid.
22. FAO, *1948-1985 World Crop and Livestock Statistics* (Rome: 1987); FAO, *Production Yearbook* (Rome: various years).
23. USDA, op. cit. note 1.

AQUACULTURE BOOSTS FISH CATCH (pages 32–33)

1. 1993 and 1994 data from Maurizio Perotti, fishery statistician, Fishery Information, Data and Statistics Service, Fisheries Department, U.N. Food and Agriculture Organization (FAO), Rome, private communications, January 19 and February 1, 1995.
2. FAO, *Yearbook of Fishery Statistics: Catches and Landings* (Rome: various years); 1993-94 data from Perotti, op. cit. note 1; population data from U.S. Bureau of Census, Center for International Research, Suitland, Md., private communication, February 6, 1995.
3. FAO, "Marine Fisheries and the Law of the Sea: A Decade of Change," Fisheries Circular No. 853, Rome, 1993.
4. Ibid., with Worldwatch estimate of growth rate.
5. FAO, op. cit. note 2; Peter Weber, *Net Loss: Fish, Jobs, and the Marine Environment*, Worldwatch Paper 120 (Washington, D.C.: Worldwatch Institute, July 1994).
6. "Asia Continues to Lead in Aquaculture Production," *Depthnews Asia*, July 1994; FAO, *Review of the State of World Fishery Resources: Aquaculture*, Fisheries Circular No. 886, Rome, 1995.
7. Perotti, op. cit. note 1.
8. Peter O'Neill, "Farming Has Expanded on World Bank Millions," *Fish Farming International*, July 1994.
9. Perotti, op. cit. note 1.
10. Ibid.
11. Ibid.
12. Ibid.
13. FAO, op. cit. note 3; Weber, op. cit. note 5.
14. Brian Groombridge, ed., *Global Biodiversity: Status of the Earth's Living Resources*, World Conservation Monitoring Center, in collaboration with the Natural History Museum of London, in association with the World Conservation Union, U.N. Environment Programme, World Wide Fund for Nature, and the World Resources Institute (New York: Chapman & Hall, 1992).
15. Matthew Gianni, press release posted on Econet in igc:env.marine, "UN Puts Pressure on Europe to Toe the Line on Driftnets," Washington, D.C., Greenpeace, December 13, 1994.
16. United Nations, *Report of the Secretary General: Law of the Sea*, General Assembly, Forty-ninth session, Agenda item 35, November 16, 1994.
17. Bruce Clark, "Law of the Sea Promises Many Disputes," *Financial Times*, November 16, 1994.
18. Ibid.
19. Chairman of the Conference, *Draft Agreement for the Implementation of the Provisions of the United Nations Convention on the Law of the Sea of 10 December 1992 Relating to Conservation and Management of Straddling Fish Stocks and Highly Migratory Fish Stocks*, delivered at the United Nations Conference on Straddling Fish Stocks and Highly Migratory Fish Stocks, General Assembly, Fourth Session, New York, Au-

gust 15-26, 1994; see also "Fate of World's Fisheries Debated," *UN Chronicle*, June 1994.
20. Brian O'Riordan, "Tangled Webs of Chaos Adrift," *New Scientist*, August 20, 1994.

WORLD FEEDGRAIN USE UP SLIGHTLY (pages 34–35)

1. U.S. Department of Agriculture (USDA), "Production, Supply, and Demand View" (electronic database), Washington, D.C., November 1994; USDA, "World Agricultural Supply and Demand Estimates," Washington, D.C., January 1995.
2. International Monetary Fund (IMF), *World Economic Growth, October 1994* (Washington, D.C.: 1994).
3. USDA (electronic database), op. cit. note 1; U.S. Bureau of the Census, Center for International Research, Suitland, Md., private communication, February 6, 1995.
4. USDA, "World Agricultural Estimates," op. cit. note 1.
5. USDA (electronic database), op. cit. note 1.
6. Ibid.; IMF, op. cit. note 2.
7. USDA (electronic database) op. cit. note 1.
8. USDA, Foreign Agricultural Service, *Livestock and Poultry: World Markets and Trade*, Washington, D.C., October 1994.
9. USDA (electronic database), op. cit. note 1.
10. Ibid.
11. Ibid.
12. Ibid.
13. Ibid.
14. Ibid.
15. USDA, *Feed Situation and Outlook Yearbook*, Washington D.C., October 1994.
16. USDA (electronic database), op. cit. note 1.
17. Ibid.
18. Ibid.
19. Ibid.
20. U.N. Food and Agriculture Organization, *Production Yearbook, 1993* (Rome: 1994).
21. USDA, op. cit. note 8.
22. Ibid.
23. Ibid.
24. Ibid.
25. USDA, op. cit. note 15.

GRAIN STOCKS DECLINE AGAIN (pages 36–37)

1. U.S. Department of Agriculture (USDA), Foreign Agricultural Service, *Grain: World Markets and Trade*, Washington, D.C., January 1995.

2. USDA, "Production, Supply and Demand View" (electronic database), Washington, D.C. November 1994.
3. USDA, op. cit. note 1.
4. USDA, op. cit. note 1; USDA, op. cit. note 2.
5. International Monetary Fund, *International Financial Statistics Yearbook* (Washington, D.C.: 1994).
6. USDA, op. cit. note 1.
7. Ibid.
8. USDA, op. cit. note 2.
9. USDA, op. cit. note 1.
10. Ibid.
11. Ibid.
12. Ibid.
13. Ibid.
14. Ibid.
15. U.S. Bureau of the Census, Center for International Research, Suitland, Md., private communication, February 6, 1995; Joseph P. Quinlan, "World Economy Ready to Surge," *Journal of Commerce*, August 31, 1994.
16. IMF, op. cit. note 5.

FERTILIZER USE CONTINUES DROPPING (pages 40–41)

1. U.N. Food and Agriculture Organization (FAO), *Fertilizer Yearbook* (Rome: various years); K.F. Isherwood and K.G. Soh, "The Agricultural Situation and Fertilizer Demand," presented at 62nd Annual Conference, International Fertilizer Industry Association (IFA), Istanbul, May 9, 1994.
2. FAO, op. cit. note 1.
3. Isherwood and Soh, op. cit. note 1.
4. K.F. Isherwood and K.G. Soh, "Short Term Prospects for World Agriculture and Fertilizer Use," presented at 19th Enlarged Council Meeting, IFA, Paris, November 22, 1993.
5. "Fertilizer Consumption and Environment Report," Information and Market Research Service, IFA, June 1994.
6. Isherwood and Soh, op. cit. note 1; "Fertilizer Growth in Asia," *Far Eastern Agriculture*, July/August 1994.
7. "Fertilizer Growth in Asia," op. cit. note 6.
8. "Fertilizer Consumption and Environment Report," op. cit. note 5.
9. Ibid.
10. Isherwood and Soh, op. cit. note 1.
11. Ibid.
12. Ibid.
13. Ibid.
14. Ibid.

15. Ibid.
16. Isherwood and Soh, op. cit. note 4.

GRAIN YIELD REMAINS STEADY (pages 42–43)

1. U.S. Department of Agriculture (USDA), "Production, Supply, and Demand View" (electronic database), Washington, D.C., November 1994.
2. Ibid.
3. Ibid.
4. Ibid.
5. Ibid.
6. USDA, *World Grain Situation and Outlook*, Washington, D.C., November 1994.
7. USDA, op. cit. note 1.
8. Ibid.
9. Boyce Rensberger, "New 'Super Rice' Nearing Fruition," *Washington Post*, October 24, 1994.
10. USDA, op. cit. note 1.
11. Ibid.
12. USDA, "World Grain Database" (unpublished printout), Washington, D.C., March 1989.
13. USDA, op. cit. note 1.
14. U.N. Food and Agriculture Organization (FAO), *Production Yearbooks* (Rome: various years); K.F. Isherwood and K.G. Soh, "The Agricultural Situation and Fertilizer Demand," presented at 62nd Annual Conference, International Fertilizer Industry Association, Istanbul, May 9, 1994.
15. FAO, op. cit. note 14.
16. Sandra Postel, *Last Oasis: Facing Water Scarcity* (New York: W.W. Norton & Company, 1992).
17. FAO, op. cit. note 14; U.S. Bureau of the Census, published in Francis Urban and Ray Nightingale, *World Population by Country and Region, 1950–90, with Projections to 2050* (Washington, D.C.: USDA, Economic Research Service, 1993).

OIL PRODUCTION UP (pages 46–47)

1. "Worldwide Oil Flow Up, Reserves Steady in '94," *Oil & Gas Journal*, December 19, 1994. The figures used in this *Vital Sign* are for crude oil, and exclude natural gas liquids from estimates of total oil production and use.
2. British Petroleum (BP), *BP Statistical Review of World Energy* (London: 1994).
3. "Worldwide Oil Flow Up," op. cit. note 1.
4. Ibid.
5. BP, op. cit. note 2.
6. U.S. Department of Energy (DOE), Energy Information Administration, *Monthly Energy Review January 1995* (Washington, D.C.: 1995).
7. Ibid.
8. Ibid.
9. BP, op cit. note 2.
10. Ibid.
11. Worldwatch Institute estimate.
12. DOE, op. cit. note 6.
13. Worldwatch estimate based on BP.
14. Worldwatch Institute estimate.
15. "Saudi Arabian Sands," *Energy Economist*, November 1993.
16. Ibid.
17. Ibid.
18. Ibid.
19. BP, op. cit. note 2.

NATURAL GAS PRODUCTION STALLS (pages 48–49)

1. Worldwatch Institute estimate based on British Petroleum (BP), *BP Statistical Review of World Energy* (London: 1994), and other sources; the Worldwatch figures include natural gas liquids as well as methane.
2. Matt Sagars, PlanEcon, Inc., Washington, D.C., private communication, February 8, 1995.
3. Worldwatch, op. cit. note 1.
4. International Monetary Fund, *World Economic Outlook, October 1994* (Washington, D.C.: 1994).
5. Sagars, op. cit. note 2; Michael S. Lelyveld, "Neighbors Siphoning Pipeline Gas from Russia," *Journal of Commerce*, December 2, 1994.
6. Sagars, op. cit. note 2.
7. Bhushan Bahree, "Siberian Natural Gas Could Solve Energy Needs of Europe, But It Poses a Threat to Oil Industry," *Wall Street Journal*, April 16, 1993; Gregory F. Ulmishek and Charles D. Masters, "Oil and Gas Resources Estimated in the Former Soviet Union," *Oil and Gas Journal*, Decmeber 13, 1995; "Turkey Does Deal with Iraq, Iran and Turkmenistan," *Energy Economist*, August 1994.
8. "Turkey Does Deal," op. cit. note 7; John J. Maresca, "The New Silk Road," *Wall Street Journal*, January 26, 1995.
9. John D. Grace, "Russian Gas Resource Base Large, Overstated, Costly to Maintain," *Oil and Gas Journal*, February 6, 1995.
10. Alanna Sullivan, "Exxon Enters $40 Billion Pact with Indonesia," *Wall Street Journal*, November 17, 1994.
11. David Lascelles, "Gas Discovery Lifts Philippines' Energy Hopes," *Financial Times*, January 6, 1995.
12. "China's Upstream Oil and Gas Industry Opens in

Steps to Outsiders, Awaits Big Discovery," *Oil and Gas Journal*, November 28, 1994; "Additional Details Spelled Out on Large Sichuan Gas Project," *Oil and Gas Journal*, June 13, 1994.
13. Worldwatch Institute calculations, based on BP, op. cit. note 1.
14. "Electricity," *Energy Economist*, July 1994.
15. U.S. Department of Energy (DOE), Energy Information Administration, *Monthly Energy Review January 1995* (Washington, D.C.: 1995).
16. William L. Fisher, "How Technology has Confounded U.S. Gas Resource Estimators," *Oil and Gas Journal*, October 24, 1994.
17. A.D. Koen, "Gas Demand Helps Spark Drilling Activity in U.S.," *Oil and Gas Journal*, April 11, 1994.
18. U.S. prices are for purchases from producers and are from DOE, op. cit. note 15; West European prices are for cif (cost, insurance, and freight) Europe and are from BP, *BP Statistical Review of World Energy* (London: various issues).
19. DOE, op. cit. note 15.
20. Ibid.
21. Charles D. Masters, David H. Root, and Emil D. Attanasi, "World Petroleum Assessment and Analysis" (draft), U.S. Geological Survey, Reston, Va., January 1994. (These figures include natural gas liquids.)
22. Robert A. Hefner III, "New Thinking About Natural Gas," in David G. Howell, ed., *The Future of Energy Gases* (Washington, D.C.: U.S. Geological Survey, 1993).
23. Subroto quoted in Bahree, op. cit. note 7.

COAL USE REMAINS FLAT
(pages 50–51)

1. United Nations (UN), *World Energy Supplies* (New York: various years); UN, *Yearbook of World Energy Statistics* (New York: 1983); UN, *Energy Statistics Yearbook* (New York: various years); 1993 figure is a Worldwatch estimate, based on UN and on British Petroleum (BP), *BP Statistical Review of World Energy* (London: 1994); 1994 figure is a Worldwatch estimate based on UN, on BP, on U.S. Department of Energy, Energy Information Administration, *Monthly Energy Review January 1995* (Washington, D.C.: 1995), on V. Luque Cabal, Industries and Markets, Fossil Fuels, European Commission, Brussels, private communication and printout, February 8, 1995, on Paul Hunt, PlanEcon, Inc., Washington, D.C., private communication and printout, January 31, 1995, on J.F. Erasmus, Department of Mineral and Energy Affairs, Johannesburg, South Africa, private communication, February 21, 1995, and on "Coal," *Energy Economist*, December 1994.
2. BP, op. cit. note 1.
3. European Union totals exclude the former East Germany, and are from Gerhard Semrau, Gesamtverband des Deutschen Steinkohlenbergbaus, Essen, private communication and printout, January 23, 1995, from Cabal, op. cit., note 1, from Charlotte Griffiths, World Coal Institute, London, private communication and printout, January 17, 1995, and from BP, op. cit. note 1.
4. U.K. trend based on BP, op. cit. note 1, and on Griffiths, op. cit. note 3.
5. Nathaniel C. Nash, "German High Court Bans Energy Subsidy on Utility Bills," *New York Times*, December 8, 1994.
6. Coal use based on BP, op. cit. note 1, and on Hunt, op. cit. note 1.
7. "Russian Miners Warn of Strike," *Financial Times*, February 3, 1995.
8. BP, op. cit. note 1.
9. Ibid.
10. Jonathan E. Sinton, ed., *China Energy Data Book* (Berkeley, Calif.: Lawrence Berkeley Laboratory, 1992).
11. "Coal," *Energy Economist*, July 1994.
12. Sinton, op. cit. note 10.
13. M.J. Chadwick and M. Hutton, *Acid Depositions in Europe: Environmental Effects, Control Strategies, and Policy Options* (Stockholm: Stockholm Environment Institute, 1991); Li Xiguang, "China Actively Controls Acid Rain Pollution, 16 Renown Experts Report to the Government," *People's Daily (Overseas Edition)*, January 9, 1995, translated by Jessica Hamburger, Battelle Pacific Northwest Laboratory, Washington, D.C., February 2, 1995.
14. Vaclav Smil, *China's Environmental Crisis: An Inquiry into the Limits of National Development* (New York: M.E. Sharpe Inc., 1993); H. Keith Florig, "The Benefits of Air Pollution Reduction in China" (draft), Resources for the Future, Washington, D.C., November 24, 1993.
15. Gregg Marland, "Carbon Dioxide Emission Rates for Conventional and Synthetic Fuels," *Energy*, Vol. 8, No. 12, 1983; coal's contribution to carbon dioxide totals is a Worldwatch estimate based on various sources listed in note 1.

NUCLEAR POWER FLAT (pages 52–53)

1. Installed nuclear capacity is defined as reactors connected to the grid as of December 31, 1994, and is based on Worldwatch Institute database compiled from Mycle Schneider and Assad Kondakji, WISE-

Notes

Paris, private communication and electronic file, January 14, 1994, from Nuclear Engineering International, *The World Nuclear Industry Handbook* (London: 1994), from "World List of Nuclear Power Plants," *Nuclear News*, September 1994, from International Atomic Energy Agency, *Nuclear Power Reactors in the World* (Vienna: 1994), from Greenpeace International, WISE-Paris, and Worldwatch Institute, *The World Nuclear Industry Status Report: 1992* (London: 1992), and additional press clippings and private communications.
2. Worldwatch database, op. cit. note 1.
3. Ibid.
4. Ibid.
5. Ibid.
6. Figures are from U.S. Department of Energy (DOE), Energy Information Administration, *Commercial Nuclear Power* (Washington, D.C.: 1990), and from Worldwatch database, op. cit. note 1.
7. DOE, op. cit. note 6; Worldwatch database, op. cit. note 1.
8. Worldwatch database, op. cit. note 1.
9. "Nuclear Phase-out Debate," *European Energy Report*, September 2, 1994; Hans Nilsson, NUTEK, Stockholm, private communication, February 2, 1995.
10. Worldwatch database, op. cit. note 1.
11. "Thais Scrap Plans for Nuclear Plants," *Journal of Commerce*, June 3, 1994; Laura Tyson, "Taiwan Ready for N-Power Showdown," *Financial Times*, June 22, 1994; P. T. Bangsberg, "Indonesia Affirms Nuclear Power Plant to be Built on Earthquake-Prone Site," *Journal of Commerce,* February 7, 1995.
12. Douglas Frantz, "U.S. Backing Work on Czech Reactors by Westinghouse," *New York Times*, May 22, 1994; Ann MacLachlan, "Westinghouse, Russia's Minatom Team for Nuclear Product Ventures," *Nucleonics Week*, April 7, 1994; Slovakia from Debora MacKenzie, "How Safe is Safe?" *New Scientist*, August 27, 1994; "AECL Will Cut Staff 15 Percent over Two Years," *Nuclear News*, July 1994.
13. "Ukrainians Balk at Beginning Chernobyl Shutdown," *Post Soviet Nuclear & Defense Monitor*, January 4, 1995.
14. Worldwatch database, op. cit. note 1.
15. Ibid.
16. International Atomic Energy Agency, *IAEA Yearbook 1994* (Vienna: 1994).
17. "How Many More Warnings Before the Final Curtain?" *Anumukti* (Vedchhi, India), June/July 1994.
18. R. Jeffrey Smith, "U.S. Prepares Oil Shipment for N. Korea," *Washington Post*, January 6, 1995; J. Carson Mark, "Reactor-Grade Plutonium's Explosive Properties," Nuclear Control Institute, Washington, D.C., August 1990.
19. David Stipp, "Yankee Atomic Spotlights Massive Costs Needed to Decommission Nuclear Plants," *Wall Street Journal*, June 2, 1992.
20. "Officials Raise by $123 Million Estimate of Dismantling Reactor," *New York Times*, November 4, 1994.

WIND POWER SOARS (pages 54–55)

1. Estimates by Birger Madsen, BTM Consult, Ringkobing, Denmark, private communication, February 23, 1995, and by Paul Gipe and Associates, Tehachapi, Calif., private communication, February 22, 1995; the historical wind power series has been adjusted from those published in earlier *Vital Signs* to reflect more recent assessments.
2. Madsen, op. cit. note 1; Gipe and Associates, op. cit. note 1.
3. Madsen, op. cit. note 1; Gipe and Associates, op. cit. note 1.
4. J.C. Chapman, *European Wind Technology* (Palo Alto, Calif.: Electric Power Research Institute, 1993); "Germany/Wind: Further Industry Growth Predicted, But Concerns Grow on Subsidies," *Renewable Energy Report*, October 28, 1994.
5. Gipe and Associates, op. cit. note 1.
6. Anthony Luke, "Spain Processing International Projects for Several Hundred Megawatts," *Windpower Monthly*, February 1995.
7. Madsen, op. cit. note 1.
8. Janice Massy, "In the Grip of Lottery Fever," *Windpower Monthly*, February 1995.
9. Ibid.
10. Worldwatch Institute estimate, based on Birger Madsen, BTM Consult, Ringkobing, Denmark, private communication, February 10, 1995.
11. Worldwatch Institute estimates based on 660 megawatts and 3.6 billion kilowatt-hours.
12. Gipe and Associates, op. cit. note 1.
13. *Wind Energy Weekly*, various issues.
14. Ed DeMeo, Electric Power Research Institute, Palo Alto, Calif., private communication, December 1, 1994.
15. David Wright and Stephen Salaff, "Renewables Outshine Nuclear," *Windpower Monthly*, February 1995.
16. "In Wake of Great Whale, Hydro-Quebec Moves Ahead with Wind," *Wind Energy Weekly*, December 12, 1994.
17. Neelam Matthews, "Dynamic Market Rapidly Unfolds," *Windpower Monthly*, September 1994; Sanjay Mohanty, Tata Energy Research Institute, New Delhi, February 22, 1995.

18. Madsen, op. cit. note 10.
19. Madsen, op. cit. note 1.
20. Jami Hossain and Chandra Shekhar Sinha, "Limiting CO_2 Emissions in the Power Sector of India: Supply Curves for Wind and Small Hydro," *Energy Policy*, October 1993; Neelam Matthews, "Parliament Focuses on Wind," *Windpower Monthly*, February 1995.
21. *Windpower Monthly*, various issues.

SOLAR CELL SHIPMENTS EXPAND RAPIDLY (pages 56–57)

1. Paul D. Maycock, "1995 World PV Module Survey," *PV News*, February 1995.
2. Cumulative total based on ibid., and assumes a 1-percent annual failure rate of existing systems.
3. Paul Maycock, Photovoltaic Energy Systems, Inc., Casanova, Va., private communications and printout, May 8, 1992, and January 24, 1995.
4. Based on prices from Maycock, op. cit. note 3, and on production data from Maycock, op. cit. note 1.
5. Maycock, op. cit. note 1.
6. Ibid.
7. Ibid.
8. Ibid.; Koichi Yamanashi, executive managing director, New Energy Foundation, Tokyo, private communications, December 16, 1993, and February 17, 1994.
9. Maycock, op. cit. note 1; Maso Karube, New Energy Foundation, Tokyo, private communication and printout, February 10, 1995.
10. Maycock, op. cit. note 1.
11. Ibid.
12. Derek Lovejoy, "Electrification of Rural Areas by Solar PV," *Natural Resources Forum*, May 1992.
13. Neville Williams, Solar Electric Light Fund, Washington, D.C., private communication, March 9, 1995.
14. Alain Ricaud, Cythelia, "Photovoltaic Commercial Modules: Which Product for What Market?" plenary lecture, Twelfth European Photovoltaic Solar Energy Conference, Amsterdam, April 11-15, 1994.
15. Robert van der Plas, "Solar Energy Answer to Rural Power in Africa," *Lessons* (World Bank, Washington, D.C.), April 1994.
16. Alan Paradis and Daniel S. Shugar, "Photovoltaic Building Materials," *Solar Today*, May/June 1994; "PV Metal Curtain Wall Among Many Concepts for Building Integration," *The Solar Letter*, January 6, 1995; Taylor Moore, "Emerging Markets for Photovoltaics," *EPRI Journal*, October/November 1994; "PV for Remote Homes and Livestock Water Pumping," Utility PhotoVoltaic Group, Washington, D.C., press release, October 24, 1994.
17. "Photovoltaic Bidders Please SMUD with Lower Prices," *The Solar Letter*, June 24, 1994; "SMUD Predicts Prices to Drop Under PV Pioneer, Utility Says," *The Solar Letter*, December 23, 1994.
18. "Siemens Boosts Production Capability 50% at Camarillo to Meet Demand," *The Solar Letter*, January 20, 1995.
19. "Amoco, Enron Link Up to Advance PV Modules, Develop Power Plants," *The Solar Letter*, December 23, 1994.
20. Ibid.

COMPACT FLUORESCENTS REMAIN STRONG (pages 58–59)

1. Evan Mills, Lawrence Berkeley Laboratory, Berkeley, Calif., private communication, February 3, 1993; 1993 and 1994 figures from Nils Borg, National Board for Industrial and Technical Development, Stockholm, Sweden, private communication, February 10, 1995.
2. Worldwatch estimate, based on 1,000-megawatt generating capacity, 19-watt CFLs replacing 75-watt incandescents, and 15-percent decay in existing CFL stock per year.
3. United Nations, *Energy Statistics Yearbook* (New York: 1994).
4. Amory B. Lovins and Robert Sardinsky, *State of the Art Technology Atlas: Lighting* (Boulder, Colo.: E SOURCE, Inc., 1988); Robert van der Plas and A.B. de Graaff, "A Comparison of Lamps for Domestic Lighting in Developing Countries," World Bank, Washington, D.C., 1988.
5. M.D. Levine et al., "Electricity End-Use Efficiency: Experience with Technologies, Markets, and Policies Throughout the World," American Council for an Energy-Efficient Economy (ACEEE), Washington, D.C., 1992.
6. "The Price of Light," *The Economist*, October 22, 1994.
7. Worldwatch estimates of net present value of the payback from replacing a 75-watt, 1,000-hour incandescent bulb with a 19-watt, 10,000-hour CFL, using a 3-percent annual real rate of return on five-year savings and a price of 75¢ for incandescent bulbs. Electricity prices from Organisation for Economic Co-operation and Development, International Energy Agency, *Energy Prices and Taxes, Second Quarter, 1994* (Paris: 1994). The Japanese price (and thus the net savings) is taken in U.S. dollars, corrected for purchasing power parities.

8. "Shedding Light on the Compact Fluorescent," *EPRI Journal*, March 1993.
9. Worldwatch estimate, based on Mills, op. cit. note 1, and on Borg, op. cit. note 1.
10. David Malin Roodman, "Power Brokers: Managing Demand for Electricity," *World Watch*, November/December 1993.
11. U.S. Department of Energy, Energy Information Administration, *Electric Power Annual 1993* (Washington, D.C.: U.S. Government Printing Office, 1994); Plexus Research, Inc., and Scientific Communications, Inc., *1992 Survey of Utility Demand-Side Management Programs, Vol. 1* (Palo Alto, Calif.: Electric Power Research Institute, 1993).
12. Roodman, op. cit. note 10.
13. Warren C. Liebold and Lindsay Audin, "Compact Fluorescents, Radioisotopes and Solid Waste," *ACEEE 1992 Summer Study on Energy Efficiency in Buildings: Proceedings* [Environment: Vol. 9] (Washington, D.C.: ACEEE, 1992).

CFC PRODUCTION PLUMMETING (pages 62–63)

1. Sharon Getamal, E.I. Du Pont de Nemours, Wilmington, Del., private communication, February 23, 1995; estimates of CFC production do not include illegally produced compounds, and therefore the global total is likely to be higher than reported here.
2. William K. Stevens, "Peril to Ozone Hastens a Ban on Chemicals," *New York Times*, November 26, 1992; "Ministers Approve Stepped Up Timetable to Phase Out Ozone Depleting Substances," *International Environment Reporter*, January 13, 1993.
3. Number of signatories from Christian Carlsson, Multilateral Fund, Montreal, Canada, private communication, December 7, 1994.
4. "Historical Global CFC Consumption-Future Demand and Supply from New Production and Recycle," *Montreal Protocol Technology Reassessment* (Nairobi: U.N. Environment Programme (UNEP), in press); 1992 China data from UNEP, "The Reporting of Data by the Parties to the Montreal Protocol on Substances That Deplete the Ozone Layer," Nairobi, July 15, 1994; 1993 China data from G.M. Bankobeza, Ozone Secretariat, UNEP, Nairobi, private communication, December 20, 1994.
5. Payments from Carlsson, op. cit. note 3.
6. "EU Illegally Importing CFCs," *Global Environmental Change Report* (Cutter Information Corp.), October 14, 1994.
7. F.A. Vogelsberg, Jr., E.I. Du Pont de Nemours, Wilmington, Del., private communication, December 9, 1994; "A Black Market in Coolants," *New York Times*, October 26, 1994.
8. UNEP, World Meterological Organization (WMO), National Aeronautics and Space Administration (NASA), and National Oceanic and Atmospheric Administration (NOAA), "Scientific Assessment of Ozone Depletion: 1994, Executive Summary," August 19, 1994.
9. Ibid.
10. Richard A. Kerr, "Antarctic Ozone Hole Fails to Recover," *Science*, October 14, 1994.
11. Ibid.
12. UNEP, WMO, NASA, and NOAA, op. cit. note 8.
13. UNEP, "Environmental Effects of Ozone Depletion: 1991 Update," Nairobi, November 1991.

GLOBAL TEMPERATURE RISES AGAIN (pages 64–65)

1. H. Wilson and J. Hansen, "Global and Hemispheric Temperature Anomolies from Instrumental Surface Air Temperature Records," in Thomas A. Boden et al., eds., *Trends '93: A Compendium of Data on Global Change* (Oak Ridge, Tenn.: Oak Ridge National Laboratory, 1994); James Hansen, NASA Goddard Institute for Space Studies, New York, private communication, January 30, 1995.
2. "The 1992 IPCC Supplement: Scientific Assessment," in Intergovernmental Panel on Cimate Change (IPCC), *Climate Change 1992: The IPCC Supplementary Report* (Cambridge: Cambridge University Press, 1992).
3. Wilson and Hansen, op. cit. note 1; Hansen, op. cit. note 1.
4. Richard A. Kerr, "Pinatubo Global Cooling on Target," *Science*, January 29, 1993; Hansen, op. cit. note 1.
5. Helene Wilson, NASA Goddard Institute for Space Studies and Columbia University, New York, private communication, February 18, 1994.
6. J.M. Barnola et al., "Historical CO_2 Record from the Vostok Ice Core," in Boden et al., op. cit. note 1; J. Jouzel et al., "Vostok Ice Temperature Record," in Boden et al., op. cit. note 1; Timothy Whorf, Scripps Institution of Oceanography, La Jolla, Calif., private communication, February 2, 1995.
7. A. Neftel et al., "Historical CO_2 Record from the Siple Station Ice Core," in Boden et al., op. cit. note 1; Barnola et al., op. cit note 6.
8. "A Problem as Big as a Planet," *The Economist*, November 5, 1994.
9. IPCC, *Climate Change: The IPCC Scientific Assess-*

ment (Cambridge: Cambridge University Press, 1990).
10. Kerr, op. cit. note 4.
11. Ibid.
12. R.A. Warrick and H. Oerlemans, "Sea Level Rise," in IPCC, op. cit. note 9.
13. U.S. Congress, Office of Technology Assessment, *Preparing for an Uncertain Climate—Vol. 1* (Washington, D.C.: U.S. Government Printing Office, 1993).
14. Ibid.
15. Ibid.

CARBON EMISSIONS RESUME RISE (pages 66–67)

1. Carbon emissions figures are from G. Marland, R.J. Andres, and T.A. Boden, "Global Regional, and National CO_2 Emissions," in Thomas A. Boden et al., eds., *Trends '93: A Compendium of Data on Global Change* (Oak Ridge, Tenn.: Oak Ridge National Laboratory, 1994); 1992 and 1993 figures are Worldwatch estimates based on ibid., on Organisation for Economic Co-operation and Development (OECD), International Energy Agency (IEA), *Energy Statistics and Balances of Non-OECD Countries 1991-1992* (Paris: 1994), and on British Petroleum (BP), *BP Statistical Review of World Energy* (London: 1994); 1994 figure is a Worldwatch estimate based on ibid., on IEA, op. cit. this note, on United Nations, *1991 Energy Statistics Yearbook* (New York: 1993), on U.S. Department of Energy, Energy Information Administration, *Monthly Energy Review January 1995* (Washington, D.C.: 1995), on V. Luque Cabal, Industries and Markets, Fossil Fuels, European Commission, Brussels, private communication and printout, February 8, 1995, on Paul Hunt, PlanEcon, Inc., Washington, D.C., private communication and printout, January 31, 1995, on J.F. Erasmus, Department of Mineral and Energy Affairs, Johannesburg, South Africa, private communication, February 21, 1995, on "Coal," *Energy Economist*, December 1994, on Tom Lewis, Department of Natural Resources, Ottawa, Ont., Canada, private communication, February 1, 1995, and on "Worldwide Production Survey," *Oil & Gas Journal*, December 26, 1994.
2. R.T. Watson et al., "Greenhouse Gases: Sources and Sinks," in Intergovernmental Panel on Climate Change (IPCC), *Climate Change 1992: The IPCC Supplementary Report* (Cambridge: Cambridge University Press, 1992).
3. IPCC, "Radiative Forcing of Climate Change: The 1994 Report of the Scientific Assessment Working Group of IPCC," Summary for Policymakers, World Meteorological Organization, Geneva, 1994.
4. I.S.A. Isaksen et al., "Radiative Forcing of Climate," in IPCC, op. cit. note 2.
5. C.D. Keeling and T.P. Whorf, "Atmospheric CO_2 Records from Sites in the SIO Air Sampling Network," in Boden et al., op. cit. note 1; Marland, Andres, and Boden, op. cit. note 1.
6. Lee Schipper and Stephen Meyers, *Energy Efficiency and Human Activity: Past Trends, Future Prospects* (Cambridge: Cambridge University Press, 1992).
7. International Monetary Fund, *World Economic Outlook, October 1994* (Washington, D.C.: 1994).
8. Ibid.
9. Figure of 0.5 tons is from Marland, Andres, and Boden, op. cit. note 1; figure of 3.0 tons is a Worldwatch estimate, based on ibid., on IEA, op. cit. note 1, on BP, op. cit. note 1, and on Population Reference Bureau, *1993 World Population Data Sheet* (Washington, D.C.: 1993).
10. OECD, IEA, *World Energy Outlook* (Paris: 1994).
11. Worldwatch estimate, based on Keeling and Whorf, op. cit. note 5, and on Timothy Whorf, Scripps Institution of Oceanography, La Jolla, Calif., private communication, February 2, 1995, and assuming that each part per million by volume of carbon dioxide corresponds to 2.12 billion tons of carbon.
12. Whorf, op. cit. note 11.
13. Worldwatch estimates, based on C.D. Keeling, "Global Historical CO_2 Emissions," in Boden et al., op. cit. note 1, on Marland, Andres, and Boden, op. cit. note 1, and on R.T. Watson et al., "Greenhouse Gases and Aerosols," in IPCC, *Climate Change: The IPCC Scientific Assessment* (Cambridge: Cambridge University Press, 1990).
14. Watson et al., op. cit. note 13.
15. "World Status: The Climate Change Treaty," *Energy Economist*, June 1992.
16. "Japan Will Substantially Overshoot Year 2000 CO_2 Emissions Target, Report Says," *International Environment Reporter*, August 10, 1994; U.S. overshoot is a Worldwatch estimate, based on "The Climate Change Action Plan," The White House, Washington, D.C., October 1993, and on Richard Stone, "Most Nations Miss the Mark On Emissions-Control Plans," *Science*, December 23, 1994.

WORLD ECONOMY EXPANDING FASTER (pages 70–71)

1. International Monetary Fund (IMF), *World Economic Outlook, October 1994* (Washington, D.C.: 1994).
2. Ibid.

Notes

3. Ibid.
4. Ibid.; U.S. Bureau of the Census, Center for International Research, Suitland, Md., private communication, February 6, 1995.
5. IMF, op. cit. note 1.
6. Richard Lawrence, "IMF Forecasts 1994 Growth of 3% in Global Economy, US Leading Way," *Journal of Commerce*, April 21, 1994; IMF, op. cit. note 1.
7. IMF, op. cit. note 1.
8. Ibid.
9. Ibid.
10. Ibid.
11. John Zarocostas, "Eastern Europe Future Bright, UN Panel Says," *Journal of Commerce*, April 8, 1994; IMF, op. cit. note 1.
12. IMF, op. cit. note 1.
13. Ibid.
14. Ibid.
15. Ibid.
16. Asian Development Bank, *Asian Development Outlook 1994* (New York: Oxford University Press, 1994); IMF, op. cit. note 1.
17. Population from Population Reference Bureau, *1994 World Population Data Sheet* (Washington, D.C.: 1994).
18. IMF, op. cit. note 1.
19. Ibid.
20. Ibid.
21. Ibid.
22. Ibid.
23. Ibid.
24. Ibid.
25. Ibid.

THIRD WORLD DEBT STILL GROWING (pages 72–73)

1. World Bank, *World Debt Tables 1994-95* (Washington, D.C.: 1994).
2. Ibid.
3. Kenneth N. Gilpin, "Foreign Debt Mop-Up," *New York Times*, April 18, 1994.
4. International Monetary Fund (IMF), *World Economic Outlook, October 1994* (Washington, D.C.: 1994).
5. John Darnton, "In Poor, Decolonized Africa Bankers are Overlords," *New York Times*, June 20, 1994.
6. Ibid.
7. IMF, *World Economic Outlook, May 1994* (Washington, D.C.: 1994).
8. "Still in the Red," *The Economist*, September 17, 1994.
9. Jane Perlez, "Western Banks to Relieve 40% of Polish Debt," *New York Times*, March 12, 1994.
10. Gilpin, op. cit. note 3.
11. Raphael Soifer, "Stealth Lending: The Quiet Return of LDC Debt," *Banking Outlook* (Brown Brothers Harriman & Co.), September 29, 1994.
12. World Bank, *World Development Report 1994* (New York: Oxford University Press, 1994).
13. Christina Cobourn, "Multilateral Debt: A Growing Crisis," *Bankchek*, June 1994.
14. Worldwatch calculation based on Debt-for-Development Coalition, Washington, D.C., private communication, October 21, 1994, and on data in World Bank, *World Debt Tables 1993-94* (Washington, D.C.: 1993).
15. Paul Siegel and Sandra Mbanefo, "Madagascar's Debt to Protect Nature," *WWF INDIA Quarterly*, April-June 1994.

WORLD TRADE CLIMBING
(pages 74–75)

1. Calculated from data in International Monetary Fund (IMF), *World Economic Outlook, October 1994* (Washington, D.C.: 1994).
2. Joseph P. Quinlan, "China Joins $100 Billion Club," *Journal of Commerce*, Jamuary 19, 1995.
3. "Happy Ever NAFTA?" *The Economist*, December 10, 1994.
4. "Northern Rumblings," *The Economist*, January 14, 1995.
5. Patrick J. Lucey, " . . . While NAFTA Speeds Right Along," *Wall Street Journal*, August 30, 1994.
6. "The World Economy in 1994-95," in IMF, op. cit. note 1.
7. Ibid.
8. "Non-Oil Commodity Prices," in IMF, op. cit. note 1.
9. Michael Windfuhr, "Who Are the GATT Winners and Losers?" *Development and Cooperation*, March/April 1994.
10. Ibid.
11. Helene Cooper and Jose de Cordoba, "Chile is Invited to Join NAFTA as U.S. Pledges Free Trade Zone for Americas," *Wall Street Journal*, December 12, 1994.
12. Ibid.
13. "Happy Ever NAFTA?" op. cit. note 3.
14. Aziz Ali Mohammed, "Push Me, Pull You into the 21st Century," *The World Paper*, October 1994.
15. Ibid.
16. Ibid.
17. "The World Economy in 1994-95," op. cit. note 6.
18. "The Opening of Asia," *The Economist*, November 12, 1994.

19. Nigel Holloway, "Waning Clout," *Far Eastern Economic Review*, November 17, 1994.
20. John Zaracostas, "Environment's Link to Trade Pits US Against Poorer Nations," *Journal of Commerce*, October 28, 1994.
21. Ibid.

TELEVISION CONTINUES TO
SPREAD (pages 76–77)

1. David Fisher, Screen Digest, private communications and printouts, February 8 and 9, 1995; half of humanity estimate from Alan Thein Durning, *How Much Is Enough?* (New York: W.W. Norton & Company, 1992).
2. Fisher, op. cit. note 1; earlier data from U.S. Bureau of the Census, *Historical Statistics of the United States: Colonial Times to 1970* (Washington, D.C.: U.S. Government Printing Office (GPO), 1975), from United Nations, *Statistical Yearbook* (New York: various years), and from "World TV Households: The Growth Continues," *Screen Digest*, March 1993.
3. Worldwatch estimate based on United Nations, op. cit. note 2, and on Bureau of the Census, op. cit. note 2.
4. Worldwatch estimates, based on United Nations, op. cit. note 2, and on Bureau of the Census, op. cit. note 2.
5. Worldwatch estimates, based on Fisher, op. cit. note 1, and on Bureau of the Census, op. cit. note 2.
6. Worldwatch estimate, based on United Nations, op. cit. note 2.
7. Ibid.
8. Ibid.
9. Figure 2 counts the former East Germany under Western Europe throughout.
10. U.S. Bureau of the Census, *Statistical Abstract of the United States* (Washington, D.C.: GPO, 1994).
11. Fisher, op. cit. note 1; figure for Asia excludes Japan.
12. Bradley Graham, "TV Opens Up Remote Villagers' World," *Washington Post*, March 10, 1988.
13. Laura Silber, "TV From Abroad Helped Open Albania's Borders," *Washington Post*, January 4, 1991; Chris Hedges, "Satellite Dishes Adding Spice to Iran's TV Menu," *New York Times*, August 16, 1994.
14. "British Watch Most Television in Europe," *Market Europe*, April 1994.
15. Nielson Media Research, *National Audience Demographics Report November 1994* (New York: 1994).
16. Marie Winn, *The Plug-In Drug* (New York: Grossman Publishers, 1977).
17. Jerry Mander, *Four Arguments for the Elimination of Television* (New York: Morrow, 1978); George Gerbner, Annenberg School for Communication, University of Pennsylvania, "Mass Media Mayhem and How to Stop It," presented at the American Medical Students Association Region III Fall Conference, Philadelphia, October 15, 1993.
18. Bill McKibben, *The Age of Missing Information* (New York: Random House, 1992).
19. Neil Postman, *Amusing Ourselves to Death: Public Discourse in the Age of Show Business* (New York: Viking, 1985).
20. Brandon S. Centerwall, "Television and Violence: The Scale of the Problem and Where to Go From Here," *Journal of the American Medical Association*, June 10, 1992.
21. Eileen Klineman, "Nine Petaluma Schools Join TV Turn-off," *The Press Democrat* (Santa Rosa, Calif.), March 2, 1994.

BICYCLE PRODUCTION
RISING (pages 80–81)

1. Author's estimate, based on *Interbike Directory 1995* (Newport Beach, Calif.: Primedia, Inc. 1995).
2. Ibid.
3. Ibid.
4. Wu Weinong, "Will Cars Push Bikes off Chinese Roads?" *China Daily*, December 5, 1994.
5. Ibid.
6. Urs Heierli, *Environmental Limits to Motorization* (St. Gallen, Switzerland: Swiss Centre for Development Cooperation in Technology and Management, 1993).
7. Ibid.
8. Karen Overton, "Women Take Back the Streets," *Sustainable Transport*, June 1994.
9. Ibid.
10. Heierli, op. cit. note 6.
11. Ibid.
12. Ibid.
13. Nancy Boyle, Kennedy Space Center, Fla., private communication, February 13, 1995.
14. Frank Meeks, Domino's Pizza, Alexandria, Va., private communication, February 13, 1995.
15. Phyllis Simmons, U.S. Postal Service, St. Petersburg, Fla., private communication, February 13, 1995.
16. "Getting Used to Sustainable Existence," *Environmental News from the Netherlands* (Ministry of Housing, Spatial Planning, and the Environment, The Hague), No. 2, 1994.
17. "New York and Amsterdam," *Sustainable Transport*, June 1994.
18. Ibid.
19. Dennis Martin, National Association of Chiefs of Po-

lice, Washington, D.C., private communication, July 12, 1994.
20. "Paramedics on Bicycles," *IBF News* (International Bicycle Fund, Seattle, Wash.), No. 2, 1994.

AUTO PRODUCTION ON THE RISE (pages 82–83)

1. Production in 1950-92 from American Automobile Manufacturers Association (AAMA), *World Motor Vehicle Data*, 1994 ed. (Detroit, Mich.: 1994); 1993 production from AAMA, *AAMA Motor Vehicle Facts & Figures '94* (Detroit, Mich.: 1994); 1994 production from John Lawson, Director, DRI/McGraw Hill, London, private communication, November 23, 1994.
2. *DRI World Car Industry Forecast Report*, DRI/McGraw-Hill, London, April 1994, as cited in Kevin Done, "Demand Likely To Accelerate," *Financial Times*, July 12, 1994.
3. Ibid.
4. Ibid.
5. Japan Automobile Manufacturers Association, Inc., *Motor Vehicle Statistics of Japan 1994* (Tokyo: 1994).
6. Walter Hook, "Eastern Europe: Paving the Way to Environmental Disaster?" *Sustainable Transport*, June 1994.
7. James Brooke, "The Metamorphosis of the Brazilian Car Industry," *New York Times*, April 23, 1994.
8. Asia/Pacific region excludes Japan; output from Lawson, op. cit. note 1; China's production from *DRI World Car Industry*, op. cit. note 2, and from "Chinese Roads Paved with Gold," *Financial Times*, November 23, 1994.
9. The "Big Three" auto makers are General Motors, Ford, and Chrysler; "Detroit Pushes Pedal to the Floor in Asia: Major Outlays Fuel Bid for Bigger Share of Auto Market," *Wall Street Journal*, June 21, 1994.
10. Susan Lawrence, "Driving on China's Road to Riches," *U.S. News & World Report*, November 28, 1994.
11. Tony Walker and Shi Junbao, "Chinese Gear Up for Huge Rise in Cars by 2010," *Financial Times*, October 26, 1994.
12. Sheila Tefft, "China Gets in Gear to Rev Up Car Production," *Journal of Commerce*, September 29, 1994.
13. "Auto Makers Hurry to Get a Piece of India's Market," *Wall Street Journal*, October 21, 1994; "Detroit Pushes Pedal," op. cit. note 9.
14. Christopher Flavin and Nicholas Lenssen, *Power Surge* (New York: W.W. Norton & Company, 1994).
15. "Electric Cars' Cost Will Fall As Production Rises, Study Says," *Journal of Commerce*, November 4, 1994.

SULFUR AND NITROGEN EMISSIONS FALL SLIGHTLY (pages 86–87)

1. Dr. J. Dignon, Lawrence Livermore National Laboratory, Livermore, Calif., unpublished data series, private communication, February 1, 1995.
2. Ibid.
3. Ibid.
4. Dr. J. Dignon, private communication, February 23, 1994; Sultan Hameed and Jane Dignon, "Global Emissions of Nitrogen and Sulfur Oxides in Fossil Fuel Combustion 1970-1986," *Journal of the Air & Waste Management Association*, February 1991.
5. Dignon, op. cit. note 4; Hameed and Dignon, op. cit. note 4.
6. Christopher Flavin and Nicholas Lenssen, *Power Surge* (New York: W.W. Norton & Company, 1994).
7. Ibid.
8. Ibid.
9. Ibid.
10. Hilary F. French, *After the Earth Summit: The Future of Environmental Governance*, Worldwatch Paper 107 (Washington, D.C.: Worldwatch Institute, March 1992).
11. Marc A. Levy, "European Acid Rain: The Power of Tote-Board Diplomacy," in Peter M. Haas, Robert O. Keohane, and Marc A. Levy, eds., *Institutions for the Earth: Sources of Effective International Environmental Protection* (Cambridge, Mass: The MIT Press, 1993).
12. Marc A. Levy, "International Co-operation to Combat Acid Rain," in *Green Globe Yearbook* (Oxford: Oxford University Press, forthcoming).
13. Ibid.
14. Ibid.
15. Megan Ryan and Christopher Flavin, "Facing China's Limits," in Lester R. Brown et al., *State of the World 1995* (New York: W.W. Norton & Company, 1995).

NUCLEAR WASTE STILL ACCUMULATING (pages 88–89)

1. Irradiated fuel figures of 10,000 and 130,000 tons are Worldwatch Institute estimates based on I.W. Leigh, *International Nuclear Waste Management Fact Book* (Richland, Wash.: Pacific Northwest Laboratory, 1994), on United Nations, *Energy Statistics Database 1992* (electronic database), New York, June 1994, on Soviet figures from G.A. Kaurov, Director of the

Notes

Center of Public Information for Atomic Energy, Moscow, in letter to Lydia Popova, Socio-Ecological Union, Moscow, August 5, 1991, on a 1993 figure based on British Petroleum, *BP Statistical Review of World Energy* (London: 1994) and above sources, and on a 1994 preliminary estimate based on U.S. Department of Energy (DOE), Energy Information Administration, *Monthly Energy Review November 1994* (Washington, D.C.: 1994) and above sources.

2. DOE, Office of Civilian Radioactive Waste Management, *Integrated Data Base for 1993: U.S. Spent Fuel and Radioactive Waste Inventories, Projections, and Characteristics* (Washington, D.C.: 1994).
3. Ibid.
4. International Atomic Energy Agency (IAEA), *IAEA Yearbook 1994* (Vienna: 1994).
5. For examples on uncertainty of geologic burial, see Konrad B. Krauskopf, "Disposal of High-Level Nuclear Waste: Is It Possible?" *Science*, September 14, 1990, and National Research Council, Board on Radioactive Waste Management, "Rethinking High-Level Radioactive Waste Disposal," National Academy Press, Washington, D.C., July 1990.
6. IAEA, op. cit. note 4.
7. Kenneth L. Whiting, "Jakarta to Build Nuclear Power Plants Despite Criticism," Associated Press, June 23, 1992.
8. "France Passes New Law on Disposal of Nuclear Waste Underground," *European Energy Report*, July 12, 1991.
9. Carl Johnson, Agency for Nuclear Projects, Nuclear Waste Project Office, Carson City, Nev., private communication, December 19, 1994.
10. Robert M. Bernaro, director, Office of Nuclear Material Safety and Safeguards, Nuclear Regulatory Commission, Washington, D.C., letter to Daniel A. Dreyfus, director, Office of Civilian Radioactive Waste Management, DOE, October 13, 1994.
11. C.K. Mertz, James Flynn, and Paul Slovic, "1994 Nevada State Telephone Survey: Key Findings," Decision Research Inc., Eugene, Oreg. December 1994.
12. "World Status of Radioactive Waste Management," *IAEA Bulletin*, Spring 1986; I.W. Leigh and S.J. Mitchell, Pacific Northwest Laboratory, *International Nuclear Fuel Cycle Fact Book* (Springfield, Va.: National Technical Information Service, 1990).
13. Quentin Peel, "Germany's Nuclear Fall-out," *Financial Times*, August 23, 1994; Rob Edwards, "Crunch Time for Nuclear Power," *New Scientist*, October 8, 1994.
14. Cumbrians Opposed to a Radioactive Environment (CORE), "A Brief Background to Reprocessing and the Thermal Oxide Reprocessing Plant (THORP)," *Thermal Oxide Reprocessing Plant: An Indepth Investigation* (Cumbria, U.K.: undated); Ronnie D. Lipschutz, *Radioactive Waste: Politics, Technology and Risk* (Cambridge, Mass.: Ballinger, 1980).
15. CORE, op. cit. note 14; Lipschutz, op. cit. note 14.
16. IAEA, op. cit. note 4; number of atomic weapons based on 8 kilograms of plutonium needed for each bomb, from Leonard Spector, with Jacqueline R. Smith, *Nuclear Ambitions: The Spread of Nuclear Weapons 1989-1990* (Boulder, Colo: Westview Press, 1990).
17. Arjun Makhijani and Scott Saleska, *High-Level Dollars, Low-Level Sense: A Critique of Present Policy for the Management of Long-Lived Radioactive Wastes and Discussion of an Alternative Approach* (New York: Apex Press, 1992); Frank L. Parker et al., *Technical and Sociopolitical Issues in Radioactive Waste Disposal, Vol. I* (Stockholm: Beijer Institute, 1987).

ENVIRONMENTAL TREATIES GROW IN NUMBER (pages 90–91)

1. U.N. Environment Programme (UNEP), *Register of International Treaties and Other Agreements in the Field of the Environment 1993* (Nairobi: 1993); Mark Labelle, legal assistant, Treaty Office, United Nations, New York, private communication, October 17, 1994.
2. Labelle, op. cit. note 1; Information Program on Sustainable Development, "Legal Agreement to Curb Desertification is Concluded," press release, United Nations, New York, July 1994; "Six Nations Adopt the Lusaka Agreement," *Our Planet*, Vol. 6 No. 5, 1994.
3. "Climate Change Treaty Comes Into Force," *International Environment Reporter*, March 23, 1994; David E. Pitt, "Biological Pact Passes Into Law," *New York Times*, January 2, 1994.
4. Anthony Goodman, "UN's Law of the Sea to Take Effect Next Year," *Journal of Commerce*, December 8, 1993.
5. Based on UNEP, op. cit. note 1, and on Labelle, op. cit. note 1.
6. Edith Brown Weiss, Paul Szasz, and Daniel Magraw, *International Environment Law: Basic Instruments and References* (Irvington-on-Hudson, N.Y.: Transnational Juris Publications, Inc., 1992).
7. Sharon Getamal, E.I. du Pont de Nemours, Wilmington, Del., private communication, February 23, 1995.
8. Michael Prather and Mack McFarland, E.I. du Pont de Nemours, Wilmington, Del., private communication, March 18, 1994. The Figure uses measured data through 1991 and projections thereafter. The top

curve assumes continued growth of 3 percent per year. The next assumes continued compliance with the original Montreal Protocol, with 3-percent growth of ozone-depleting substances not controlled by the agreement. The third assumes compliance with the London agreements, with HCFC phaseout by 2040. The bottom curve assumes global compliance with the Copenhagen agreements.
9. "Synthesis of the Reports of the Ozone Scientific Assessment Panel, Environmental Effects Assessment Panel, Technology and Economic Assessment Panel," Prepared by the Assessment Chairs for the Parties to the Montreal Protocol, November 1991.
10. Marc Levy, "European Acid Rain: The Power of Tote-Board Diplomacy," *Institutions for the Earth: Sources of Effective International Environmental Protection* (Cambridge, Mass.: The MIT Press, 1993).
11. "Protocol to Protect Antarctica Signed by 31 Nations at Meeting," *International Environment Reporter*, October 9, 1991.
12. "Historic Agreement Reached Between OECD and Non-OECD Countries to Ban Export of Hazardous Wastes," press release, UNEP, Geneva, March 28, 1994.
13. Hilary F. French, "Making Environmental Treaties Work," *Scientific American*, December 1994.
14. U.S. General Accounting Office, *International Environment: International Agreements are Not Well Monitored* (Washington, D.C.: 1992).
15. Ibid.
16. Simone Bilderbeek, Wouter J. Veening, and Ankie Wijgerde, Netherlands National Committee for the International Union for Conservation of Nature and Natural Resources, background document to the Global Consultation on the Development and Enforcement of International Environmental Law, With a Special Focus on the Preservation of Biodiversity, International Environmental Law Conference, The Hague, August 12-16, 1991.

POPULATION GROWTH STEADY (pages 94–95)

1. U.S. Bureau of the Census, Center for International Research, Suitland, Md., private communication, February 6, 1995.
2. Ibid. The Census Bureau periodically updates its historical data series, based on the most recently available numbers. For instance, in *Vital Signs 1994* the population increase for 1993 was given as 87 million, but it now appears that it was closer to 88 million. All such changes are reflected in the table.
3. Bureau of the Census, op. cit. note 1.
4. Ibid.
5. Ibid.
6. Ibid.
7. Population Reference Bureau (PRB), *1994 World Population Data Sheet* (Washington, D.C.: 1994).
8. United Nations, *World Population Prospects: The 1994 Revision* (New York: 1994); PRB, op. cit. note 7.
9. United Nations, op. cit. note 8. The figure 7.9 billion is known as the U.N.'s "low variant" projection for 2050; 9.8 billion is the standard "medium variant"; and 11.9 billion is the "high variant."
10. United Nations, "Programme of Action of the United Nations International Conference on Population and Development," final but unedited draft, September 19, 1994.
11. Ibid.
12. John Bongaarts, "Population Policy Options in the Developing World," *Science*, February 11, 1994; Charles Westoff, "Reproductive Preferences: A Comparative View," *Demographic and Health Surveys, Comparative Studies No. 3* (Columbia, Md.: Institute for Resource Development, 1991).
13. Barbara Crossette, "Population Debate: The Premises Are Changed," *New York Times*, September 14, 1994; Gita Sen, Adrienne Germain, and Lincoln C. Chen, eds., *Population Policies Reconsidered: Health, Empowerment, and Rights* (Cambridge, Mass.: Harvard Center for Population and Development Studies, 1994).
14. United Nations, op. cit. note 10.
15. Ellen Jamison and Frank Hobbs, *World Population Profile: 1994* (Washington, D.C.: U.S. Bureau of the Census, 1994); Sen, Germain, and Chen, op. cit. note 13.
16. Boyce Rensberger, "Cairo Forum Addresses Inequities Toward Women," *Washington Post*, September 11, 1994.

CIGARETTE PRODUCTION UP SLIGHTLY (pages 96–97)

1. U.S. Department of Agriculture (USDA), Foreign Agricultural Service, "World Cigarette Production By Country," private communication by facsimile, Washington, D.C., December 20, 1994.
2. Worldwatch calculation based on ibid.
3. Ibid.
4. USDA, op. cit. note 1.
5. Ibid.
6. Ibid.
7. Ibid.
8. Ibid.
9. Ibid.

Notes

10. Ibid.
11. "US, Russian Firms Form Cigarette Venture," *Journal of Commerce*, August 4, 1993.
12. USDA, op. cit. note 1.
13. Ibid.
14. Sheila Tefft, "Tobacco Companies See Huge Market in China," *Christian Science Monitor*, May 25, 1994.
15. Ibid.
16. Ibid.
17. "U.S. Makers Aiming To Get China In the Habit," *Wall Street Journal*, May 27, 1994.
18. Marcus W. Brauchle, "China Passes Law In Move to Prohibit Ads for Tobacco," *Wall Street Journal*, October 31, 1994.
19. Tefft, op. cit. note 14.
20. Kirk R. Smith, "Looking for Pollution Where the People Are," *Asia Pacific Issues: Analysis from the East-West Center*, No. 10, January 1994.
21. John Lancaster, "Military Bans Smoking in Workplace," *Washington Post*, March 8, 1994.
22. Ibid.

HIV/AIDS CASES RISE AT RECORD RATES (pages 98–99)

1. World Health Organization (WHO), Global Programme on AIDS, "The Current Global Situation of the HIV/AIDS Pandemic," 1994 and 1995 editions, Geneva; Jonathan Mann and Daniel Tarantola, eds., *AIDS in the World*, Vol. II (New York: Oxford University Press, forthcoming); Daniel Tarantola, Global AIDS Policy Coalition (GAPC), Harvard School of Public Health, Cambridge, Mass., private communication, January 19, 1995. GAPC, founded by Dr. Jonathan Mann, former head of WHO's Global Programme on AIDS, estimated new 1994 infections at 4 million; WHO's number, conservative by their own admission, was 3.5 million. GAPC's number is used since this independent organization is less constrained by the official data-reporting channels of often-evasive national governments.
2. Mann and Tarantola, op. cit. note 1; Tarantola, op. cit. note 1. There seems to be a 30-percent inheritance rate in babies born to HIV-positive mothers; UNICEF, *Children and AIDS: An Impending Calamity* (New York: 1990).
3. Mann and Tarantola, op. cit. note 1; Tarantola, op. cit. note 1. (WHO's estimate for 1994 was 1.5 million; WHO, op. cit. note 1.)
4. Mann and Tarantola, op. cit. note 1; Tarantola, op. cit. note 1.
5. Low figure from WHO 1995, op. cit. note 1; high figure from Daniel Tarantola, GAPC, Harvard School of Public Health, Cambridge, Mass., private communication, January 20, 1995. GAPC estimates are used for the Figures because WHO does not release historical estimates. GAPC's historical series are revised every year: the reconstruction of the curve that traces the development of the HIV/AIDS pandemic depends partly on the number of new AIDS cases reported (and adjusted for underreporting) for the most recent year.
6. WHO 1995, op. cit. note 1; Mann and Tarantola, op. cit. note 1; Tarantola, op. cit. note 1; Tarantola, op. cit. note 5.
7. WHO, Global Programme on AIDS, "Current and Future Dimensions of the HIV/AIDS Pandemic: A Capsule Summary," Geneva, 1992; Jonathan Mann, Daniel Tarantola, and Thomas W. Netter, eds., *AIDS in the World* (Cambridge, Mass.: Harvard University Press: 1992); The Panos Institute, *The Hidden Cost of AIDS: The Challenge of HIV to Development* (London: 1992); "Japan Opens AIDS Forum; Note of Gloom," *New York Times*, August 8, 1994.
8. "Dead Silence on AIDS," *Down to Earth*, September 30, 1994.
9. Mann and Tarantola, op. cit. note 1; Tarantola, op. cit. note 1.
10. Sven Sandstrom, Managing Director, World Bank, "AIDS and Development: A Shared Concern, A Shared Vision," presented at AIDS in the World Conference, Stockholm, November 28, 1994; Mann and Tarantola, op. cit. note 1; Tarantola, op. cit. note 1.
11. Mann and Tarantola, op. cit. note 1; Tarantola, op. cit. note 1.
12. Mann and Tarantola, op. cit. note 1; Tarantola, op. cit. note 1; Sandstrom, op. cit. note 10; Andrew Pollack, "Japan Facing Up to Its AIDS Cases," *New York Times*, August 7, 1994.
13. Phyllida Brown, "Fear and Denial as Infections Soar," *New Scientist*, August 13, 1994.
14. Mann and Tarantola, op. cit. note 1; Tarantola, op. cit. note 1.
15. Tim Brown and Peter Xenos, "AIDS in Asia: The Gathering Storm," *Asia Pacific Issues: Analysis from the East-West Center*, No. 16, August 1994; David Brown, "Fast Action Needed to Prevent Spread of AIDS in Asia, Experts Told," *Washington Post*, August 9, 1994.
16. Joel Kibazo, "Killer Virus Hits at Heart of Economy," *Financial Times*, September 1, 1993; Karen A. Stanecki and Peter O. Way, "Review of HIV Spread in Southern Africa," Center for International Research (CIR), U.S. Bureau of the Census (Washington, D.C.: 1994); Health Studies Branch (HSB), CIR, "Recent HIV Seroprevalence Levels by Country: June 1994," Research Note No. 13 (Washington,

D.C.: Bureau of the Census, 1994); HSB, CIR, "Trends and Patterns of HIV/AIDS Infection in Selected Developing Countries," Research Note No. 14 (Washington, D.C.: Bureau of the Census, 1994).
17. Sandstrom, op. cit. note 10; "The World Bank Responds to AIDS," *World Bank News*, December 1, 1994; Susan Okie, "AIDS Devouring Africa Even as Awareness Grows," *Washington Post*, August 18, 1994; J.U. Ugwuanyi, "AIDS: A Threat to African Survival," *Discovery and Innovation*, March 1994; Kate Dunn, "Killing the Ripest Crop," *Ceres*, September/October 1994.
18. Mann and Tarantola, op. cit. note 1; Tarantola, op. cit. note 1; Sandstrom, op. cit. note 10.
19. Peter O. Way and Karen A. Stanecki, *The Impact of HIV/AIDS on World Population* (Washington, D.C.: Economics and Statistics Administration, Bureau of the Census, 1994).
20. WHO estimate from Brown, op. cit. note 13.

URBANIZATION SPREADING
(pages 100–01)

1. United Nations (UN), *World Population Prospects: The 1992 Revision* (New York: 1993).
2. Ibid.
3. UN, *Propsects of Urbanization 1988*, Population Studies No. 112 (New York: 1989).
4. Ibid., with updates from UN, op. cit. note 1.
5. UN, *Estimates and Projections of Urban, Rural and City Populations, 1950-2025: The 1982 Assessment* (New York: 1985).
6. U.N. Development Programme, *Human Development Report 1994* (New York: Oxford University Press: 1994).
7. UN, op. cit. note 5, with updates from UN, op. cit. note 1.
8. Ibid.
9. Ibid.
10. Gordon McGranahan and Jacob Songsore, "Wealth, Health and the Urban Household: Weighing Environmental Burdens in Accra, Jakarta, and São Paulo," *Environment*, July/August 1994.
11. Ibid.
12. Ibid.
13. Sarah Richardson, "The Return of the Plague," *Discover*, January 1995.
14. Ibid.
15. McGranahan and Songsore, op. cit. note 10; Global Environment Monitoring Systems (GEMS), U.N. Environment Programme (UNEP), and the World Health Organization (WHO), *Urban Air Pollution in Megacities of the World* (Cambridge, Mass.: Blackwell Publishers, 1992), as excerpted in *Environment*, March 1994.
16. "Thailand: Growing Mounds of Garbage Creating Crisis for Nation's Second Largest City," *International Environment Reporter*, October 5, 1994.
17. GEMS, UNEP, and WHO, op. cit. note 15.
18. U.S. Bureau of the Census, *Statistical Abstract of the United States: 1994* (Washington, D.C.: 1994).
19. GEMS, UNEP, and WHO, op. cit. note 15.
20. Ibid.

REFUGEE FLOW UNABATED
(pages 102–03)

1. U.N. High Commissioner for Refugees (UNHCR), Geneva, private communication, February 10, 1995.
2. Rosemarie Rogers and Emily Copeland, *Forced Migration: Policy Issues in the Post–Cold War World* (Medford, Mass.: The Fletcher School of Law and Diplomacy, Tufts University, 1993).
3. Calculation based on data from UNHCR, *The State of the World's Refugees* (New York: Penquin Books, 1993), and from UNHCR, op. cit. note 1.
4. UNHCR, op. cit. note 1.
5. U.S. Committee for Refugees, *1994 World Refugee Survey* (Washington, D.C.: 1994).
6. UNHCR, op. cit. note 1.
7. Ibid.
8. Howard W. French, "Liberia's War Refugees Now United in Misery," *New York Times*, September 17, 1994.
9. UNHCR, op. cit. note 1.
10. Worldwatch calculation based on Aaron Segal, *An Atlas of International Migration* (London: Hans Zell Publishers, 1993).
11. UNHCR, op. cit. note 1.
12. Ibid.
13. Ibid.
14. Ibid.
15. Ibid.
16. Ibid.
17. Ibid.
18. Ibid.
19. World Bank, *World Development Report 1994* (New York: Oxford University Press, 1994).
20. Organisation for Economic Co-operation and Development, "Sharp Changes in the Structure of Financial Flows to Developing Countries and Countries in Transition," Press Release, Paris, June 20, 1994.
21. Erskine Childers with Brian Urquhart, "Renewing the United Nations System," *Development Dialogue* (Dag Hammarskjöld Foundation/Ford Foundation), 1994:1.

Notes

22. Ad de Rad, U.N. Development Programme, New York, private communication, October 19, 1994; Heather Courtney, public information officer, UNHCR, Washington, D.C., private communication, October 4, 1994.
23. Francis Ghilès, "Last Chance in Algeria," *New York Times*, October 1, 1994.

NUCLEAR ARSENALS DECLINE AGAIN (pages 106–07)

1. These numbers include warheads that are deployed, held in reserve, or retired and awaiting dismantlement. Calculated from Robert S. Norris and William M. Arkin, "Estimated U.S. and Soviet/Russian Nuclear Stockpiles, 1945-94," *Bulletin of the Atomic Scientists*, November/December 1994, from Robert S. Norris and William M. Arkin, "Estimated Nuclear Stockpiles, 1945-1993," *Bulletin of the Atomic Scientists*, December 1993, and from Patrick E. Tyler, "As China Upgrades Its Nuclear Arsenal, It Debates Need for Guns vs. Butter," *New York Times*, October 26, 1994.
2. William Arkin and Robert S. Norris, "The Nuclear Follies, Post–Cold War," in Ruth Leger Sivard, *World Military and Social Expenditures 1993* (Washington, D.C.: World Priorities, Inc., 1993).
3. Calculated from Norris and Arkin 1993, op. cit. note 1, and from Norris and Arkin 1994, op. cit. note 1.
4. Norris and Arkin 1993, op. cit. note 1.
5. Arkin and Norris, op. cit. note 2.
6. Norris and Arkin 1994, op. cit. note 1.
7. Institute for Defense and Disarmament Studies (IDDS), *Arms Control Reporter 1994* (Cambridge, Mass.: 1994), sheet 614.A.1.
8. The White House, Office of the Press Secretary, "Background Briefing by Senior Administration Official," Press Release, Washington, D.C., December 5, 1994.
9. Ibid.
10. The White House, Office of the Press Secretary, "Joint Statement on Strategic Stability and Nuclear Security by the Presidents of the United States and Russia," Press Release, Washington, D.C., September 28, 1994.
11. Peter Gray, *Briefing Book on the Nonproliferation of Nuclear Weapons* (Washington, D.C.: Council for a Livable World Education Fund, 1993).
12. IDDS, *Arms Control Reporter 1993* (Cambridge, Mass.: 1993), sheet 455.B.73.
13. Michael Renner, "Nuclear Arsenal Decline on Hold," in Lester R. Brown, Hal Kane, and Ed Ayres, *Vital Signs 1993* (New York: W.W. Norton & Company, 1993).
14. Matthew Kaminski, "Ukraine Approves Treaty to Abandon Nuclear Weapons," *Financial Times*, November 17, 1994; IDDS, op. cit note 7.
15. White House, op. cit. note 8; IDDS, op. cit. note 7, sheet 611.E-0.3.
16. White House, op. cit. note 8; IDDS, op. cit. note 7, sheet 611.E-0.3.
17. IDDS, op. cit. note 7, sheet 608.A.1.
18. Verification Technology Information Centre (London), "China Detonates Nuclear Bomb," Press Release, October 7, 1994, as posted on the APC electronic conference igc:disarm.ctb-npt on October 10, 1994.
19. Jim Wurst, "The Non-proliferation Treaty," *The Nonviolent Activist*, January/February 1995, as posted in the APC electronic conference igc:disarm.ctb-npt on December 20, 1994.

PEACEKEEPING EXPENSES REACH NEW HIGH (pages 108–09)

1. U.N. Department of Peace-Keeping Operations, Field Operations Division, Field Finance and Budget Section, New York, private communication, September 15, 1994.
2. Calculated from ibid., from Joseph Preston Baratta, *International Peacekeeping: History and Strengthening* (Washington, D.C.: Center for U.N. Reform Education, 1989), and from U.N. Department of Public Information, *United Nations Peace-keeping* (New York: 1993).
3. United Nations, General Assembly and Security Council, "Supplement to an Agenda for Peace: Position Paper of the Secretary-General on the Occasion of the Fiftieth Anniversary of the United Nations," A/50/60 and S/1995/1, January 3, 1995. During May and June 1994—the duration of the brief but successful Libya-Chad mission—the number of peacekeeping operations reached 18; U.N. Daily Highlights Press Release DH/1805, New York, January 9, 1995.
4. Michael Renner, *Budgeting for Disarmament: The Costs of War and Peace*, Worldwatch Paper 122 (Washington, D.C.: Worldwatch Institute, November 1994).
5. Ibid.
6. Calculated from U.N. Secretariat, "Status of Contributions" (issued monthly), New York, various editions.
7. U.N. Daily Highlights Press Releases DH/1701, August 4, 1994, and DH/1804, New York, January 6, 1995.

8. U.N. Press Release DH/1701, op. cit. note 7; U.N. Secretariat, "Status of Contributions as of 31 December 1994," ST/ADM/SER.B/458, January 5, 1995.
9. U.N. Secretariat, op. cit. note 8.
10. U.N. General Assembly and Security Council, "Improving the Capacity of the United Nations for Peace-keeping. Report of the Secretary-General," A/48/403 and S/26450, New York, March 14, 1994.
11. U.N. Daily Highlights Press Release, DH/1717, New York, August 26, 1994.
12. U.N. Department of Peace-Keeping Operations, op. cit. note 1.
13. U.N. Security Council, 3447th Meeting, AM Summary, Press Release SC/5926, "Security Council Extends UNOSOM II for Final Period Until 31 March 1995," New York, November 4, 1994.
14. Roger Cohen, "U.N. to Withdraw Unless the Firing in Bosnia Ceases," *New York Times*, November 30, 1994; Michael R. Gordon, "Paris Ends Threat to Drop its Role in Bosnian Force," *New York Times*, December 13, 1994; Roger Cohen, "Croatia Is Set to End Mandate of U.N. Force on Its Territory," *New York Times*, January 12, 1995.
15. Paul Lewis, "U.S. Forces U.N. to Put Off Plan to Send 5,500 Troops to Rwanda," *New York Times*, May 17, 1994; Milton Leitenberg, "Anatomy of a Massacre" (op-ed), *New York Times*, July 31, 1994.
16. The Security Council voted to end the Mozambique operation on January 31, 1995; U.N. Security Council, 3479th Meeting, Press Release SC/5964, "Security Council Welcomes Installation of President, Inauguration of Assembly in Mozambique," New York, December 14, 1994; U.N. Daily Highlights, op. cit. note 3.
17. U.N. Security Council, "Report of the Secretary-General on the United Nations Angola Verification Mission (UNAVEM III). Addendum," S/1995/97/Add.1, New York, February 6, 1995; U.N. Security Council, "Report of the Secretary-General on the Question Concerning Haiti. Addendum," S/1995/46/Add.1, New York, January 25, 1995.

WARS REACH A PLATEAU (pages 110–111)

1. Worldwatch calculations based on data from Milton Leitenberg and Nicole Ball, "Appendix I. Wars and Conflicts in Developing Economies and Estimates of Related deaths since the End of World War II," in Robert S. McNamara, "The Post–Cold War World: Implications for Military Expenditure in the Developing Countries," *Proceedings of the World Bank Annual Conference on Development Economics 1991* (Washington, D.C.: World Bank, 1992), from Milton Leitenberg, private communications, various dates, and from Peter Wallensteen and Karin Axell, "Conflict Resolution and the End of the Cold War, 1989-93," in Ylva Nordlander, ed., *States in Armed Conflict 1993*, Report No. 38 (Uppsala, Sweden: Department of Peace and Conflict Research, Uppsala University, 1993). Data for 1994 are Worldwatch estimates based on newspaper reports.
2. Worldwatch estimate based on newspaper reports during 1994.
3. Worldwatch calculations, op. cit. note 1.
4. Ibid.
5. Jim Wurst, "Mozambique Disarms," *Bulletin of the Atomic Scientists*, September/October 1994.
6. Dan Connell, "Eritrea: An Island of Stability in Strife-Filled Africa," *Christian Science Monitor*, November 30, 1994.
7. Judith Matloff, "Angola Edges Toward Cease-Fire As UN Brokers New Peace Accord," *Christian Science Monitor*, October 21, 1994; Wallensteen and Axell, op. cit. note 1.
8. Wallensteen and Axell, op. cit. note 1.
9. Jo-Marie Burt and Jose Lopez Ricci, "Update Peru: Shining Path After Guzman," *NACLA Report On The Americas*, November/December 1994.
10. Cesar Chelala, "Haiti: Fighting for Survival," *Swiss Review of World Affairs*, September 1994.
11. Steve Watrous, "Nobody Here But Us Roadbuilders: The Pentagon Keeps Busy in El Salvador," *The Progressive*, October 1994.
12. James F. Clarity, "Former Irish Leader Is Criticized for Remarks on I.R.A. Talks," *New York Times*, December 19, 1994.
13. Clyde Haberman, "Israel Yields Land to Jordan In Keeping With Peace Pact," *New York Times*, January 31, 1995.
14. Philip Shenon, "U.S. Considers Providing Arms To Cambodia to Fight Guerillas," *New York Times*, January 30, 1995.
15. Michael Specter, "Rebel Capital in the Caucasus Now a City of Living Wraiths," *New York Times*, January 30, 1995.
16. Institute of Peace and Conflict Studies, Conrad Grebel College, *Armed Conflicts Report 1993* (Waterloo, Ont.: Project Ploughshares, 1994).
17. Ibid.
18. Ibid.
19. Ibid.
20. Worldwatch calculations, op. cit. note 1.
21. Ruth Leger Sivard, *World Military and Social Expenditures 1993* (Washington, D.C.: World Priorities, 1993).
22. Leitenberg and Ball, op. cit. note 1.

Notes

23. Sivard, op. cit. note 21.
24. Michael Renner, *Critical Juncture: The Future of Peacekeeping*, Worldwatch Paper 114 (Washington, D.C.: Worldwatch Institute, May 1993).
25. Barbara Crossette, "Unicef Optimistic About Saving More Children From Disease," *New York Times*, December 16, 1994.
26. Howard W. French, "War Engulfs Liberia, Humbling the Peacekeepers," *New York Times*, October 7, 1994.
27. Worldwatch calculations, op. cit. note 1.

TROPICAL FORESTS VANISHING (pages 116–17)

1. U.N. Food and Agriculture Organization (FAO), *Forest Resources Assessment 1990: Tropical Countries*, Forestry Paper 112 (Rome: 1993).
2. Norman Myers, *The Primary Source: Tropical Forests and Our Future* (New York: W.W. Norton & Company, 1992); Nels Johnson and Bruce Cabarle, *Surviving the Cut: Natural Forest Management in the Humid Tropics* (Washington D.C.: World Resources Institute, 1993).
3. Species percentage from World Conservation Monitoring Centre, *Global Diversity: Status of the Earth's Living Resources* (New York: Chapman & Hall, 1992).
4. Kenton Miller and Laura Tangley, *Trees of Life: Saving Tropical Forests and Their Biologial Wealth* (Boston: Beacon Press, 1991).
5. World Wide Fund for Nature (WWF), *Conservation of Tropical Forests, Special Report 1* (Gland, Switzerland: 1988).
6. Chris C. Park, *Tropical Rainforests* (New York: Routledge, 1992).
7. World Conservation Monitoring Centre, op. cit. note 3.
8. FAO, op. cit. note 1.
9. Ibid.
10. Park, op. cit. note 6.
11. Sandra Postel and John C. Ryan, "Reforming Forestry," in Lester Brown et al. *State of the World 1991* (New York: W.W. Norton & Company, 1991).
12. FAO, op. cit. note 1.
13. Park, op. cit. note 6; Miller and Tangley, op. cit. note 4.
14. Arnold Newman, *Tropical Rainforest: A World Survey of Our Most Valuable and Endangered Habitat with a Blueprint for Its Survival* (New York: Facts on File, 1990).
15. World Conservation Monitoring Centre, op. cit. note 3.
16. Park, op. cit. note 6.
17. World Resources Institute, *World Resources 1990–91* (New York: Oxford University Press, 1990).
18. Park, op. cit. note 6.
19. Myers, op. cit. note 2; *Vanishing Eden: The Plight of the Tropical Rainforest* (Hong Kong: Barron's, 1991).
20. FAO, op. cit. note 1.
21. These figures are predictions based on theory rather than tallies of individual extinctions, but as measures of the erosion of life worldwide, they may be considered conservative; Wilson cited in John C. Ryan, *Life Support: Conserving Biological Diversity*, Worldwatch Paper 108 (Washington, D.C.: Worldwatch Institute, April 1992).
22. Miller and Tangley, op. cit. note 4.
23. *Vanishing Eden,* op. cit. note 19; WWF, op. cit. note 5.
24. Park, op. cit. note 6.
25. Deforestation emissions estimate from Intergovernmental Panel on Climate Change, *Climate Change 1992: The IPCC Supplementary Report* (Cambridge: Cambridge University Press, 1992); share of total emission is a Worldwatch estimate, based on ibid., and on G. Marland, R.J. Andres, and T.A. Boden, "Global Regional, and National CO_2 Emissions," in Thomas A. Boden et al., eds., *Trends '93: A Compendium of Data on Global Change* (Oak Ridge, Tenn.: Oak Ridge National Laboratory, 1994).
26. Alan Thein Durning, "Redesigning the Forest Economy," in Lester Brown et al., *State of the World 1994* (New York: W.W. Norton & Company, 1994).

SOIL EROSION'S TOLL CONTINUES (pages 118–19)

1. U.S. Department of Agriculture (USDA), Soil Conservation Service, "Summary Report, 1992 National Resources Inventory," Washington, D.C., July 1994.
2. U.S. Government Accounting Office (GAO), "Soil and Wetlands Conservation: Soil Conservation Service Making Good Progress But Cultural Issues Need Attention," Gaithersburg, Md., September 1994.
3. USDA, op. cit. note 1.
4. GAO, op. cit. note 2.
5. Robert L. Paarlberg, "The Politics of Agricultural Resource Abuse," *Environment*, September 1994.
6. David Pimentel, ed., *World Soil Erosion and Conservation* (New York: Cambridge University Press, 1993).
7. Berman D. Hudson, "Soil Organic Matter and Available Water Capacity," *Journal of Soil and Water Conservation*, March/April 1994.

8. Robert Herrscher, "'Granary of the World' is Becoming a Desert," *Subtext*, December 1992.
9. J.S. Molina Buck, "Soil Erosion and Conservation in Argentina," in Pimentel, op. cit. note 6.
10. Ibid.
11. Wen Dazhong, "Soil Erosion and Conservation in China," in Pimentel, op. cit. note 6; K.F. Isherwood and K.G. Soh, "The Agricultural Situation and Fertilizer Demand," presented at 62nd Annual Conference, International Fertilizer Industry Association, Istanbul, May 9, 1994.
12. S.A. El-Swaify, "Soil Erosion and Conservation in the Humid Tropics," in Pimentel, op. cit. note 6.
13. Yacob Maul, Victor Garmanov, and J. Sanford Rikoon, "Soil Conservation and Agricultural Land Issues in Kazakhstan," *Journal of Soil and Water Conservation*, September/October 1993.
14. Ibid.
15. Michael A. Zöbisch, "Erosion Susceptibility and Soil Loss on Grazing Lands in Some Semiarid and Subhumid Locations of Eastern Kenya," *Journal of Soil and Water Conservation*, September/October 1993.
16. U.N. Food and Agriculture Organization, *Production Yearbooks* (Rome: various years); Zöbisch, op. cit. note 15.
17. Wen, op. cit. note 11.
18. Ibid.
19. Ibid.
20. David Pimentel et al., "Soil Erosion and Agricultural Productivity," in Pimentel, op. cit. note 6.

AMPHIBIAN POPULATIONS TAKE A DIVE (pages 120–21)

1. James L. Vial and Loralei Saylor, *The Status of Amphibian Populations: A Compilation and Analysis* (Milton Keynes, U.K.: Declining Amphibian Populations Task Force, World Conservation Union, 1993); Andrew R. Blaustein, "Chicken Little or Nero's Fiddle? A Perspective on Declining Amphibian Populations," *Herpetologica*, Vol. 50, No. 1, 1994.
2. Chris Bolgiano, "Unearthing Salamander Secrets," *Defenders*, September/October 1989.
3. John G. Palis, "*Rana utricularia* (Southern Leopard Frog) Road Mortality," *Herpetological Review*, Vol. 25, No. 3, 1994.
4. John Ryan, "Conserving Biological Diversity," in Lester R. Brown et al., *State of the World 1992* (New York: W.W. Norton & Company, 1992).
5. John M.R. Baker and Verina Waights, "The Effects of Nitrate on Tadpoles of the Tree Frog *Litoria caerulea*," *Herpetological Journal*, Vol. 4, No. 3, 1994.
6. "UV to Blame for Amphibian Decline?" *Oryx*, July 1994; "UV-B Linked to Declines," *Froglog*, March 1994.
7. Kathryn Phillips, *Tracking the Vanishing Frogs* (New York: St. Martin's Press, 1994).
8. Trevor Beebee, "Nuclear Power? Yes Please! It Could Be the Best Option for Wildlife," *New Scientist*, December 2, 1989.
9. Phillips, op. cit. note 7.
10. Vial and Saylor, op. cit. note 1.
11. "UV-B Linked to Declines," op. cit. note 6; Boyce Rensberger, "Sunlight and Fungus as Amphibian Hazards," *Washington Post*, March 7, 1994.
12. Beth Livermore, "Amphibian Alarm: Just Where Have All the Frogs Gone?" *Smithsonian*, October 1992.
13. Phillips, op. cit. note 7.
14. Vial and Saylor, op. cit. note 1; Alegra Filio and Asimakopoulos Byron, "On the Legal Status Concerning the Protection of Amphibians and Reptiles in Greece," *Herpetological Review*, Vol. 21, No. 2, 1990.
15. Phillips, op. cit. note 7.
16. "Postmetamorphic Death Syndrome," *Froglog*, September 1993.
17. "Virus Studies," *Froglog*, March 1994.
18. J. Alan Pounds and Martha L. Crump, "Amphibian Declines and Climate Disturbances: The Case of the Golden Toad and the Harlequin Frog," *Conservation Biology*, March 1994.
19. Ibid.
20. Ronald Heyer, Smithsonian Institution, Washington, D.C., private communication, November 10, 1994.
21. Vial and Saylor, op. cit. note 1.

WATER TABLES FALLING
(pages 122–23)

1. World Resources Institute (WRI), *World Resources 1994-95* (New York: Oxford University Press, 1994); World Bank, Environment Division, Middle East and North Africa Region, "Forging a Partnership for Environmental Action," December 1994.
2. WRI, op. cit. note 1; World Bank, op. cit. note 1.
3. Worldwatch estimates, based on water consumption rates from WRI, op cit. note 1, and on population growth rates from Population Reference Bureau, *1994 World Population Data Sheet* (Washington, D.C.: 1994).
4. World Bank, *A Strategy for Managing Water in the Middle East and North Africa* (Washington, D.C.: 1993).
5. Saudi Arabia from Abdulla Ali Al-Ibrahim, "Exces-

sive Use of Groundwater Resources in Saudi Arabia: Impacts and Policy Options," *Ambio*, February 1991; Jordan, Israel, and the West Bank from Bruce Stutz, "Water & Peace," *Audubon*, September/October 1994.
6. Ministry of the Environment, Israel, "Israel Environment Bulletin," Tel Aviv, Spring-Summer 1994.
7. World Bank, op. cit. note 4.
8. You Wen-Rui, "Environmental Issues in Water Development of China," *Environmental Issues in Land and Water Development* (Bangkok: Regional Office for Asia and the Pacific, U.N. Food and Agriculture Organization, 1992).
9. *Beijing Review*, July 30-August 5, 1990.
10. Patrick E. Tyler, "China Lacks Water to Meet its Mighty Thirst," *New York Times*, November 7, 1993.
11. Xie Yicheng, "Minister in Urgent Bid to Preserve Water," *China Daily*, June 16, 1993.
12. A. Vaidyanathan, "Second India Series Revisted: Food and Agriculture," Madras Institute of Development Studies, Madras, India, 1994.
13. Marcus Moench, "Approaches to Groundwater Management: To Control or Enable," *Economic and Political Weekly*, September 24, 1994.
14. Raj Chengappa, "India's Water Crisis," *World Press Review*, August 1986.
15. Moench, op. cit. note 13.
16. Chengappa, op. cit. note 14.
17. Rodney Smith, "Sinking or Swimming in Water Policy?" *Regulation*, No. 3, 1994; Department of Water Resources, *State Drought Water Bank: Program Environmental Impact Report*, State of California, Sacramento, November 1993.
18. Department of Water Resources, op. cit. note 17.
19. Daniel B. Wood, "Stakes Rise in Vegas Water Dispute," *Christian Science Monitor*, May 2, 1991; John McPhee, "Water War," *The New Yorker*, April 26, 1993.
20. McPhee, op. cit. note 19.
21. "Drying Out," *The Economist*, February 12, 1994.
22. "Wet and Dry," *The Economist*, April 10, 1993.
23. Ibid.
24. "Drying Out," op. cit. note 21.
25. Eduardo Monteverde, "Mexico City Runs Dry," *World Press Review*, December 1991.
26. Sandra Postel, *Last Oasis: Facing Water Scarcity* (New York: W.W. Norton & Company, 1992).
27. Rhona Mahony, "Deep Water," *Reason*, February 1992; Monteverde, op. cit. note 25.
28. "Drying Up," *The Economist*, September 29, 1990.
29. Mahony, op. cit. note 27.
30. "Drying Up," op. cit. note 28.

DAM STARTS UP (pages 124–25)

1. International Commission on Large Dams (ICOLD), "Status of Dam Construction in 1993," Paris, January 16, 1995; ICOLD, "Status of Dam Construction in 1992," Paris, October 4, 1993. ICOLD figures do not include data from the former Soviet Union, or from nonmember countries.
2. ICOLD, "Status in 1993," op. cit. note 1; ICOLD, "Status in 1992," op. cit. note 1.
3. Sandra Postel, *Last Oasis: Facing Water Scarcity* (New York: W.W. Norton & Company, 1992).
4. ICOLD, "Status in 1992," op. cit. note 1.
5. ICOLD, "Status in 1993," op. cit. note 1.
6. Figure for 1950 from Jan A. Veltrop, "Importance of Dams for Water Supply and Hydropower," in Asit K. Biswas, Mohammed Jellali, and Glenn Stout, eds., *Water for Sustainable Development in the 21st Century* (Delhi: Oxford University Press, 1993); current figure from Patrick McCully, International Rivers Network, Berkeley, Calif., private communication, February 17, 1995.
7. *International Water Power and Dam Construction Handbook 1993* (Sutton, Surrey, UK: Reed Business Publishing, 1994).
8. Calculated from data in ICOLD, "Status in 1993," op. cit. note 1.
9. United Nations, *Energy Statistics Yearbook 1992* (New York: 1992).
10. Ibid.
11. Postel, op. cit. note 3.
12. Sandra Postel, The Global Water Policy Project, Cambridge, Mass., private communication, February 16, 1995.
13. "The Beautiful and the Dammed," *The Economist*, March 28, 1992.
14. Veltrop, op. cit. note 6.
15. Asit K. Biswas, "The Aswan High Dam Revisited," *Ecodecision*, September 1992.
16. Sanjay Kumar, "Indian Dams Will Drive Out Rare Animals . . ." *New Scientist*, February 4, 1995.
17. "Rotting Reservoirs," *New Scientist*, July 24, 1993.
18. Katherine P. Ransel, "The Last Salmon Run," *New York Times*, February 18, 1995.
19. John A. Dixon, Lee M. Talbot, and Guy J.-M. Le Moigne, "Dams and the Environment: Considerations in World Bank Projects," World Bank Technical Paper No. 110 (Washington, D.C.: World Bank, 1989).
20. Fred Pearce, "A Dammed Fine Mess," *New Scientist*, May 4, 1991.
21. Robert Goodland, "Ethical Priorities in Environmentally Sustainable Energy Systems: the Case of Tropi-

cal Hydropower," Environment Working Paper No. 67 (Washington: World Bank, 1994).
22. Ibid.
23. E. Goldsmith and N. Hildyard, *The Social and Environmental Effects of Large Dams* (Camelford, U.K.: Wadebridge Ecological Center, 1984).
24. Ibid.
25. Ibid.
26. Goodland, op. cit. note 21.
27. Ibid.
28. Robert Goodland, "Environmental Sustainability in the Power Sector and the 'Big Dams' Debate" (draft), World Bank, Washington, D.C., June 1, 1994.
29. Veltrop, op. cit. note 6.

LEAD IN GASOLINE SLOWLY PHASED OUT (pages 126–27)

1. Data for 1970 from Jerome O. Nriagu, "The Rise and Fall of Leaded Gasoline," *Science of the Total Environment 92*, 1990, as cited in Environmental Defense Fund (EDF), "Lead in Gasoline: Exposures and Alternatives," Washington, D.C., September 1994; 1993 estimate from Valerie Thomas, "The Elimination of Lead in Gasoline," *Annual Review of Energy and Environment* (Palo Alto, Calif.: Annual Reviews, Inc., forthcoming). The Natural Resources Defense Council (NRDC), on the other hand, estimates that more than 200,000 tons of lead were added to gasoline in 1993; Jared E. Blumenfeld, NRDC, Washington, D.C., private communication, February 13, 1995.
2. Carl M. Shy, "Lead in Petrol: The Mistake of the XXth Century," *World Health Statistic Quarterly*, Vol. 43, No. 3, 1990.
3. Alliance to End Childhood Lead Poisoning and EDF, *The Global Dimensions of Lead Poisoning: An Initial Analysis* (Washington, D.C.: 1994).
4. Shy, op. cit. note 2.
5. Sandra Blakeslee, "Concentrations of Lead in Blood Drop Steeply," *New York Times*, July 27, 1994; William Driscoll et al., "Reducing Lead in Gasoline: Mexico's Experience," *Environmental Science and Technology*, Vol. 26, No. 9, 1992.
6. Organisation for Economic Co-operation and Development, *Risk Reduction Monograph No. 1: Lead*, Paris, 1993, as cited in EDF, op. cit. note 1.
7. Earth Summit Watch, "Four in '94. Two Years After Rio: Assessing National Actions to Implement Agenda 21," NRDC and Campaign for Action to Protect the Earth (CAPE 21), New York, December 1994.
8. Hugh Carneey, "Sweden Bans Lead in Petrol," *Financial Times*, March 1, 1995.
9. Guatemala, Suriname, and Antigua are also reported to have eliminated leaded gasoline, but this information has not been confirmed. Various sources cited in EDF, op. cit. note 1.
10. Earth Summit Watch, op. cit. note 7.
11. "U.S. and 33 in Hemisphere Agree to Build Free Trade," *New York Times*, December 11, 1994.
12. The leaded gasoline used in the United States has 0.026 grams per liter (0.1 grams per gallon) of lead; this is the residual level that allows cars built before 1975 to operate, in which lead serves to lubricate engine valves; Driscoll et al. op. cit. note 5; Clean Air Act from EDF, op. cit. note 1.
13. In Greece, excluding Athens, and in Portugal a lead content of up to 0.4 grams per liter is still allowed, although in all other countries the maximum level is limited at 0.15 grams per liter. CONCAWE, *Motor Vehicle Emissions and Fuel Specifications—1992 Update*, Report No. 2/92, Brussels, November 1992.
14. Ibid.
15. "Unleaded Gasoline Takes Larger Share of EU Market, Statistics Agency Reports," *International Environment Reporter*, May 4, 1994.
16. Earth Summit Watch, op. cit. note 7.
17. Estimate of hypertension cases caused by lead exposure from World Bank, *World Development Report 1992* (New York: Oxford University Press, 1992); Driscoll et al, op. cit. note 5.
18. Driscoll et al., op. cit. note 5.
19. Earth Summit Watch, op. cit. note 7; Anirudh Bhattacharyya, "Exhausting Concerns," *Down To Earth*, August 31, 1994.
20. Valerie Thomas and Thomas G. Spiro, "Emission and Exposure to Metals: Cadmium and Lead," in R. Socolow et al., eds., *Industrial Ecology and Global Change* (Cambridge: Cambridge University Press, 1994).
21. Michael Walsh, consultant, Arlington, Va., private communication, January 30, 1995; Valerie Thomas, Center for Energy and Environmental Studies, Princeton University, Princeton, N.J., private communication, January 30, 1995.
22. Walsh, op. cit. note 21; Thomas, op. cit. note 21.
23. China from Walsh, op. cit. note 21; Venezuela and Trinidad and Tobago from EDF, op. cit. note 1.
24. Robert E. Ottenstein and Albert H. Tsuei, "Ethyl Corporation," CS First Boston, May 10, 1994; Walsh, op. cit. note 21.
25. EDF, op. cit. note 1.
26. Earth Summit Watch, op. cit. note 7.
27. CONCAWE, op. cit. note 13.
28. Earth Summit Watch, op. cit. note 7.
29. The South African government introduced unleaded gasoline in January 1995; "Unleaded Fuel, Legisla-

tion on Emissions Slated for Introduction at the Start of 1995," *International Environment Reporter*, October 19, 1994.

30. Valerie Thomas, Center for Energy and Environmental Studies, Princeton University, Princeton, N.J., private communication, February 1, 1995; estimates from U.S. Environmental Protection Agency, *Costs and Benefits of Reducing Lead in Gasoline* (Washington, D.C.: 1985).

STEEL RECYCLING RISING (pages 128–29)

1. F. Katrak et al., "Outlook for Steel, Scrap and Alternative Iron Supply/Demand," presented at the MBM Eighth Mini-Mill Conference, Bangkok, Thailand, March 1994. Inclusion of mill scrap in recycling figures can be misleading: while it reduces the need for virgin material inputs, mill scrap also implies a lower level of steel output; its contribution to the net reduction in materials flows can be small. Mill scrap production is a better measure of steel production inefficiency than of resource reuse.
2. William Chandler, *Materials Recycling: The Virtue of Necessity*, Worldwatch Paper 56 (Washington, D.C.: Worldwatch Institute, October 1983).
3. Calculated from data in "Ferrous Markets: Hot This Winter," *Commodities* (Institute of Scrap Recycling Industries, Washington, D.C.), January 12, 1995. If mill scrap is included, the figure increases to 65 percent, according to the Steel Recycling Institute.
4. Steel Recycling Institute, "A Few Facts About Steel" (factsheet), Pittsburgh, Pa., 1994.
5. Nicholas Lenssen and David Malin Roodman, "Making Better Buildings," in Lester R. Brown et al., *State of the World 1995* (New York: W.W. Norton & Company, 1995).
6. Calculated from data in John E. Young, *Mining the Earth*, Worldwatch Paper 109 (Washington, D.C.: Worldwatch Institute, July 1992).
7. Jose Guilherme de Heraclito Lima, *Restructuring the U.S. Steel Industry* (Boulder, Colo.: Westview Press, 1991).
8. Bill Heenan, "Missing the (Steel) Mark: EPA Procurement Guidelines Fail to Recognize Steel," *The Recycling Magnet* (Steel Recycling Institute, Pittsburgh, Pa.), Fall 1994.
9. Ibid.
10. "100 Million Tons of Chinese Steel by 2000," *New Steel*, August 1994; William T. Hogan, *Global Steel in the 1990s: Growth or Decline* (Lexington, Mass.: Lexington Books, 1991).
11. Hogan, op. cit. note 10.
12. "World: Raw Steel Production Projection, 2003," *Skillings Mining Review*, (D.N. Skillings, Inc., Duluth, Minn.), April 16, 1994.
13. Global figure from ibid; U.S. figure from Bill Heenan, Steel Recycling Institute, Pittsburgh, Pa., private communication, January 6, 1995; China figure from "100 Million Tons," op. cit. note 10.
14. "A Troubled Russian Steel Industry," *New Steel*, August 1994; Economic Commission for Europe, *The Steel Market in 1991* (New York: United Nations, 1992).
15. Lower figure for 2003 is from "World: Raw Steel Production Projection," op. cit. note 12; estimate of 40-45 percent for 2000 from William Hogan, *Steel in the 21st Century: Competition Forges a New World Order* (New York: Lexington Books, 1994).
16. Hogan, op. cit. note 10.
17. Ted Kuster, "Wanted: Low-Residual Scrap," *New Steel*, April 1994.
18. Philip Burgert, "What Goes Up Must Come Down? When?" *New Steel*, January 1994.
19. Ibid.
20. Hogan, op. cit. note 10.
21. Heenan, op. cit. note 13.
22. F. Katrak et al., "Is the Steel Scrap Crisis Real or Imagined?" *33 MetalProducing*, July 1994.
23. "World: Raw Steel Production Projection," op. cit. note 12.
24. Ibid.
25. Steel Recycling Institute, op. cit. note 4.
26. Greg Crawford, Steel Recycling Institute, Pittsburgh, Pa., private communication, January 6, 1995.
27. Steel Recycling Institute, op. cit. note 4.
28. Bob Garino, Institute of Scrap Recycling Industries, Washington, D.C., private communication, January 18, 1995.

COMPUTERS MULTIPLYING RAPIDLY (pages 132–33)

1. Egil Juliussen and Karen Petska-Juliussen, *Computer Industry Almanac 1994-95* (Lake Tahoe, Nev.: Computer Industry Almanac, Inc., 1994).
2. Ibid.
3. Ibid.
4. Ibid.
5. Ibid.
6. Ibid.
7. Ibid.; Population Reference Bureau, *1994 World Population Data Sheet* (Washington, D.C.: 1994).
8. Institute for Global Communications (IGC), "IGC Brochure," San Francisco, Calif., IGC Gopher (gopher.igc.apc.org).

9. Ibid.
10. Ibid.
11. John E. Young, *Global Network: Computers in a Sustainable Society*, Worldwatch Paper 115 (Washington, D.C.: Worldwatch Institute, September 1993).
12. John E. Young, "Asleep on the Job," *World Watch*, March/April 1993.
13. Young, op. cit. note 11.

WOMEN SLOWLY ACCEPTED AS POLITICIANS (pages 134–35)

1. Inter-Parliamentary Union (IPU), "Distribution of Seats Between Men and Women in the 178 National Parliaments Existing as at 30 June 1994: And in One International Parliamentary Assembly Elected by Direct Vote," Geneva, 1994.
2. United Nations, *The World's Women 1970-1990: Trends and Statistics* (New York: 1991).
3. IPU, "Women and Political Power: Survey Carried Out Among the 150 National Parliaments Existing as of 31st October 1991," Geneva, 1992.
4. Ibid.
5. United Nations, *Women in Politics and Decision-Making in the Late Twentieth Century: A United Nations Study* (Boston: Martinus Nijhoff Publishers, 1992).
6. Molly Moore, "Paths to Power for Asian, Latin Women," *Washington Post*, November 13, 1994.
7. Olga S. Opfell, *Women Prime Ministers and Presidents* (Jefferson, N.C.: McFarland & Co., 1993); *Information Please Almanac: Atlas and Yearbook 1995* (New York: Houghton Mifflin Company, 1995).
8. IPU, "Distribution of Seats Between Men and Women National Parliaments: Statistical Data from 1945 to 30 June 1991," Geneva, 1991.
9. Calculated from IPU, op. cit. note 1.
10. Ibid.
11. Ibid.
12. Ibid.
13. United Nations, *Women: Challenges to the Year 2000* (New York: 1991).
14. IPU, op. cit. note 1.
15. Ingmarie Froman, "Sweden for Women," *Current Sweden*, November 1994.
16. Kathy Kleeman, "Women and the 1994 Elections: Outcomes," *CAWP News and Notes*, Winter 1994.
17. Nuita Yoko, Yamaguchi Mitsuko, and Kubo Kimiko, "The U.N. Convention on Eliminating Discrimination Against Women and the Status of Women in Japan," in Barbara J. Nelson and Najma Chowdhury, eds., *Women and Politics Worldwide* (New Haven, Conn.: Yale University Press, 1994).
18. IPU, op. cit. note 1.
19. Sharon Wolchik, "Women and the Politics of Transition in the Czech and Slovak Republics," in Marilyn Rueschemeyer, ed., *Women in the Politics of Postcommunist Eastern Europe* (New York: M.E. Sharpe, Inc., 1994).
20. Fatos Tarifa, "Disappearing from Politics: Social Change and Women in Albania," in Rueschemeyer, op. cit. note 18.

BREAST AND PROSTATE CANCER RISING (pages 136–37)

1. M.P. Coleman et al., eds., *Trends in Cancer Incidence and Mortality*, International Agency for Research on Cancer (IARC) Scientific Publications No. 121 (Lyon, France: World Health Organization's International Agency for Research on Cancer, International Union Against Cancer, and the International Association of Cancer Registries, 1993).
2. Joe Thornton, *Chlorine, Human Health and the Environment: The Breast Cancer Warning* (Washington, D.C.: Greenpeace, 1993).
3. John Maurice, "Cancer Will 'Overwhelm' the Third World," *New Scientist*, December 14, 1991.
4. Coleman et al., op. cit. note 1.
5. P.J. Skerrett, "Screening for Prostate Cancer," *Technology Review*, August/September 1994.
6. David G. Hoel et al., "Trends in Cancer Mortality in 15 Industrialized Countries, 1969-1986," *Journal of the National Cancer Institute*, March 4, 1992.
7. J. Kelsey and M. Gammon, "The Epidemiology of Breast Cancer," *CA: A Cancer Journal for Clinicians*, Vol. 41, 1991, as cited in Thornton, op. cit. note 2.
8. "Closing In on a Serial Killer," *Financial Times*, November 29, 1994.
9. Abigail Trafford, "Breast Cancer," *Washington Post*, April 19, 1994; Thornton, op. cit. note 2.
10. Michael Castleman, "Breast Cancer and the Environment," *Mother Jones*, May/June 1994.
11. Marc B. Garnick, "The Dilemmas of Prostate Cancer," *Scientific American*, April 1994.
12. Dr. D.M. Parkin, Chief, Unit of Descriptive Epidemiology, International Agency for Cancer Research, World Health Organization, Lyon, France, private communication, December 8, 1994.
13. Ibid.
14. Ibid.
15. Coleman et al., op. cit. note 1.
16. Ibid.
17. Ibid.
18. Ibid.; changes in diet from T. Colin Campbell, "The Dietary Causes of Degenerative Diseases: Nutrients vs Foods," in N. J. Temple and D.P. Burkitt, *Western*

Diseases: Their Dietary Prevention and Reversibility (Totowa, N.J.: Humana Press, 1994).
19. Samuel Epstein, "Breast Cancer and the Environment," *The Ecologist*, September/October 1993.
20. Campbell, op. cit. note 18; Leslie Bernstein et al., "Physical Exercise and Reduced Risk of Breast Cancer in Young Women," *Journal of the National Cancer Institute*, September 21, 1994.
21. Ann Misch, "Assessing Environmental Health Risks," in Lester R. Brown et al., *State of the World 1994* (New York: W.W. Norton & Company, 1994).
22. Jerome B. Westin and Elihu Richter, "The Israeli Breast-Cancer Anomaly," in Devra Lee Davis and David Hoel, eds., "Trends in Cancer Mortality in Industrial Countries," *Annals of the New York Academy of Sciences*, Vol. 609, 1990.
23. Charles C. Mann, "The Prostate-Cancer Dilemma," *Atlantic Monthly*, November 1993.
24. Ibid.
25. Ibid.
26. Skerrett, op. cit. note 5.
27. Ibid.; Mann, op. cit. note 23; T. Adler, "Just Say No to Prostate Cancer Screening," *Science News*, September 17, 1994.
28. Castleman, op. cit. note 10; Mann, op. cit. note 23.
29. Malcolm Gladwell, "How Safe Are Your Breasts?" *New Republic*, October 24, 1994.
30. Castleman, op. cit. note 10.
31. Ibid.; American Cancer Society, "Breast Cancer: Questions and Answers," Washington, D.C., 1992.

CIGARETTE TAXES SHOW UPS AND DOWNS (pages 138–39)

1. Non-Smokers' Rights Association (NSRA) of Canada, "Consumption of Cigarettes Per Capita and Real Price of Tobacco," Ottawa, unpublished printout and private communication, November 17, 1994; David Sweanor and Luc Martial, NSRA of Canada, private communication, December 12, 1994.
2. Charles Trueheart, "Canada Cuts Tobacco Tax to Halt Smuggling," *Washington Post*, February 9, 1994; Clyde Farnsworth, "Canada Cuts Cigarette Taxes to Fight Smuggling," *New York Times*, February 9, 1994.
3. NSRA of Canada, op. cit. note 1.
4. NSRA of Canada, Ottawa, private communication, January 4, 1993; NSRA of Canada, op. cit. note 1.
5. Jimmy Carter, "A Healthy Tobacco Tax Could Help Farmers Too," *Washington Post*, February 9, 1994.
6. John Schwartz, "Change Is in the Air For Tobacco Industry," *Washington Post*, November 11, 1994.
7. Ibid.
8. Robert Pear, "Panel Supports $1.25 Increase For Cigarettes," *New York Times*, March 23, 1994.
9. John Schwartz, "Institute Seeks Strong Steps To Prevent Yough Smoking," *Washington Post*, September 14, 1994.
10. Action on Smoking and Health, "ASH Review," *Ash Smoking and Health Review*, November-December 1994.
11. Sweanor and Martial, op. cit. note 1.
12. Luc Martial, NSRA of Canada, Ottawa, private communication, December 5, 1994.
13. Ibid.
14. NSRA of Canada, op. cit. note 1.
15. Martial, op. cit. note 12.
16. William V. George, "Import Requirements and Restrictions for Tobacco and Tobacco Products In Foreign Markets" (draft), U.S. Department of Agriculture, Foreign Agricultural Service, Washington, D.C., unpublished, June 1992.
17. Julie Chao, "Smoke Signals: China's Choice on Cigarettes: Public Health or Revenues," *Far Eastern Economic Review*, November 3, 1994.
18. Ibid.
19. "CDC Report Boosts Clinton In Call for Cigarette Tax," *Journal of Commerce*, July 11, 1994.
20. Ibid.
21. Ibid.
22. Ibid.
23. John Darnton, "Report Says Smoking Causes a Global Epidemic of Death," *New York Times*, September 21, 1994.
24. Ibid.
25. Philip J. Hilts, "Children of Smoking Mothers Show Carcinogens in Blood," *New York Times*, September 21, 1994; "Surgeon General Warns About Children, Secondhand Smoke," *Washington Post*, January 7, 1994; K.A. Fackelmann, "Mother's Smoking Linked to Child's IQ Drop," *Science News*, February 12, 1994.

ACCESS TO SAFE WATER EXPANDS (pages 140–41)

1. World Bank, *World Development Report 1992* (New York: Oxford University Press, 1992).
2. Ibid.
3. World Resources Institute, *World Resources 1988-89* (New York: Basic Books, Inc., 1988).
4. Daniel Campbell, librarian, Environmental Health Project, Rosslyn, Va., private communication, December 6, 1994.
5. World Health Organization (WHO), *World Health Statistics Report* (Geneva: 1976).

6. WHO, *The International Drinking Water Supply and Sanitation Decade (1981-1990)* (Geneva: 1992).
7. Ibid.
8. "Drinking Problems," *Asiaweek*, September 7, 1994.
9. WHO, op. cit. note 6.
10. John Briscoe, "When the Cup is Half Full: Improving Water and Sanitation Services in the Developing World," *Environment*, May 1993.
11. World Bank, op. cit. note 1.
12. Briscoe, op. cit. note 10.
13. United Nations, *World Urbanization Prospects: The 1992 Revision* (New York: 1993).
14. Ibid.
15. Pan American Health Organization, *Health Conditions in the Americas* (Washington D.C.: 1994).
16. Briscoe, op. cit. note 10.
17. Ibid.
18. "All Human Beings Should Have The Right to Water," *Development Hotline*, March 1994.
19. Deborah Moore, "Think Small to Solve the World's Drinking Water Crisis," *Environmental Defense Fund Letter*, November 1994.
20. World Bank, op. cit. note 1.

HOMELESSNESS REMAINS A PROBLEM (pages 142–43)

1. Joel Audefroy, "Eviction Trends Worldwide—And the Role of Local Authorities in Implementing the Right to Housing," *Environment and Urbanization*, April 1994.
2. "The Problem of Homelessness," *Building for the Homeless* (New York: U.N. Department of Public Information, 1987).
3. Ibid.
4. "The Housing Indicators Program, Vol. II: Indicator Tables," U.N. Centre for Human Settlements and World Bank, Nairobi, October 1993.
5. Alan Gilbert, "Human Resources: Work, Housing and Migration," Independent Commission for Population and Quality of Life, Paris, August 1994.
6. "How Many People Are Homeless in the U.S.?" fact sheet, National Coalition for the Homeless, Washington D.C., September 1994.
7. Ibid.
8. Ibid.
9. Ibid.
10. Marjorie Hope and James Young, "The Politics of Displacement: Sinking into Homelessness," in Jon Erickson and Charles Wilhelm, eds., *Housing the Homeless* (New Brunswick, N.J.: Center for Urban Policy Research, 1986).
11. Mary Daly, *European Homelessness—The Rising Tide* (Berchem, Belgium: European Observatory on Homelessness, 1992).
12. Ibid.
13. William Brown, "Hidden Homeless Who Came to Stay . . . ," *New Scientist*, September 18, 1993.
14. United Nations, *World Urbanization Prospects: The 1992 Revision* (New York: Department of Economic and Social Information and Policy Analysis, 1993).
15. Charles Correa, *The New Landscape: Urbanisation in the Third World* (London: Concept Media Ltd., with Butterworth Architecture, 1989).
16. Gill-Chin Lim, "Housing Policies for the Urban Poor in Developing Countries," *Journal of the American Planning Association*, Spring 1987.
17. Jorge Hardoy and David Satterthwaite, "Shelter, Infrastructure and Services in Third World Cities," presented to the World Commission on Environment and Development, São Paulo, October 1985.
18. Audefroy, op. cit. note 1.
19. Annick Billard, "A Roof for Refugees . . . ," *World Health*, July 1987.
20. U.N. High Commissioner for Refugees, Geneva, private communication, February 10, 1995.
21. Aaron Segal, *An Atlas of International Migration* (London: Hans Zell Publishers, 1993).
22. International Federation for Housing and Planning, "Homelessness in Industrialised Countries," The Hague, Netherlands, October 1987.
23. "The City Summit," U.N. Centre for Human Settlements, Nairobi, undated.

INCOME GAP WIDENS
(pages 144–45)

1. U.N. Development Programme (UNDP), *Human Development Report 1994* (New York: Oxford University Press, 1994).
2. Ibid.
3. Population Reference Bureau, *1994 World Population Data Sheet* (Washington, D.C.: 1994).
4. UNDP, op. cit. note 1.
5. Alan Durning, *How Much Is Enough?* (New York: W.W. Norton & Company, 1992).
6. Ibid.; International Monetary Fund (IMF), *World Economic Outlook* (Washington, D.C.: October 1994).
7. UNDP, *Human Development Report 1993* (New York: Oxford University Press, 1993).
8. Durning, op. cit. note 5.
9. IMF, op. cit. note 6; K.F. Isherwood and K.G. Soh, "Short Term Prospects For World Agriculture and Fertilizer Use," 19th Enlarged Council Meeting, In-

ternational Fertilizer Association, Paris, November 22, 1993.
10. Aaron Segal, *An Atlas of International Migration* (London: Hans Zell Publishers, 1993).
11. United Nations, *World Urbanization Prospects, The 1992 Revision* (New York: 1993).
12. National Academy findings cited in "China's Next Revolution," *Financial Times*, August 26, 1994.
13. IMF, op. cit. note 6.
14. "Latin American Speedup Leaves Poor Behind," *New York Times*, September 7, 1994.
15. Helene Cooper, "Sub-Saharan Africa is Seen as Big Loser in GATT's New World Trade Accord," *Wall Street Journal*, August 15, 1994.
16. John Darnton, " 'Lost Decade' Drains Africa's Vitality," *New York Times*, June 19, 1994.
17. World Bank, *World Development Report 1994* (New York: Oxford University Press, 1994).
18. Ibid.

HUNGER STILL WIDESPREAD
(pages 146–47)

1. U.N. Administrative Committee on Coordination, Subcommittee on Nutrition, *Second Report on the World Nutrition Situation, Vol. I: Global and Regional Results* (Geneva: United Nations, 1992).
2. Ibid.
3. Ibid.
4. Ibid.
5. U.N. Food and Agriculture Organization (FAO), *International Conference on Nutrition: Nutrition and Development—A Global Assessment 1992* (Rome: FAO and World Health Organization, 1992).
6. Ibid.
7. Patricia Allen, "The Human Face of Sustainable Agriculture: Adding People to the Environmental Agenda," Issue Paper No. 4, Center for Agroecology and Sustainable Food Systems, University of California, Santa Cruz, November 1994.
8. Ibid.
9. Bread for the World Institute on Hunger and Development, *Hunger 1992: Second Annual Report on the State of World Hunger* (Washington, D.C.: 1991).
10. FAO, op. cit. note 5.
11. Ibid.
12. Ibid.
13. Ibid.
14. Ibid.
15. Ibid.
16. Ibid.
17. Ibid.
18. World Bank, *Enriching Lives: Overcoming Vitamin and Mineral Malnutrition in Developing Countries* (Washington, D.C.: 1994).
19. Ibid.
20. U.N. Administrative Committee on Coordination, Subcommittee on Nutrition, *Second Report on the World Nutrition Situation, Vol. II: Country Trends, Methods and Statistics* (Geneva: United Nations, 1993).

THE VITAL SIGNS SERIES

Some topics are included each year in Vital Signs; others, particularly those in Part Two, are included only in certain years. The following is a list of the topics covered thus far in the series, with the year or years each appeared indicated in parentheses. See page 6 for information on ordering the Worldwatch Database Diskette.

Part ONE: KEY INDICATORS

FOOD TRENDS
  Grain Production (1992, 1993, 1994, 1995)
  Soybean Harvest (1992, 1993, 1994, 1995)
  Meat Production (1992, 1993, 1994, 1995)
  Fish Catch (1992, 1993, 1994, 1995)
  Grain Stocks (1992, 1993, 1994, 1995)
  Grain Used for Feed (1993, 1995)
  Aquaculture (1994)

AGRICULTURAL RESOURCE TRENDS
  Grain Area (1992, 1993)
  Fertilizer Use (1992, 1993, 1994, 1995)
  Irrigation (1992, 1994)
  Grain Yield (1994, 1995)

ENERGY TRENDS
  Oil Production (1992, 1993, 1994, 1995)
  Wind Power (1992, 1993, 1994, 1995)
  Nuclear Power (1992, 1993, 1994, 1995)
  Solar Cell Production (1992, 1993, 1994, 1995)
  Natural Gas (1992, 1994, 1995)
  Energy Efficiency (1992)
  Geothermal Power (1993)
  Coal Use (1993, 1994, 1995)
  Hydroelectric Power (1993)
  Carbon Use (1993)
  Compact Fluorescent Lamps (1993, 1994, 1995)

ATMOSPHERIC TRENDS
  CFC Production (1992, 1993, 1994, 1995)
  Global Temperature (1992, 1993, 1994, 1995)
  Carbon Emissions (1992, 1994, 1995)

ECONOMIC TRENDS
  Global Economy (1992, 1993, 1994, 1995)
  Third World Debt (1992, 1993, 1994, 1995)
  International Trade (1993, 1994, 1995)
  Steel Production (1993)
  Paper Production (1993, 1994)
  Advertising Expeditures (1993)
  Roundwood Production (1994)
  Gold Production (1994)
  Television Use (1995)

TRANSPORTATION TRENDS
  Bicycle Production (1992, 1993, 1994, 1995)

The Vital Signs Series

Automobile Production (1992, 1993, 1994, 1995)
Air Travel (1993)

ENVIRONMENTAL TRENDS
Pesticide Resistance (1994)
Sulfur and Nitrogen Emissions (1994, 1995)
Environmental Treaties (1995)
Nuclear Waste (1995)

SOCIAL TRENDS
Population Growth (1992, 1993, 1994, 1995)
Cigarette Producton (1992, 1993, 1994, 1995)

Infant Mortality (1992)
Child Mortality (1993)
Refugees (1993, 1994, 1995)
HIV/AIDS Incidence (1994, 1995)
Immunizations (1994)
Urbanization (1995)

MILITARY TRENDS
Military Expenditures (1992)
Nuclear Arsenal (1992, 1994, 1995)
Arms Trade (1994)
Peace Expenditures (1994, 1995)
Wars (1995)

Part Two: SPECIAL FEATURES

ENVIRONMENTAL FEATURES
Bird Populations (1992, 1994)
Forest Loss (1992, 1994, 1995)
Soil Erosion (1992, 1995)
Steel Recycling (1992, 1995)
Nuclear Waste (1992)
Water Scarcity (1993)
Forest Damage from Air Pollution (1993)
Marine Mammal Populations (1993)
Paper Recycling (1994)
Coral Reefs (1994)
Energy Productivity (1994)
Amphibian Populations (1995)
Large Dams (1995)
Water Tables (1995)
Lead in Gasoline (1995)

ECONOMIC FEATURES
Wheat/Oil Exchange Rate (1992, 1993)
Trade in Arms and Grain (1992)

Cigarette Taxes (1993, 1995)
U.S. Seafood Prices (1993)

SOCIAL FEATURES
Income Distribution (1992, 1995)
Maternal Mortality (1992)
Access to Family Planning (1992)
Literacy (1993)
Fertility Rates (1993)
Traffic Accidents (1994)
Life Expectancy (1994)
Computer Production and Use (1995)
Women in Politics (1995)
Breast and Prostate Cancer (1995)
Access to Safe Water (1995)
Homelessness (1995)
Hunger (1995)

MILITARY FEATURES
Nuclear Arsenal (1993)
U.N. Peacekeeping (1993)

Also from The Worldwatch Institute and Earthscan

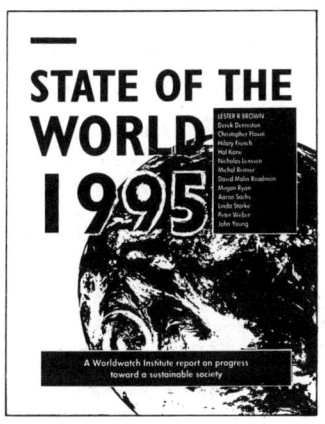

State of the World 1995
A Worldwatch Institute Report on Progress Toward a Sustainable Society
Lester Brown et al

This 12th edition of *State of the World* appears at a time when more and more people are aware of the effects of our rapidly rising population on the earth's support systems. The seemingly sudden collapse of the oceanic fishing economy, the rising expectations of China's 1.2 billion consumers, deforestation of the Indian subcontinent and the increase in refugees around the world all point to a need for understanding the interrelationship of population and environmental forces.

This book opens with a hard look at the economic and social costs of the unsustainable harvesting of the earth's natural resources, from the decimated hardwood forests of the Ivory Coast to the idle fishing fleets of Newfoundland. The Worldwatch team have also researched and reported the trends that can lead us to a more sustainable future, and this year's volume covers the welcome growth in the number of global environmental treaties; the growing revolution in the energy industry – from new transport technologies to the shift to hydrogen; and the growing awareness that future economic growth will come from more efficient use of materials. There are also essays on China's economic and environmental future; constructing sustainable buildings; the state of the world's fisheries; the need to conserve mountain ecosystems and societies; creating a sustainable materials economy; the crisis in refugees; and budgeting for disarmament.

State of the World is the flagship publication of The Worldwatch Institute, and is translated into 27 languages around the world. National governments, UN agencies, the international development community and law-makers all rely on this annual for the most current authoritative and well-reasoned policy analysis and information available. Its integrative and interdisciplinary approach make it ideal for students, and it has been adopted on a wide variety of courses, ranging from biology to political science.

Available from:
Earthscan Publications Ltd
120 Pentonville Road
London N1 9JN
Tel: 0171 278 0433
Fax: 0171 278 1142

The Worldwatch Environmental Alert Series:
Introductions to the Basic Issues Confronting Humanity

Full House
Reassessing the Earth's Population Carrying Capacity
Lester Brown and Hal Kane

All the projections show that the world's population is set to continue to increase rapidly. The obvious question is: will there be enough to go round? So far, improvements in technology and crop yields have enabled food output to keep pace with population growth in most of the world – just. But for how long can this continue? *Full House* sets out the main issues in the population debate, and the steps to avoid future disaster.

Power Surge
A Guide to the Coming Energy Revolution
Christopher Flavin and Nicholas Lenssen

The world energy economy is poised to shift away from imported crude oil and environmentally damaging coal during the next few decades. *Power Surge* describes the move towards more efficient, decentralised and cleaner energy sources, and forecasts the energy sources of the future.

How Much is Enough?
The Consumer Society and the Future of the Earth
Alan Thein Durning

Standards of living in the developed world have never been higher, but are we happy? Alan Thein Durning argues that the voracious consumption of the world's affluent minority not only causes more environmental damage than any other factor, but that, as a substitute for community values and meaningful leisure activities, it does not contribute significantly to human happiness.

'Excellent survey of the consumer society and the toll it is taking on the earth'
The Guardian

The Last Oasis
Facing Water Scarcity
Sandra Postel

Sandra Postel gives a graphic and alarming account of the rapidly growing crisis in the global fresh water supply, which is resulting in falling water tables, the spread of disease and the threat of international conflict over diminishing reserves. This is an excellent general introduction to one of the most pressing environmental issues.

Saving the Planet
How to Shape an Environmentally Sustainable Global Economy
Lester Brown, Christopher Flavin and Sandra Postel

Lester Brown has been called one of the world's most influential thinkers. In this book he answers such questions as 'how should fossil fuels be replaced?', and 'how can a growing population feed itself?'. He describes the major political decisions needed, including the ways in which taxation systems need to be restructured to promote the shift to a sustainable economy.